THE ORGANISATION IN ITS ENVIRONMENT

Stephen Huntley

Edward Arnold

A division of Hodder & Stoughton

LONDON   BALTIMORE   MELBOURNE   AUCKLAND

© 1988 Stephen Huntley

First published in Great Britain 1988

British Library Cataloguing Publication Data

Huntley, Stephen
  The organisation in its environment.
  1. Organization
  I. Title
  302.3'5'024658   HM131

  ISBN 0–7131–3630–8

Typeset in 10/11 pt Cheltenham medium by Colset Private Limited, Singapore
Printed and bound in Great Britain for Edward Arnold, the educational academic and medical publishing division of Hodder and Stoughton Limited, 41 Bedford Square, London WC1B 3DQ by Butler & Tanner Ltd, Frome and London

CONTENTS

INTRODUCTION

to abstract – to reduce to a manageable size. The organisational world is none the less for that, but *we* may gain a little wisdom.

Students will find this book appropriate for a wide range of business studies courses, in particular BTEC National 'The Organisation in its Environment', A-level business studies, BTEC Higher National conversion courses, BTEC Higher National 'People and Organisations', first-year Institute of Personnel Management 'Introduction to Organisational Behaviour', and relevant parts of National Examinations Board for Supervisory Studies courses.

The text has been prepared with the BTEC National Core Unit especially in mind. Each chapter is divided into two parts: an exploratory section covering the central themes of the general objectives with suggestions for short assignments throughout (indicated by •); and a section of suggested assignments with an indication of skills assessable. These assignments will be useful to all students in giving them the opportunity to apply their knowledge in a practical way.

Although skill areas are shown with the assignments it must be emphasised that BTEC policy is for the learning strategy and skill development to be undertaken by colleges prior to the start of courses. Given that colleges will be developing their own learning strategies taking account of student need in their individual areas, it is unlikely that a general pattern of skill assessment will develop throughout the country, such that specific skills will be assigned the same weight at the same stage in the course by all the centres providing BTEC National courses. It is therefore inappropriate that weighting of skills for assessment purposes is given with the assignments, and so only an indication of the skills which could be assessed by each assignment is given.

In preparing this book, every effort was made to ensure that the information, data and examples given were accurate at the time of writing. However, conditions change, laws change, attitudes change, and inevitably some information will no longer be up to date. This in no way detracts from the accuracy of the general principles of the subject, which do not alter. Any example given is used only as a means of illustrating these principles.

Anyone studying organisations and their environment needs to have a sense of proportion. Just as there are individuals who are larger than life so there are also organisations which do not operate in the way theory predicts and yet are successful. To make sense of our environment we sometimes have

Skills which can be assessed

(All lists indicate least complex (1) to most complex skills)

1. Identifying and tackling problems

1. Identifying that a problem exists.
2. Defining the nature of a problem.
3. Formulating task objectives.
4. Using appropriate techniques and procedures.
5. Using initiative and creative modes of thinking/working to help develop a range of approaches to a problem.
6. Preparing a strategy and plan which is feasible in terms of time and resources.
7. Determining priorities for implementation, and being able to do so under pressure.
8. Organising activities and implementing action.
9. Monitoring and adjusting the plan as necessary.
10. Evaluating results of action taken.

2. Learning and study skills

1. Identify which questions to ask and break questions and problems into smaller parts.
2. Select relevant information.
3. Use a range of less complex study aids (including written, audio, visual, and electronically stored material) and techniques.
4. Complete assignment/work schedules on time and review work produced to ensure it meets the requirements of the task.
5. Manage own time effectively (prioritise).
6. Take appropriate action when circumstances prevent completion of a task within its time limits.
7. Take advantage of advice and counselling.
8. Use a more complex range of study aids (e.g. skimming, sifting, etc.).

3. Working with others

1. Present oneself in a manner appropriate to the situation.
2. React confidently in familiar and unfamiliar situations.
3. Respond constructively to instructions received from more senior staff.

4. Accept criticism of own contribution and/or modification of own findings.
5. Consult others and exchange information.
6. Negotiate realistic allocation of tasks in a group.
7. Contribute to formulation of a group plan of action.
8. Identify and undertake a variety of group roles.
9. Organise and direct individuals and groups to achieve given objectives.
10. Put others at ease, listen and help them to communicate.
11. Constructively criticise the contribution of others.
12. Recognise situations in which agreement cannot or should not be reached.

4. Communicating

1. Determine the purpose of a communication.
2. Relate a sequence of events by a visual and/or oral, and/or written presentation.
3. Structure and present information in a manner and at a time suited to its purpose and its recipient.
4. Design a structured communication (e.g. a stock record).
5. Use appropriate technical terms effectively.
6. Use appropriate tone for, and medium of, communication.
7. Listen, question, and respond in order to obtain information.
8. Recognise, use, and respond to non-verbal elements in communication.
9. Assess the effectiveness of a communication and take additional or remedial action as necessary.
10. Present a cogently argued case for specific action which incorporates:
    - a definition of the problem;
    - analysis and evaluation of relevant information, together with a description of sources;
    - application of appropriate principles and technique;
    - formulation and evaluation of solution(s).

5. Numeracy

1. Present numerical data in tabular and graphical forms.
2. Use appropriate indicators to establish performance or trends, e.g. percentages and averages.
3. Estimate an approximate result and use this as a guide to how reasonable the solution to a calculation is.

4. Assess the reliability and validity of information presented numerically or graphically.
5. Apply a range of techniques to analysing business information in terms of money, time, and resources.
6. Use appropriate equipment/technology to process business-related information.
7. Recognise those aspects of business tasks which would benefit from the application of quantitative techniques.
8. Select the appropriate techniques which contribute to solution of a problem.
9. Establish the degree of accuracy appropriate to a situation.
10. Communicate the results and implications in appropriate format with regard to the audience and desired effect.

6. Information gathering

1. Obtain information from appropriate means or analyse reasons for failure.
2. Identify what is required or likely to be of assistance.
3. Identify and select likely sources of information.
4. Identify situations when more or better information is required.
5. Recognise cost and other barriers to obtaining information.
6. Assess the limitations of the information obtained and the effect on the situation or task.

7. Information processing and technology

1. Set up a micro to process application packages.
2. Use computers and appropriate software as an aid in collecting, storing, etc.
3. Use a variety of methods for input of information into computer.
4. Select and use appropriate computer packages to help identify and tackle business problems.
5. Use a range of business equipment associated with document production and reprographic services.

8. Design and visual discrimination

1. Communicate with design professionals and others through the use of appropriate terminology.
2. Develop a critical awareness of products, procedures, services, and environments, and identify those elements which are particularly influenced by the design process.

3. Compare and evaluate the suitability of items and environments to their purpose.
4. Explore such design elements as colour, shape, space, and texture, and identify how they may be used to achieve specific objectives.
5. Investigate physiological, psychological and cultural factors that may affect human perception and appraisal of products, services, and environments.
6. Use images and symbols to communicate a particular message or value.

ACKNOWLEDGEMENTS

The publishers would like to thank the following for their permission to reproduce copyright material:

Business Top Thousand (1986) for a table; *Financial Times* for articles; *The Guardian* for articles; Her Majesty's Stationery Office for material from *Notes for Guidance on Business Names and Ownership* which is Crown Copyright and is reproduced by permission; *The Independent* for articles; *The Observer* for articles and Times Newspapers Limited for articles and illustrations.

The author would also like to acknowledge and give thanks for the contributions freely given by colleagues and students at Croydon College:

'In general conversations; in team meetings; in course evaluations, etc both the staff and students mentioned have contributed to this book.

'I would especially like to thank John Capper and Greg Smith for enticing me into writing this book; Gareth Leeves for listening to some of my ideas and giving valuable criticism; Richard Taylor for his encouragement.

'I want to thank Rob Matthews, Colin Holmes, Tony Ornial and Ted Hyett for their contributions many years ago.

'Finally, I want to thank my wife, daughter and our families for the encouragement and patience they have shown me, in this as in all else.'

1
THE NATURE, PURPOSE AND CHARACTERISTICS OF ORGANISATIONS

We work in, interact with, and live in organisations. We were born into an organisation, played in organisations, went to school in them, and now socialise in them. It is important that we understand how organisations develop and operate, given that much of our lives are taken up with them.

This chapter will consider the development, purposes and characteristics of organisations.

What is an organisation?

- *Make a list of the characteristics which you feel are common to organisations that you are familiar with. Examples of organisations that could be considered are school, clubs, teams, family, workplace, etc.*

Of all the organisations that you consider, you may be surprised to find that none is really unique – they will all have something in common, which is that organisations are made up of people who are *interdependent*. This implies that there will be the need for some form of *structure*. Also, a *decision-making* process will necessarily have to be at work. We therefore have:

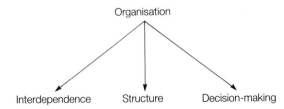

Fig. 1.1

Interdependence

- *Consider the organisations depicted in Fig. 1.2 overleaf and make brief notes on how the people concerned with these organisations are interdependent.*

People are interdependent, whether they work together or not, whether they know each other or not. What I do may have an impact on you even though we may never have met, even though we may not live in the same town or even the same country. If we work for the same organisation and I fail to do something at work, you may have to work a little harder to compensate – you may not even be able to carry on without my help. Consider the time when you and others had to do something and one person (a free-rider) did not pull his or her weight.

- *Read the articles on page 3 and list all of the people you can think of who would have been affected by the action mentioned in each case.*

Structure

- *Using the organisation you work in or study at as an example, make a brief presentation on what you think is meant by the structure of an organisation.*

Did you find that very difficult? What do you think is meant by the *structure* of an organisation? Is it the organisation of the organisation?

The structure of an organisation is the framework within which objectives have to be met. Organisations have objectives and they need to be organised, as does any group, to have a chance of achieving those objectives.

An organisation's structure is the organisational set-up as set out in its organisation chart. It is who reports to whom and who is responsible for what. The structure needs to provide an environment in which management can carry out long-term plans without being bogged down by day-to-day problems of running an organisation. Organisational *structures need to be flexible* in order to cope with a world facing constant *change* and innovation. In fact, in organisations such as the paper product manufacturer, Kimberly-Clark, there are permanent members of staff whose job is to find out how parts of the organisation relate to other parts – these members of staff then try to figure out how the various parts *ought* to relate.

Decision-making

- *Working in pairs, make a decision about a piece of furniture or a video that you might wish to purchase if you were sharing the same home.*

Fig. 1.2

Teachers' union rejects 'final' 6.9 pc pay offer

**By Sarah Boseley,
Education Correspondent**

THE National Union of Teachers rejected immediately a 'final offer' from local authorities yesterday aimed at ending this year's pay dispute.

The only prospect in sight last night for an end to nine months of classroom disruption was the plan by Sir Keith Joseph, the Education Secretary, to change the representation of the teachers' panel on the Burnham negotiating committee at the end of the year. This will cost the NUT – the largest union – its majority vote.

Phone rise threat

BRITISH Telecom, which raised telephone charges only 10 days ago, claimed yesterday that further increases will be necessary because of the terms on which it must allow the new Mercury system access to its line network.

M-way pile-ups in fog

By John Pearcey

A report on yesterday's multiple pile-ups on fog-bound motorways has been requested by the Department of Transport after nearly 120 vehicles were involved in a string of collisions which closed sections of the M1 in the Midlands for up to eight hours. At least 19 people were injured.

Peace hopes ruined

**By Patrick Keatley and
Jonathan Steele**

BRITAIN'S hopes of breathing life into the stalled Jordanian-PLO initiative for Middle Eastern peace lay in ruins last night after Sir Geoffrey Howe cancelled what would have been the first meeting between a British Foreign Secretary and representatives of the PLO.

He failed to obtain assurances from them about their policies after a storm of protest from Israel and dissuasion from the United States.

Select the type of item you are both interested in purchasing and visit three or four retail outlets that supply this item. Make a joint decision as to which of the many brands/types on offer you would purchase. Note what information you had to obtain before making the decision. What had to be considered before the decision could be made? How did you (as a pair) decide among the many alternatives on offer?

When you are with friends trying to decide what to do or where to go, what happens when you all try to voice an opinion at the same time? What attempts, if any, are made to reconcile conflicting objectives?

Decision-making is discussed in more detail in Chapter 9, but for now it is enough that you are aware that someone (notwithstanding that this 'someone' could be a group or a committee), somewhere, has to make a decision – is charged with responsibility. Whatever the mechanism, decisions have to be made. You may find other writers suggesting that organisations consist of a number of people who have specific goals and who work according to a body of rules. Clearly, if an organisation had no goal there would little point in its existence. Similarly, to imply that people must work to a set of rules merely recognises that organisations must have order or be thrown into chaos. An enlarged version of Fig. 1.1 could thus look like Fig. 1.4 (overleaf).

Fig. 1.3   Can you see how the people shown in these pictures are interdependent?

Fig. 1.3b

Fig. 1.3a

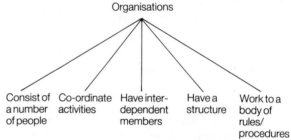

Fig. 1.4

Organisations

Consist of a number of people | Co-ordinate activities | Have interdependent members | Have a structure | Work to a body of rules/ procedures

Why have organisations?

Some organisations develop in an evolutionary way – without the trappings of legal regulation relating to establishment and membership. For example, even an informal gathering of hooligans at a football match could be considered to be an organisation. But is this really an organisation? There are a number of people who rely on each other (are interdependent), who do things together (are co-ordinated), who act and react in a particular way – as accepted by the group because of 'norms' of agreed behaviour being established (a body of rules) – and everyone in the group knows what is expected of them – where they 'belong' (structure). Let us say, then, that this informal group is an organisation which developed in an evolutionary way. If the members of the group were asked why or how this group developed, they might have little idea – it just happened. There might be agreement that the membership shared, or appeared to share, a common objective. However, if we look at more formal organisations, such as those depicted in Fig. 1.2, we may be able to see why such organisations are formed.

We have seen that organisations have a goal – it is this that gives us the major reason for their development. To achieve their objective, it may be necessary for people to establish a *form which lends itself to that particular objective*. There are many types of objective (economic, social, political, etc.), and it should come as no surprise that there are a number of types of organisation established to achieve similar objectives, since it is doubtful that everyone will agree on the 'best' format. (Equally, not everyone will have the same resources with which to develop an organisation.)

Organisational objectives can range from profit-making to providing welfare benefits for the needy.

It is possible to classify organisations in a number of ways, and this process is useful in its own right since it enables us to introduce some order into a situation where we have many types of organisation. We could, for example, classify according to

a) the sector of the economy the organisation operates in, or
b) the nature of the work undertaken.

The above are not the only means of classification – in fact, when it comes to classifying, the first issue is: what is the classification for? The basis of the classification will be determined by the requirements of those investigating the lists produced. We could classify according to size, in terms of the size of profits or turnover (sales) or the number of people employed or the value of capital assets. We could classify according to the market served or according to the stage of production – primary, secondary, or tertiary. Organisations could even be classified according to the form of ownership.

One generally very useful means of classification is to arrange organisations as indicated in (a) above – according to the sector of the economy to which they belong. To do this, you must first know something of the sectors of the economy. Let us start with the simplistic notion that there are two sectors of the economy and everything falls neatly into one of these sectors. There is a *private* sector, where organisations are owned privately, and a *public* sector where they are owned by the State (and administered by the Government).

The distinction between the private and public sectors of the economy is in most cases a useful one, although there are some problem areas. Organisations do not always exclusively belong to the private or public sector of the economy: there are some that are often described as being 'grey' in that they cannot be classified as private or public, just as we sometimes hear that not all arguments are about things that are 'black' or 'white'. Such organisations would belong to that sector where the distinction between private and public is somewhat blurred. Some examples of organisations that fall into this category will follow later.

- *Consider those organisations depicted in Figs 1.2 and 1.7 (pp 2 and 7) under the following headings:*
  a) *who owns them?*
  b) *who controls them?*
  c) *where does the money come from?*
  d) *how was the organisation formed?*
  e) *what financial risk is involved if the organisation cannot meet its financial obligations?*

Before we consider some examples of grey-area organisations, let us first briefly consider the distinction between Government and business.

In nineteenth-century Britain, the distinction between 'business' and 'Government' was a clear one: 'business' concerned activities undertaken for a profit, while 'Government' concerned itself with a very limited range of activities such as defence and law and order, which were clearly not commercial. This distinction which once prevailed has, however, become obscured during this century, with successive governments becoming increasingly involved in what can only be described as 'commercial' activities. Even the Conservative Government under Mrs Thatcher – which had the clear objective of privatising large sectors of the State-run 'businesses' – is heavily involved in economic activities.

Observation of the working of our economy reveals the close links between Government and business, with governments requiring the co-operation of finance, industry, and the trade unions to successfully implement policy, while businesses, for their part, attempt to persuade the Government to adopt particular policies which will benefit them. Businesses rely on the government of the day and the policies it pursues, while the Government relies on the activities of businesses in the running of the economy. Sounds familiar? The concept of interdependence in a family can be applied here. This notion of interdependence within an economy is,

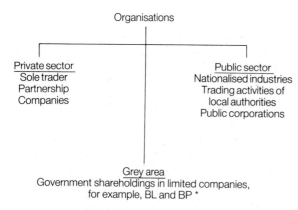

*In the 1984 BP Annual Report and Accounts, it was stated that the British Government held 31.7% of the ordinary shares.

Fig. 1.5

however, unfortunately lost on many of those in a position to affect matters of economic and social life!

The *grey area* previously mentioned has developed as a result of the growth of government involvement in business. Consider the chart in Fig. 1.5. This depicts those organisations that clearly fall into the private or public sector of the economy, along with those organisations that are not entirely State-run nor completely privately owned. There are many privately owned enterprises which undertake a number of activities normally assumed to be those of Government and which are not always concerned with the profit motive, such as the providers of voluntary social services. It may therefore be useful to consider another means of classifying organisations, namely, according to whether they are concerned with profit or with social/public welfare (Fig. 1.6 below).

Do not be alarmed if some of the above organisations are not familiar to you at this stage – an explanation of each will follow in another chapter.

- *What percentage of BP ordinary shares are held by the Government today?*

Assignments

Student activity 1.1

This is an individual assignment. The task relates to the characteristics of an organisation as depicted in Figure 1.4.

Write an informal report illustrating these characteristics, with respect to a business or educational organisation with which you are familiar.

Student activity 1.2

This is an individual assignment. You have been asked to address a meeting of the local Chamber of Commerce. The theme of the talk you have been asked to give is, 'interdependence in an organisation'. With reference to the organisation in

Fig. 1.6

Fig. 1.7

which you work or study, prepare the speech you will give, outlining the areas where interdependence occurs and the significance of that interdependence.

Student activity 1.3

This is an individual assignment. Because of the nature of production and distribution in the society in which we live, it is often suggested that we all depend on others for survival. Apart from those few extreme cases of people adopting a self-sufficient style of life, many would suggest that the great mass of the population will always necessarily be interdependent.

List all the examples you can think of from everyday life which illustrate the interdependence you feel exists between people in society, and say how you think this situation came about.

Student activity 1.4

This is a group assignment suitable for groups of three or four.

'This distinction which once prevailed has, however, become obscured during this century, with successive governments becoming increasingly involved in economic activities . . .'

While the statement claims that Government has become increasingly involved with economics, many people would argue for a broadening of this statement to reflect the extent to which government is now involved with the operations of organisations in general.

Working in small groups, conduct a survey of your town (or at least a reasonable part of it) and note all of the instances where you see that Government in some way interferes with, regulates, promotes, or finances organisational activity. Such examples might include the existence of local hospitals, parks, constabulary; the control of development, planning applications, and the protection of the environment; restrictions on trading, employment; etc.

Categorise the type of interference, etc., and present your findings (with suitable charts) to the rest of the group.

Student activity 1.5

This is a group assignment, suitable for groups of three or four.

By observation and investigation in the vicinity of your college or place of work, obtain a database of all organisations within a segment of that vicinity. Classify the organisations discovered under one of the four main headings in which organisational types are found (see Fig. 1.6).

Present the information obtained to the rest of your course group.

Skills assessable

	Skill							
	1	2	3	4	5	6	7	8
Assignment								
1	1.8	2.1 2.2 2.5		4.3		6.2		
2	1.3 1.4 1.8	2.4		4.3 4.5 4.6		6.1		
3	1.10	2.2 2.4 2.5		4.3		6.1		
4	1.5 1.6 1.7 1.8 1.9	2.1 2.2 2.4 2.5	3.5 3.7 3.6 3.10	4.3 4.5 4.6	5.1	6.1	7.1 7.2	8.6
5	1.4 1.6 1.8 1.9	2.2 2.4 2.5 2.6	3.5 3.6 3.7	4.2 4.3 4.5 4.6		6.1 6.2	7.1 7.2 7.4	8.6

2

THE NATURE OF AND RELATIONSHIP BETWEEN OBJECTIVES, STRUCTURE, AND POLICIES

Fig. 2.1 There is considerable variety in the types of organisation in the UK, but they all have at least one thing in common – objectives. What would you say are the objectives of these organisations?

All organisations have particular objectives – some may only have one or two while others may have many – and they need to be geared in such a way as to be able to achieve those objectives. In other words, the structure of organisations may determine the methods by which they attempt to achieve those objectives. The achievement of objectives is the purpose of policies. We therefore need to know something about organisational objectives, structure, and policies.

Objectives

- *Consider the organisation where you work or study. What do you think are the objectives of that organisation? Why do you think your organisation needs to set objectives?*

It is usually suggested that organisations have objectives because of the benefits those objectives yield – such as

a) *better management* – since management can use the results of past efforts and performance standards, it can manage more effectively.
b) *comparison* – the setting of objectives provides a mechanism for planning and control.
c) *motivation* – the members of an organisation may become more committed when they are aware of just what the organisation's objectives are.

Put simply then, objectives give you something to aim at and also give you something to compare actual performance with, so that plans can be reformulated to meet objectives.

The growth of government involvement in business has already been noted in Chapter 1. Such growth has led to the fact that a number of organisations that may be 'business' in nature are State organisations (nationalised industries). Such organisations will often have objectives not pursued by private-sector businesses, and some of these objectives are usually thought of as the roles of these organisations. It is therefore easier if we look at objectives first from the point of view of private-sector businesses and then from the point of view of nationalised industries (as these will indicate the constraints on public-sector organisations in general).

- *Working individually, note as many objectives as*

you can think of that a business is likely to have. When you have completed your list, exchange it with the list of another person in your group and note how many and which objectives are on both lists.

Objectives of private-sector businesses

At this stage it is sufficient to indicate that there are a number of different organisational types of private-sector business (these are discussed in Chapter 3). Those at the smaller end of the scale (sole traders and partnerships) will probably have personal objectives such as making a living, survival, making profits, etc. Larger organisations may have other, perhaps more wide-ranging, objectives. Such objectives can be thought of in terms of

a) the central purpose of the organisation,
b) responsibilities to shareholders,
c) the field of activities within which the organisation operates.

Bear in mind that every organisation operates within an environment, and if this changes in some way it will almost certainly have an impact on the organisation and its objectives, in terms of both the nature of the objectives and the methods to achieve those objectives. For example, in order to survive, organisations (particularly in the manufacturing sector) have had to adapt and improve products, services, and technology. Objectives should never be regarded as being sacred: they must be changed when they can no longer fulfil the organisation's current desires. When considering the objectives of these private-sector businesses, it should be noted that those of growth and profitability – favourites among teachers for so long – have in many cases tended to recede as organisations have become, or have been forced to become, more aware of their social/ethical obligations to employees and society in general. For example:

i)   the need to prevent pollution,
ii) conservation (of both raw materials and energy resources),
iii) the need to help find a solution to industrial/ecological problems,
iv) the problems of recycling waste products,
v)   aid with community development programmes.

Any of these objectives of private-sector business organisations could be valid; however, let us consider the objectives thought to be more commonly held by larger businesses:

a) profit maximisation,
b) profit security,
c) sales maximisation, and
d) security and power.

Profit maximisation

This is the basic goal of the free-enterprise system. Firms are in business to make profits. They could be *short-run profits*, such as those one would expect to make in a short period of time through an activity undertaken today; or they could be *long-run profits*, such as those which accrue as a result of investment or, say, research and development – which may in fact reduce short-run profits.

There are four implications attached to the notion of profit maximisation:

1. Those who control the organisation *are able* to maximise profits. *Do they have the necessary expertise and technique?*
2. Controllers of the organisation have the necessary information to enable them to make valid judgements about strategy which will allow them to maximise profits. *Do they have up-to-date information on costs and market demand?*
3. The objective of the organisation is in fact to maximise profits. *Could there be some other objective?*
4. The controllers of the organisation want to maximise profits. *Do they? Why should they?* In a small organisation, owned by the person who runs it, profit is no doubt the motive; but, in large organisations that are run by people who may have no share ownership, are such controllers likely to burst a blood vessel in order to make money for others? Such people may be 'satisficers' – that is, they (controllers/managers) do just enough to satisfy the desires of the shareholders, which permits them (managers) to maximise some other objective, for example, an easy life, more free time to play golf, longer business lunches, ...

The objective of profit maximisation has been tainted by the image of exploitation, child labour, profit regardless of employee well-being, and profit regardless of social environment. The notion of profit maximisation may need to be couched in more acceptable terms. To this end, profit is now often being regarded as a measure of efficient resource use. When resources are used, wealth is created and this can be used to reward those who originally contributed capital. Without this investment there would be fewer jobs. While no amount of investment can guarantee to create jobs, employment will only be maintained by the reinvestment of profits.

There are still those who argue against profits on the basis that we should be looking to the wider implications, for the whole community and our environment, of more production. To this end it is interesting to note the activities of organisations such as BP who often go to great lengths to protect and restore the environment – and, equally, go to such lengths to let us know about it! (BP have developed techniques for dealing with dangers in their own field of activities. The dangers of environmental damage anywhere in the world through oil spillage at sea can be met by the Oil Spill Response Unit, based at Southampton; while spills in rivers can be dealt with by using their Fasflow Unit equipment.) Disasters such as the massive chemical explosion at Bhopal (India, 1985) bring home to us the risks faced as a result of profit-geared production.

Profit security

Firms may appear to be attempting to achieve the goal of profit security, by pursuing policies designed to strengthen control over the market. The type of policies that lend themselves to this activity normally involve merger with or takeover of other organisations. Rather than going for profit maximisation, firms seem to be striving for a smaller though more sustainable/stable level of profits.

Sales maximisation

Since success in business is sometimes thought to be measured by the market share of the organisation, the objective of managers may be to maximise sales revenue. This may in turn have the effect of increasing the manager's salary and prospects for promotion. It would not be difficult for managers in many cases to successfully maximise sales while keeping within minimum profit constraints – provided such levels of profit were sufficient to keep shareholders satisfied.

Security and power

This could well be an objective of non-shareholding managers in public companies. The objective of profit maximisation involves risk. You should bear in mind that, to increase sales, a firm must make its products look more attractive than those of competitors – an easy way to do this is to reduce the price. Although likely to lead to a corresponding reduction in profits, it *should* lead to greater sales. (In the section concerned with how markets enable organisations to meet customer demands, you will find a

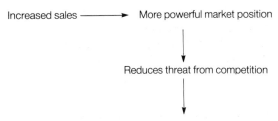

Such expansion widens the power and responsibility of managers (and possibly helps to increase salary)

Fig. 2.2

brief mention of demand elasticity, which explains why I have qualified this statement with the word 'should'.) A manager's salary could thus be greater than it might have been in a smaller though more profitable company. The *status and prestige* of the manager could also be boosted by the knowledge that his or hers was the largest or one of the largest organisations in that market.

- *Working in small groups (three or four) consider the activities of one nationalised industry and list what you think are the objectives of that organisation.*

Objectives of public-sector 'businesses'

There are a number of public-sector 'businesses', ranging from nationalised industries to trading organisations such as Her Majesty's Stationery Office and local-authority-controlled car parks. Some local authorities also own race courses and golf courses which are revenue earners. However, the largest of the public-sector businesses are the nationalised industries, such as the British Steel Corporation (turnover of £3,231,000,000 in 1984), British Railways Board (1984 turnover of £3,188,800,000), and the British Gas Corporation (with a turnover of £5,930,300,000 in 1984).

- *Working individually, locate a source(s) of information that will yield the turnover figures for every year since those quoted for the nationalised industries mentioned. Calculate the percentage change in these turnover figures for the time period concerned and show the information on a suitable chart.*

Because the nationalised industries are so large and dominant in the public sector, it is useful – when considering the objectives of public-sector businesses – to discuss the objectives of those nationalised industries themselves. It is useful to appreciate that the role a nationalised industry was intended to fulfil, at the time of nationalisation, may differ from the aims of successive boards and governments. Roles, in terms of social and environmental aims, for example, have certainly altered in the recent past. As a result, the objectives of such organisations have, to some extent, also altered.

The 1978 White Paper on Nationalised Industries (Cmnd 7131) gave a framework for accountability and assessment which had three elements:

1. *A financial target* as the primary expression of financial performance, to be decided industry by industry. The target was expected to take account of a number of factors, including the expected returns from effective, cost-conscious management of assets; counter-inflation policy; and social/sectoral objectives, for example, for energy and transport industries.
2. *A real rate of return*, given as a percentage. To be based on pre-tax real returns achieved by private-sector companies and the likely trend in return on private investment.
3. *Non-financial performance indicators*, 'so that the public can be better informed on the industries' success' in controlling costs and increasing efficiency. On performance and service standards, 'published financial targets should be supplemented by publication of performance indicators'. 'The Financial and Economic Framework for Nationalised Industries' by Andrew Likierman, *Lloyds Bank Review*, Oct 1979 (No 134).

In proposing the framework for accountability and assessment, the Government has given guidance as to the objectives of the organisations concerned. The National Economic Development Office, in its report on the nationalised industries in 1976, suggested that, 'because they [nationalised industries] are not subject to the same market disciplines as the private sector there is more scope for argument about their proper role and objectives'.

Since nationalised industries are often subjected to ad-hoc Government intervention, it is sometimes difficult to appreciate what their objectives are. An illustration of this intervention is the situation regarding pricing, downward (government) pressure on which has, in a number of cases, prevented organisations from fulfilling statutory obligations to *break-even*. Government intervention has thus ensured that nationalised industries cannot achieve the financial targets set (even though they may have been set by that very Government!).

- *What are the so-called 'socio-political' objectives of public-sector organisations?*

Structure

Organisation charts are much like underground maps. I remember once being in Omonia Square (Athens) and, wanting to get to Pireas, I decided to go via the underground. It didn't look that far on the map but, in the heat of the day, I was thankful for the cool, slatted, wooden seats on that train. I remember profusely demonstrating the Englishman's use of sweat glands to the amused locals. The point is, the journey, as shown on my underground map, was not to scale. We can see that some of our heritage comes from the Greeks, since much the same sort of thing happens in this country in connection with the underground – though without the same degree of heat.

- *Obtain a map of the London Underground. Note the graphical relationship between Euston and Charing Cross. Note also the distance shown on the map between Sloane Square and South Kensington and the distance between Waterloo and Kennington. Now obtain a scale map of the same area and discover what the geographical relationship between Euston and Charing Cross is. Also, with the scale map, see if the distances between Sloane Square and South Kensington and between Waterloo and Kennington are the same.*

Organisation charts are like maps of the underground in that they are simplified and only have to show relationships – such as who is superior to whom (which station follows which) – rather than actual distance.

Historically, organisation charts show more people at the base than at the top of the organisation – they look like pyramids. There is, however, a lot more to the structure of an organisation than those issues concerned with the way such a structure is depicted. The structure will be concerned with issues such as the relationships between people at work (line and staff relationships); the relationships those people have between themselves and others in terms of power, authority, and decision-making (centralisation/decentralisation); and the number of subordinates people are expected to control (flat and tall structures – span of control).

Organisations are *systems* (a set of connected

parts which together form a complex whole). Such systems are composed of many *subsystems* (departments). Each of the subsystems of an organisation has a part to play, a function to perform. Such areas (Production, Personnel, Finance, Marketing, etc.) are commonly referred to as *functional* areas.

Some functions of organisations can also be viewed as being those activities within an organisation that are part of the whole structure but which cannot be compartmentalised. Functions such as planning, organising, controlling, staffing, etc. cut across the organisational structure – that is, all departments perform these activities.

First, though, an indication and explanation of some of the technical terms:

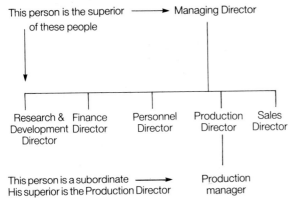

Fig. 2.3

The relationship between the Production Director and the Production Manager in Fig. 2.3 is said to be a *line relationship*. A line relationship is a direct line of hierarchical authority running from a superior to a subordinate.

The relationship between the Finance Director and the Sales Director in Fig. 2.3 is said to be a *staff relationship*. The nature of a staff relationship is advisory – there is no responsibility or accountability between these or any other points where a staff relationship exists.

Line and staff are distinguished by their authority relationships, not by what the holders of various positions do in their job.

- *Consider the organisation chart of the place where you study or work. Identify six positions which illustrate a line relationship and six which illustrate a staff relationship.*

Note that the Legal Department in an organisation, for example, is *advisory* in its role and as

such is a *staff* function. However, within that department, just as with other departments, there will be *line* relationships between superiors and subordinates.

Centralisation/decentralisation

This can be considered from three viewpoints:

a) *Geographically* – do we have operations for the organisation dispersed (decentralised) or concentrated (centralised)?

b) *Functional* – concerns various departments. Take personnel as an example. The question would be, do we have a separate Personnel Department which performs the personnel functions for all other departments (centralised) or do we allow each functional department to take care of its own personnel functions (decentralised)?

c) *Retention/delegation of decision-making* – this is the option we shall be concerned with in terms of organisation structure. The determining factor is: how much decision-making is retained at the top (of the organisation) and how much is delegated to lower levels?

Centralisation implies close control of operations, ensuring uniformity of policy and action, resulting in less risk of error by subordinates.

Decentralisation implies greater participation by subordinates in the decision-making process, which should increase motivation. It also leads to invaluable decision-making experience and hopefully ensures effective decisions, since those making decisions will have first-hand knowledge.

Span of control is the number of subordinates a superior is expected to manage. Suggestions as to the ideal maximum number for effective control vary from author to author, but a reasonable figure would be in the region of six.

Flat and tall structures describe the patterns of span of control in an organisation and the levels of management. The degree of control exercised over subordinates varies with the number of subordinates. If the span of control is wide (many subordinates) then the organisation may be depicted as in Fig. 2.4 (overleaf).

In an organisation where the span of control is wide, the organisation would of necessity need to delegate. Thus, flat structures encourage decentralisation.

If the span of control is narrow (a few subordinates) then the organisation may be depicted as in Fig. 2.5 (overleaf).

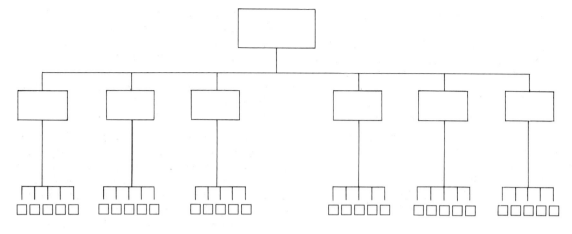

(There are 37 people in this part of the organisation)

Fig. 2.4

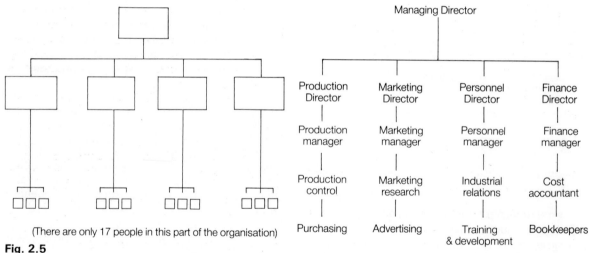

(There are only 17 people in this part of the organisation)

Fig. 2.5

Managing Director

Production Director	Marketing Director	Personnel Director	Finance Director
Production manager	Marketing manager	Personnel manager	Finance manager
Production control	Marketing research	Industrial relations	Cost accountant
Purchasing	Advertising	Training & development	Bookkeepers

Fig. 2.6

In an organisation where the span of control is narrow, the organisation would be able to exercise considerable control over subordinates, since each person in a position to exercise control has few subordinates.

In terms of the organisation of an organisation, then, we should expect to see a number of different types of organisation chart, depending in the main on (a) what the organisation does and (b) the degree of control exercised by the superiors in that organisation.

Some organisations find it beneficial to structure themselves according to *functional* areas, in which case we may expect to see the organisation chart looking like the one depicted in Fig. 2.6.

• *Construct a functional organisation chart for an organisation such as a local hospital.*

There will be other organisations that have adopted a *product-based* structure and their organisation chart may look like Fig. 2.7 (opposite).

• *Construct a product-based structure for an organisation such as might be found in the high-technology microcomputer industry.*

Finally there are the organisations that have developed a geographical approach to organisation, and they may thus find themselves structured as shown in Fig. 2.8 (opposite).

• *Consider four examples of organisations that*

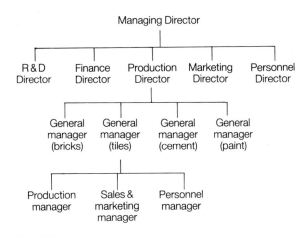

Fig. 2.7

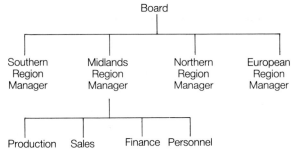

Fig. 2.8

would probably opt for an organisational structure that was geographical in nature.

Policy

This final part of Chapter 2 is concerned with the *statement of conduct* adopted by an organisation. We have seen that organisations have objectives (*what* they want to achieve – *ends*) and are organised in particular ways, according to how they hope to attain those objectives. They also devise plans or frameworks within which action takes place (the *means* to achieving success). Policies ensure that people behave in particular ways – they are not in themselves actions.

Before we discuss policy, we need to emphasise that much goes into policy-making before the announcement of the policy alternatives and the one(s) selected. Since policy needs to be based on requirements, it is necessary that facts are gathered and analysed. Various areas within the organisation will need to be consulted and drafts of policy must be prepared and circulated.

- *Working with at least three colleagues, prepare a plan concerned with methods of obtaining finance for a trip to a college in Amsterdam, to be undertaken by a group of twenty BTEC National-level students*
- *Working with three different colleagues from those in the task above, devise a policy statement concerned with the above plan.*

The above task should give you some idea of the problems encountered in producing policy statements. You probably found that the decisions which you had to make were made easier by the effective use of quantitative data, since you ought to have started by finding out how much you needed to raise. This in itself tells you something about policy-making, namely, that you have to make use of as much information as is practicable in the situations concerned. You were asked to produce a *policy statement*, which is an indication to those concerned of what they will do and what they will not do to pursue the overall purpose of an enterprise. Similarly, organisations produce policy statements that, in effect, do much the same sort of thing, while also expressing the culture and belief-system of the organisation.

It is difficult to give an indication of types of policy without falling into the trap of merely listing the policies that have been executed by various organisations in response to particular circumstances. It is more useful to consider, initially, general examples of the types of policy that could be adopted by organisations in different sectors of the economy. For example, organisations in the public sector of the economy usually exist with the objective of serving the public in one way or another. It may be then that the broad policy issue is that *all decisions concerning the provision of goods/services by the organisation be taken regardless of cost.*

Another policy objective, also concerned with those organisations that have the objective of serving society, may be that employees adopt specific patterns of behaviour (perhaps even a code of ethics) and a set of rules, which will ensure that all actions taken by the many individuals in the organisation are consistent, while being in sympathy with the broad objectives of the organisation.

In both the public and the private sector of the economy, an important policy decision for organisations, in general, is that they should endeavour to make as much use as possible of long-term projections and planning. Those organisations in the private sector of the economy are likely to be following a framework or plan which will enable them to make profits or maintain a healthy turnover position. What then would we expect their policy statements to contain?

- *Assume you were the owner of a small business which hired out video films. Your objective is to make as much money as possible while staying within the law and without upsetting local residents. What would you include in your policy statement (assuming you are forward thinking enough to produce one!)?*

Organisations in the private sector of the economy will predominantly be concerned with the profit motive and, as such, apply themselves to the task of obtaining as much revenue as possible, while keeping costs as low as possible. Let us consider each of these actions in turn: to operate at minimum cost and to maximise revenue.

Operating at minimum cost will require constant information concerning issues such as competitive costs, methods of reducing current costs, areas of possible cost saving, etc. A policy decision to ensure that the organisation achieves as much of this as possible should therefore be something along the lines of 'set up a system for obtaining and processing information concerning all aspect of costs'.

Increasing revenue to the highest possible point will mean selling as much as possible at the highest price possible. What policy decisions would you take in these circumstances?

In the above task concerning the policy statement produced for the video business, the guidelines for behaviour that you *could* have suggested (which would have permitted activity within the law and activity acceptable to local residents) might have included statements to the effect that

a) no employee should ever handle any material which, it is suspected, has been produced contrary to copyright legislation;
b) the business should on no account stock material which is likely to cause offence to the average person. (If you think this is too strong, then your policy could be couched in terms of not permitting such 'X-rated' material to be openly displayed/advertised or accessible to people under the age of 18.)

These suggestions are by no means the only options – a range of possibilities exists, along with the probability that many other items ought to be included.

Types and levels of policy

It should now be apparent that there are many types of policy, each depending on the various objectives that the organisation establishes for itself. Just as there are many types, there are also various levels at which policy can be produced. From the previous discussion on policy for the video business you can see (item b) that the degree of severity of policy can be altered to suit circumstances.

From earlier in this chapter, you will remember that organisations are composed of many levels of superior/subordinate relationships. Just as the levels of management differ, so will levels of policy. Policy-making functions exist at each level of management. Such policy may be concerned with the way we conduct business (relationships with customers/suppliers) or the way we conduct our internal affairs (relationships between employees within the organisation). It is unlikely that those at the top of the organisation will do little more than create broad policy, allowing each level of management to make the specific policy necessary to ensure that this broad policy is effective.

There are a number of stages in the process of policy-making. They include:

a) *formulation* – determining what the policy should be and, possibly, analysing the issue(s);
b) *communication* – dissemination of policy information to appropriate personnel;
c) *application* – putting policy into effect (with consistency);
d) *review* – periodic assessment to avoid retention of policies that have become obsolete.

A feature running through all organisations, from the smallest to the largest, is the impact of change. How will rapid changes in, say, technology affect organisations?

- *Consider the changes you expect to take place in banking services as a result of technological change.*
- *Consider the changes you could reasonably expect to take place in the nature of full-time employment as a result of potential changes in the social structure and the law as it relates to employment.*

This chapter has been concerned with the objectives, structure, and policy of organisations. Change – the one certainty – will have an impact on all of these issues. We can expect the captains of industry, administrators in public welfare programmes, the small retailer, the local authority, etc. all to feel the impact of change, particularly in the need to amend/alter objectives. It may be that previous objectives are no longer feasible in the light of changes in the political, social, legal, technological, or environmental sphere. It could conceivably be the case that we revise objectives in an 'upward' manner, particularly if we find that we originally underestimated potential or demand or some other salient factor.

Organisations must be so structured as to be able to survive the effects of the ever-increasing tide of change. If change affects objectives, as it must surely do, then organisational structure may need to be amended to reflect such change(s).

Finally, policy will be subjected to changes in circumstances. In the example given earlier of policy for the video shop in connection with 'X-rated' material, it might be that changes in moral attitude occur such that the handling of this material becomes expected of dealers. Anyone in this line of business would therefore need to revise policy in connection with this issue to have at least the hope of maintaining a healthy competitive position.

Assignments

Student activity 2.1

This is an activity designed for two people working together. Your objective, through interviewing the person you have been paired with, is to discover what objective(s) he/she had before starting the BTEC course you find yourselves on. When you have completed your interview, reverse roles, so that the interviewee now questions the interviewer, on the same basis as before. From any notes you have made, both prepare a presentation to be given to the whole group to deal with what you consider to be the objectives of your partner. After the presentation, the person whose objectives have just been discussed has the right to clarify/deny the observations – with an explanation.

Student activity 2.2

This is an individual assignment. Select an organisation in a busy street near the college where you study. With regards to this organisation, you have to prepare a presentation in which you suggest what you think are the objectives of two of the personnel. Go on to suggest what you think may be the objectives of the organisation that employs them. Say whether or not there appears to be any conflict between the objectives so cited and, if conflict/incompatibility appears to exist between

the objectives, say what the likely outcome of such conflict might be.

Student activity 2.3

This is an individual assignment. Obtain data which shows the cost of running your local social services department. From research that you conduct into the areas with which the department concerns itself, prepare an informal report on what you consider to be the four major objectives of the department.

Student activity 2.4

This is a group assignment for three or four students. Collect information from whatever sources you consider relevant, e.g. college prospectus, staff/student interviews, surveys of the college, etc., with a view to producing an organisation chart which illustrates the organisational structure of your college.

Suggest ways in which (a) the college structure could be improved, from the point of view of (i) first-year students, (ii) staff, (iii) visitors to the college who want information on a specific course, and (b) the new college structure could be made known to all those concerned in (a) above.

Student activity 2.5

This assignment is suitable for two or three students working together. Obtain the company reports for Marks & Spencer, Dixons, and Storehouse plc (the Habitat Mothercare group). With reference to these reports and other research (visits to the stores if possible, newspaper and magazine features), prepare an article for a business magazine which outlines the differences in management approach adopted by these organisations.

Student activity 2.6

This is a group assignment designed for the whole group (class). In April 1986 the Nationwide Building Society showed that home-owners in the South had to pay twice as much as home-owners in the North to obtain similar property. Similarly, the Halifax Building Society was reporting on the escalating value of residential property in the South East. With house prices rising by about 10% elsewhere but by about 20% p.a. in Greater London (with some properties rising by 16% in six months), there were calls for a move to build on the Green Belt.

First, find out what is meant by the *Green Belt*. Secondly, whether you live in or around London or not, the principle involved is significant. Decisions have to be made to protect valuable open space around towns or encourage development to ease the burden on the homeless or those hoping to enter the property-owning market. Conduct a local inquiry into the possibility of granting planning permission to build on what is currently an area of outstanding natural beauty. The group can be divided into representatives of:

a) the local council,
b) the land owner,
c) the property developer,
d) local residents,
e) a prospective home-owners action group.

After the discussion, the entire group must agree on a policy for the use of similar existing open space in your environment.

Skills assessable

Assignment	Skill 1	2	3	4	5	6	7	8
1	1.8	2.1 2.2 2.5	3.1 3.5	4.3 4.6 4.7		6.2		
2	1.3 1.4 1.8	2.4		4.3 4.6		6.1		
3	1.6 1.8	2.2 2.4 2.5		4.3 4.7		6.1 6.2		
4	1.4 1.6 1.8 1.9 1.10	2.1 2.2 2.4 2.5	3.5 3.6 3.7 3.10	4.3 4.4 4.6		6.1 6.2 6.3		8.3 8.4 8.6
5	1.8 1.9	2.2 2.4 2.5 2.6		4.3 4.6		6.1 6.2 6.3		
6	1.8		3.1 3.2 3.10	4.6 4.8 4.10				

3
THE CONTRIBUTION MADE BY DIFFERENT FORMS OF ORGANISATION IN A MIXED ECONOMY

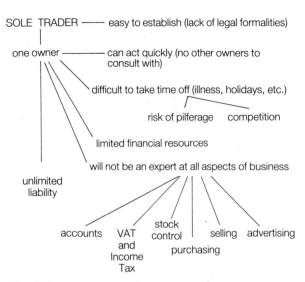

Fig. 3.1

When you finish the course you are studying, some of you may work in the public sector of the economy – for nationalised industries or local government or a quango (see page 27) – while others may find employment in the private sector of the economy – in a company or partnership or working for yourself. This unit will consider the essential features of organisations in the private and public sectors of the economy and will enable you to form a more accurate impression of the nature of such organisations in the UK.

Choice between business units

In Chapter 1 it was stated that a useful method of classifying organisations is to arrange them according to the sector of the economy to which they belong. In that chapter you were introduced to the notion of the *private* and *public* sectors of the economy and to the 'grey' area, where there are private-sector-type organisations that are State-owned (either wholly or in part).

In Chapter 2, the objectives of organisations were considered and, again, a distinction was drawn between private-sector and public-sector organisations.

On p. 6 Fig. 1.5 depicts types of organisation that are to be found in the economy, and it will be useful later if, at this stage, we consider these organisations in a little more detail.

Private-sector businesses

Sole trader (see Fig. 3.1)

This is an organisation owned and controlled by one person, requiring no legal formality for establishment other than that concerning disclosure of information connected with the ownership of the business, as specified in the Business Names Act 1985 (see page 20). Sole-trader businesses are thus easy and cheap to establish. The major disadvantage is the existence of *unlimited liability* for the owner, which effectively means that he or she will be liable for business debts to the full extent of all personal wealth.

The fact that there is only one owner does not necessarily mean that there is only one person engaged in the business – sole traders can employ as many people as they wish.

- *In some localities it is necessary to obtain a licence before setting up businesses concerned with particular types of work. Find out, from your local authority, what businesses need to obtain such a licence before trading.*

Partnerships (see Fig. 3.2)

These are organisations established by a minimum of two people, who enter into a *Partnership Agreement*. This agreement does not have to be written down, although it ought to be, since partners may disagree at a future date. If this Agreement does not help solve particular problems, the partners can

1.   INTRODUCTION

The Business Names Act 1985 came into effect on 1st July 1985 and consolidated previous business names provisions contained in the Companies Act 1981 (which itself replaced the Registration of Business Names Act 1916 on 26th February 1982).

The Business Names Act 1985 provides for the control of business names and the disclosure of business ownership which are explained in detail in these Notes.

The Notes are a guide to the current Business Names Act. They are **not** a guide to a law relating to the use of names generally. In particular there are a number of Acts which regulate the use of certain words/expressions and there is also a body of law which protects rights which persons may already have in relation to names or words. Anyone wishing to use a business name should consider consulting a solicitor.

> THERE IS NO REQUIREMENT FOR OWNERS OF BUSINESS TO REGISTER THEIR BUSINESS NAMES WITH ANYBODY.

2.   CONTROL OF NAMES

Where business is carried on in Great Britain under a name other than that of the owner, or owners (whether an individual, a partnership, or a company), the name may require the written approval of the Secretary of State.

Names which require approval are those containing words and expressions set out in statutory regulations, or names which give the impression that the business is connected with Her Majesty's Government or a local authority.

However, where such a name was registered under the Registration of Business Names Act 1916 no further approval is required, unless there has been a change of ownership. Where there has been a change in ownership, approval of the business name must be obtained within 12 months of that change.

In addition, no further approval is needed for a name which was approved under the business names provisions of the Companies Act 1981. But in the case of such a name and also in the case of a name approved under the Business Names Act 1985, a new owner of a business must obtain further approval within 12 months of acquiring the business.

A copy of the full Business Names Act 1985 can be obtained by writing to HMSO Publications Centre, 51 Nine Elms Lane, London SW8 5DR.

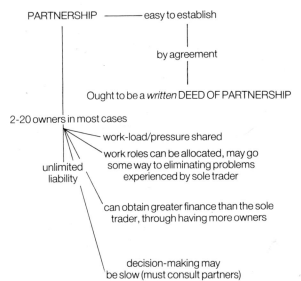

Fig. 3.2

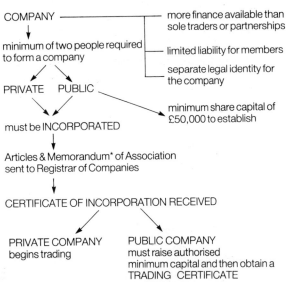

*   The Memorandum of Association states what the objectives of the company are Anything done by the company outside of these objectives is said to be *ultra vires*. Contracts thus entered into are unenforceable.

Fig. 3.3

resort to the conditions laid down in the Partnership Act 1890.

Just as with sole traders, the partnership also suffers from the drawback of unlimited liability, but in this case each partner is liable for the debts incurred in connection with the partnership by all of the other partners.

Partnerships are relatively simple and quick to establish and therefore fairly cheap to set up. The immediate and most obvious advantage is that there is more than one person involved, thus work is shared. There is a limitation on the number of partners that may be involved in a partnership, but this really depends on the nature of the business concerned – usually the limit is twenty.

Information in connection with the ownership of the business must be made known for compliance with the Companies Act 1981 (see p. 20, opposite).

*   *Find a suitable source giving the names and addresses of solicitors and dentists. Say what type of business organisation generally appears to be formed by these businesses and why such a type should be so common.*
*   *Prepare a 200 word (maximum) informal report on what is understood by a limited partnership.*

Companies (see Fig. 3.3)

These may be *private* or *public*, although both belong in the private sector of the economy. The major difference between this form of organisation and the sole trader or partnership is that there is a

procedure which must be followed before the organisation can begin its activities as a company (see Fig. 3.3) – following this procedure ensures that the company has a separate legal identity from that of its owners.

*   *What is meant by the term* incorporated *in Fig. 3.3? What is the significance of incorporation?*
*   *Familiarise yourself with the actions surrounding the case of* Salomon v. Salomon & Co. Ltd (1897). *Bearing in mind the facts and judgment in the Salomon case, can you see why Sir Freddie Laker was not charged with bankruptcy when Laker Airways crashed?* (See page 108 for a clue.)

Since the Companies Act 1981, the only important differences between private and public companies are that the public company must have a minimum share capital of £50,000 and it must either have the words 'public limited company' or the initials 'plc' after its name. As has always been the case with companies, it is only a public company which can appeal directly to the public for funds – its shares are the only ones that are freely transferable.

*   *Obtain a report of the legal case of Ashbury Railway Carriage Company Ltd* v. *Riche (1875). Familiarise yourself with the actions surrounding*

this case and satisfy yourself that you know why the decision went the way it did. Compare the situation in the Ashbury case with what you predict might be the outcome of a similar case heard today. Bear in mind the effects of the European Communities Act 1972 (section 9(1)) which gives protection to a person entering into a contract with a company acting ultra vires provided that the person entered the contract in good faith.

Companies, then, are organisations that require specific procedures to have been complied with before they are permitted to operate in the economy. Some organisations that are companies require compliance with additional requirements before they can trade – these include businesses such as banks (regulated by the Banking Act 1979); insurance companies (Insurance Acts 1958–80); and building societies (although one of the larger societies is a co-operative, these all have to be registered under the Building Societies Acts).

- *Prepare a 200 word (maximum) report on what is understood by an unlimited company.*

Co-operatives

Co-operatives exist in many fields, from production (worker co-operatives) to retail (the 'Co-op'), insurance (the Co-operative Insurance Society), and banking (the Co-operative Bank). In the field of production, the idea of worker co-operatives/worker control tends to be more of a political strategy rather than a settled industrial-relations system – more by way of vote-catching than a means by which shop-floor workers can influence the operations of their firm. Such experiences in the UK are not, however, the same for co-operatives in other countries, where they have proved successful. A good example is that of the Mondragon Co-operatives situated in the Basque provinces of Spain. Here there is a group of enterprises centred on Mondragon which embraces a range of different ventures: agriculture, schools, a polytechnic, a chain of co-operative consumer stores, and a social welfare service. This group also has its own banking and management-services institution (the Caja Laboral Popular).

- *Working in groups of three or four, research the area of UK worker co-operatives and present your findings to the rest of your group.*
- *Working in groups of four or five, conduct research on the development, growth, and subse-*

quent decline of the retail co-operative in this country from the time of the Rochdale Pioneers. Prepare a 700 word (maximum) article on this issue for inclusion in a retail trade magazine.

With the growth of Government encouragement, in the first half of the 1980s, for people to start small businesses, it is interesting to note the help and advice available for those willing to begin such a venture. The major banks all publish information and offer advice for prospective businessmen and, in the field of co-operatives for example, the Manpower Services Commission, through its Careers and Occupational Information Centre, has produced a booklet entitled *Co-operating for work*. Useful information about co-operatives can also be obtained from the Co-operative Development Agency in London, Scotland, or Wales. The addresses are as follows:

The Co-operative Development Agency, Broadmead house, 21 Panton St. London, SW1Y 4DR (01–839 2988).
The Scottish Co-operative Development Committee, Templeton Business Centre, Templeton St. Bridgetown, Glasgow, G40 1DA (041–54 3797).
Wales Co-operative Development and Training Centre, 55 Charles St. Cardiff, CF1 4ED (0222 372237).

Franchises

Although a franchise is not a type of business unit, franchising is important since it has made a significant contribution to the development of some business organisations in the UK. It therefore warrants a mention here. It has allowed the creation of some 5000 businesses in the UK, employing over 31,000 people.

A franchise is a licence to manufacture and/or sell particular products or brands of goods or to provide a 'trademarked' service. There are many companies in the UK that provide a licensing system, enabling you to market a tried and tested product with the back-up of their trade name, business know-how, advertising, etc. The process is relatively simple to get into: you pay an initial premium (a sum of money) to the franchise company and pay them royalties on sales. For this you are given a franchise. The amount which has to be invested varies from a few hundred pounds to several thousand, but this will often be reflected in the quality and level of support from the franchising company. There is an Association which can help with advice – The British Franchise Association,

Fig. 3.4

Grove House, 628 London Road, Slough, Berkshire, SL3 8QH (02812 4909).

Many people view franchising as an effective means of entering a market. Take, for example, the Wimpy (hamburger) franchise. You agree to buy only Wimpy hamburgers and rolls (at a reduced price) and have your outlet decorated in the Wimpy style and you get free television advertising and the additional benefit that customers recognise your trade name and associate it with particular food.

The idea is not a new one – the original concept began in the UK in the late eighteenth century through the brewery-tied public house. Second-generation franchising (business format franchising) has, however, been developed in the USA over the past century and has been reintroduced and developed in the UK.

Franchising is a useful contributor to business growth and, with the following advantages, should become a powerful force in UK business development:

a) It eliminates as far as possible the inherent risks in setting up a new business, because one is usually buying a marketable existing product.
b) Businesses can be established along the lines of already successful pre-designed formats – with support from the franchiser.
c) Detail necessary on how the business should be run is often provided in the form of an operations manual.
d) Products/services franchised are generally easily identifiable because of an existing brand image/mark.

Public-sector businesses

The 'businesses' that appear in the public sector are public corporations in the form of nationalised industries. Public corporations outside the business sector have been around for much longer than nationalised industries, most of which were created after 1945. For example, the Port of London Authority was established in 1908, and one of the more famous of our public corporations, the British Broadcasting Corporation (BBC), came into existence in 1926.

A public corporation has its own legal identity, with its own constitution, powers, and duties being prescribed by law. It is therefore a statutory body.

Public corporations can be divided into three categories:

i) industrial or commercial – e.g. the British Steel Corporation or the Post Office;

ii) social service organisations – e.g. the National Health Service;
iii) regulatory/advisory organisations – e.g. the Equal Opportunities Commission.

A public corporation is publicly owned and independent in respect of operations, although there is some degree of Government control.

- *Using newspapers and magazines of the time, conduct research on the issue of BBC news coverage of the Falklands conflict. Conduct similar research on the issue of union membership by employees of the Government Communications HQ at Cheltenham. Prepare an argument that shows that there was some degree of Government control over (a) news coverage and (b) vetting of staff.*
- *Having completed the previous task, now prepare an argument to show that such control was necessary.*

Nationalised industries are created by Act of Parliament. Although Parliament (effectively the Government of the day) is ultimately responsible for their operations, the day-to-day management of each industry is in the hands of a *Board*. In many respects this Board operates in much the same way as a board of directors for a private or public limited company. The organisation is, however, much more complex than might be appreciated at first sight, since it is an industry – that is, it is a collection of what were previously separate firms. A glance at the capital-employed statistics of three nationalised industries and three of the largest public limited companies (the largest of the private-sector organisations) will show just how large the nationalised industries are (Table 3.1).

Table 3.1

Organisation	Sector of the economy	Capital employed 1984 (£000)
Electricity Council	Public	33,830,500
British Gas Corp.	Public	12,375,100
National Coal Board	Public	3,223,000
British Petroleum Co.	Private	19,223,000
B.A.T. Industries	Private	4,893,000
Imperial Chemical Industries	Private	5,541,000

Source: *Times 1000* (1984–5)

- *Using the examples in Figs. 3.4 and 3.5 (pp. 23 and 25), say which belong to the private sector and which to the public sector. Also, give an*

Fig. 3.5

indication of the type of business organisation (sole trader/partnership/public limited company etc.) which you think is involved.

- *Obtain the capital-employed statistics for the organisations in Table 3.1 for later as well as earlier years and compare the growth/decline in these figures over time. What do you find interesting/significant in these figures?*

Accountability of organisations

- *Select one local business and list all the other organisations and people with whom it will have contact. Say in what way(s) this organisation may be thought to be accountable to these other groups.*

When we say that organisations are 'accountable', what do we mean? Accountable for what? To whom? Perhaps the best way to think of accountability is to think of it in terms of responsibility – responsibility to various people/groups/organisations.

- *Assume you own and run a small newsagents. Who would you say you were accountable to, and in what way?*

If we are to consider to whom organisations are accountable and what they may be responsible for, we ought to begin by distinguishing between the accountability faced by private organisations and that faced by public-sector organisations. Let us first consider accountability from the point of view of private-sector organisations and then follow this with a view of public-sector accountability.

All private-sector organisations can be said to face accountability from two points of view:

i)   that which is internal to the organisation,
ii) that which is external to the organisation.

Internal accountability is apparent in all private-sector organisations and appears in many guises. For example, we could say that a sole trader is responsible to his staff for their health and safety (as any employer would be); a partner in a partnership has a responsibility not to make private profits; people in organisations are accountable for their actions to superiors – the Production Manager in Fig. 2.3 (p. 13) is accountable for his actions, and those of his subordinates, to the Production Director. Companies have shareholders and these expect their companies to perform particular

actions in a specific way. Companies are accountable to shareholders.

- *Assume that you have shares in a large public limited company. What do you think the company must do to ensure that you are happy with its conduct of affairs? For what types of things would you expect the company to be accountable to you?*

As for external accountability, we are here considering the responsibility a business has towards groups/organisations such as:

1.   Creditors – people to whom money is owed.

- *What is the nature of the accountability that exists between a company and its creditors?*

2.   Consumers/customers – responsibility not only for not breaching a contract but also for ensuring that products sold are safe for use.

- *Consider the legal case of* Donoghue v. Stevenson *(1932). What does this tell you about manufacturers and the safety of their products?*

3.   Other organisations. In what way can an organisation be said to have a responsibility towards other organisations? In fact there are a number of areas where just such a situation arises. If, for example, my organisation performs a particular act on my land which affects the operation of another organisation, then my business may be guilty of a negligent act, or one which is a nuisance, or one which contravenes a law such as anti-pollution legislation.

- *Consider the legal case of* Sturges v. Bridgman *(1879). In what way was one of the businesses concerned said to be accountable to the other?*

4.   Government – organisations are accountable in terms of the *legal* framework within which they must operate and the *financial*. The legal framework will include areas such as employment or redundancy issues; whereas the financial framework within which organisations will be accountable to the State includes the areas of taxation, Government grants, and State investment.

Accountability in the public sector tends to be wider than in the private sector, since a public-sector organisation not only has a responsibility towards customers, creditors (the State also borrows, as well as you and I!), and private-sector organisations, but will also be subject to *public* accountability. Government departments are subject to Parliamentary control. These departments, as well as the National Health Service and local authorities, are also subject to public observation of activities through an independent Commissioner for Administration (Ombudsman). There is also public accountability through the checks and controls on expenditure of public funds.

- *For what is the Public Accounts Committee of the House of Commons responsible?*

Public/private-sector interface

When we talk about the mixed economy we are referring to the combination of public and private-sector organisations that produce and allocate goods and services amongst those who demand them. We have seen that the private sector contains many types of business unit and that the public sector has nationalised industries within it. We have not yet considered some of the other public-sector organisations that play an important part in our lives, when we are both customers as well as producers/workers. Such organisations are *quangos* and *local government*.

Quangos are independent public-sector agencies established to perform a service or to carry out some administrative function free from direct government control, although Ministers may exercise some restraint. These agencies are Quasi-Autonomous National Governmental Organisations (as opposed to Quasi-Autonomous Non-Governmental Organisations, a definition which is much more restrictive than the original and which would thus not include some of the bodies which are, in fact, accepted as quangos). The term 'quasi-autonomous' implies that the body is independent of the government machine itself, which is of importance to organisations such as the Arbitration, Conciliation and Advisory Service (ACAS), which must always appear independent of the State.

- *It has just been stated that ACAS must always appear independent of the State. What does ACAS do and why is it important that it should be, and should be seen to be, independent of the State?*

Local government in the UK is the system whereby Parliament authorises other bodies (local authorities) to perform specific functions, so that these duties are carried out by local administration rather than by central government. Some duties are the sole responsibility of county councils (such as environmental health in relation to animal diseases; construction of roads; and Town and Country Planning issues involving major developments), while others remain the sole responsibility of district councils (for instance, maintenance of roads, and town and country planning issues concerning local plans). There are several duties shared by both councils, such as responsibility for museums and galleries, public health, and sewerage.

- *Find out which type of council administers the area where you work/go to college. What are the main functions of that council?*

The relationship between local government and central government, or between 'town hall' and 'Whitehall', has undergone considerable change over the years, especially with the involvement of the Thatcher Government in local-authority expenditure. Final power rests with Parliament, although many authorities have questioned central government's ability to provide what local communities want.

- *What is meant by rate-capping? What are the arguments in favour and against such action?*

Councillors must undergo elections every four years, and in most cases party politics is a central issue with the electors. The machinery of local government is operated by salaried staff – much the same situation as in central government, which is operated by the Civil Service. The work of a local authority is thus conducted through a council, which is assisted by a number of committees working in collaboration with the senior officers of the local authority. These senior officers are employed by the council and head the various departments, within which full-time employees work. Departments cover areas such as education (teachers, school caretakers, school-meals-service employees), social services, libraries, recreation (parks attendants, swimming-pool attendants, etc.), street cleaners, refuse collectors, fire service, police, the courts and probation staff, etc. The occupational groups in local government are:

- chief officers
- administrative, professional, and clerical staff
- teachers, police, and firemen
- manual workers

- *Find out how many employees your local authority has and present the information in a table and a diagram which illustrates how many are employed in each of the above occupational groups.*

Finance, as far as local authorities are concerned,

is obtained from a number of sources. For example, some own race courses, others own golf courses, while most operate municipal car-parks and leisure centres. However, most of the resources used by a local authority will come either from the rates or from central-government funds through a grant. The renting of council houses and the income received from investments is not normally of major significance to local authorities.

- *Obtain the financial information from your local authority which will enable you to produce a diagram showing the components of income and expenditure for that authority. Produce the diagram and give a brief oral explanation of your findings to the rest of the group.*
- *What is meant by a* rate poundage? *How is the domestic rate on your home calculated?*

The economic system in the UK is, as we have seen, made up of private- and public-sector organisations. An important feature of all of these organisations is that none operates in isolation; private-sector businesses will affect each other by their actions and they will in turn be affected by, and affect, public-sector organisations.

Private-sector organisations are concerned specifically with the allocation of products and services in return for money (payment), while public-sector organisations do not always operate in this way. The allocation process for a National Health Service hospital bed, for example, is not conducted in terms of competitive-payment bids by patients for that bed – although we do have a thriving private medical sector where just such occurrences happen. The system that operates in the UK, whereby private- and public-sector organisations can work side-by-side, says something about the political nature of the environment which can sustain such provision.

- *Name three other situations where there is both private and public provision of the same commodity.*

In terms of an *interface* – a situation where interaction occurs, a common boundary between two parts – the private and public sectors of the UK economy appear to operate remarkably well. It would be misleading to suggest that the two sectors are completely independent of each other, since there is often interaction between them. Consider the three public sector industries shown at the top of Table 3.1. The Electricity Council does not operate in isolation from private-sector organisations – there is, in fact, a thriving private-sector provision

of electrical appliances. Without this private-sector provision the Electricity Council would not sell as much electricity, while the appliance manufacturers would be lost without the power source provided by the investment of the Electricity Council. The British Gas Corporation would find itself in a similar situation with regard to manufacturers of gas appliances; and these manufacturers would also be lost were it not for the activities of the British Gas Corporation. Finally, we have British Coal, a large nationalised industry which generates work for thousands in the private-sector of the economy from private coal hauliers, to fireplace manufacturers, to other totally unrelated producers who use electricity generated by coal-fired power stations, to those manufacturers in the private sector who produce goods which are derivatives of coal.

Very often the common boundary between the public and private sectors of the economy is the consumer. In the majority of cases we find it quite acceptable that goods and services are provided by organisations which allocate them via a price mechanism – that is, if you can pay the price you can buy the good or the service; if you cannot pay, you go without. However, it is recognised in the UK, as in many other countries, that the State is responsible for the well-being of its citizens. Clearly, this implies a system of law and order to maintain internal stability in a country and a system of defence to protect a country from attack. It does imply a little more, though – the suggestion is that control must be exercised over the pricing/allocation of certain necessary goods and services in order that the well-being of the population is maintained. This control can only be effectively exercised if the organisation is within the public sector, rather than the private sector (which is goaded by the profit motive).

- *From research into the area of nationalisation, prepare a set of notes which outline the major arguments in favour of nationalisation of an industry.*

The public/private sector interface is suitably demonstrated by the evidence of 'mixed enterprises' (referred to on page 5 as 'grey' organisations). These organisations represent a distinct form of public ownership which came into existence by the acquisition of companies which were in such serious financial difficulties that they were likely to have gone out of business as private-sector organisations. Since these organisations (such as British Leyland, Rolls Royce and Ferranti Limited) were helped by the then National Enterprise Board,

-the Board has been combined with the National Research and Development Corporation to form the British Technology Group. The result of this amalgamation, which came about as a result of a policy change aimed at altering the kinds of organisation the Government wanted to help, was that the new body should acquire shares in firms in particular fields.

- *The National Enterprise Board was established in 1975. What was the original conception behind its introduction?*
- *The idea was for the new British Technology Group to acquire shares in firms such as Celltech and Inmos. Prepare a brief informal report on the activities of these two organisations.*

Value systems

The systems employed throughout the world by which economies are operated vary according to value systems, that is, they vary according to the way in which people would like to see the world operating; according to what they think is an acceptable/unacceptable means of ownership and control of resources. At one end of the spectrum of views concerned with the way an economy should operate is that commonly referred to as *capitalism*. This is a situation which emphasises freedom and incentive for the 'individual' in order that he can pursue his own self-interest as worker, consumer, and possibly investor, or person who starts and runs businesses (an entrepreneur). The underlying assumption of capitalism is that the interests of society at large will best be served by productive economic activity which has been generated by self-interest. It is not possible to point to any country and claim that it totally supports or is reflective of one particular economic system, since all countries vary in the degree to which they ascribe to a particular view. However, for want of a better example, it is often claimed that the economy of the USA is capitalist in nature – although we must bear in mind that there is a large 'State sector'.

It is sometimes useful to distinguish between the abstract *laissez-faire*-competitive model of capitalism and the mixed capitalistic system to be found, for example, in the UK.

- *Research the area of* laissez-faire *capitalism and prepare short notes for an oral presentation which should last ten minutes.*
- *List as many examples as you can which show that the USA is not a pure capitalist economy.*

At the other extreme is the economic system which regards 'society' as being all-important in the process of organising, planning, and conducting economic activity, rather than the individual. In this situation it is assumed that the individual will become so accustomed to working for society that he will do so without the need for an incentive such as a wage. A situation like this would be described as 'complete communism'. Again, it is not possible to give an example of a country entirely given over to such a system, though the most significant voice in this area must be that of the Union of Soviet Socialist Republics (USSR). Since it has not totally ascribed to the ideals of a complete or full communist system, we refer to the USSR as a 'socialist' economy.

Socialism can be used to describe the system which permits free markets for consumer goods and labour, but with government ownership of capital (liberal socialism) or the situation where the Government owns all productive capital *and* makes the decisions concerning employment and the production of consumer goods (authoritarian socialism/communism). Liberal socialism is variously referred to as 'limited socialism', 'market socialism', and 'democratic socialism'. Socialist economies such as those existing in the USSR are known as 'command' economies.

- *List as many examples as you can which show that the USSR is not a full communist system.*

Between these two extremes we have all of the examples of economies throughout the world. Such economies tend to be capitalistic in nature or socialistic in nature in that they exhibit varying degrees of capitalism/socialism. The economy in the UK is said to be a 'mixed economy', which indicates that there is a mix of both private ownership and control of capital resources, and public ownership and control.

There is an economic system where the principle of private ownership of capital is upheld but, and this is where it differs from traditional capitalism, great emphasis is placed upon co-operation and mutuality of interests between employers and employees. Such a system is termed 'corporatism' and it has been variously associated in the past with the efforts of religious groups; with attempts by capitalists to prevent the growth of socialism; and with nationalistic movements.

Romantic political thinkers in nineteenth-century Western Europe put forward the notion that a system of corporatism sponsored by strong national states would best achieve desired social harmony. This view was expressed since it was thought that individualism would promote disruption in society through greed and personal ambition. However, these thinkers had little influence and it was not until Catholic and Protestant religious groups, aiming to produce better economic and social conditions for workers in a harsh capitalist system, advocated corporatism that things began to change. An extreme type of corporatism, that of 'authoritarian capitalism' or 'fascism', was seen to develop in countries such as Italy, Germany, Spain and Portugal after World War I.

Competition and planning

Competition and planning in a mixed economy need to be considered in a little detail. Competition exists between manufacturers, wholesalers and retailers in the private sector of the economy, since these are all led by the incentive of making a profit. To this end, all organisations are in competition with each other for the consumers' scarce resources.

As a consumer I have limited resources (money) and must therefore decide what I am to spend it on. For example, I can either spend it with one retailer on a new stereo system or with another on a new surf board. Although the products are not directly substitutable for each other, I must decide where my scarce income is going to be spent. So when I buy my new surf board, the hi-fi retailer has failed to capture my expenditure. These retailers may not appear to have been in direct competition, but they were competitors for my scarce resources.

There are other organisations that are in direct competition with each other – for example, competition will exist between a number of butchers' shops in the same vicinity (or even in the same street, see Fig. 3.6), so it is normally this type of area that we think of immediately when we consider competition.

A good example of how businesses are affected by the *amount* of money we have in our pockets is the hairdressing trade. Whenever there is a change in the economic situation of a country, watch what happens to the finances of hairdressers – they are a very good barometer of economic life. When we enter an economic slump and money is scarce, hairdressers are among the first to notice that people are not spending as much as usual on their hair. People do not go to the hairdressers so frequently, and they do not spend as much when they are there. Similarly, when the economy picks up and people find they have more money to spare, it is hair-

Fig. 3.6   This picture was taken in the town of Barnstaple (North Devon) where there is one 'street' in which almost all the shops are butchers

dressers and people like them who are among the first to notice that their takings go up.

Because competition is an inevitable fact of life for those operating in the private sector of the economy, businessmen must plan. We saw at the beginning of Chapter 2 that organisations have objectives. Later in the same chapter it was emphasised that these organisations must develop a plan or framework within which action takes place. The task on page 16 gave you an insight into what has to be taken into account when planning and producing policy statements.

- *You intend to open a small wine bar near the centre of the town where you live. At the moment you are still at the planning stage. What issues can you foresee would have to be resolved before you purchased the lease on a property and began work? Produce a plan showing what must be done and in what order.*

It is not only the private-sector organisations which have to plan. Those in the public sector also have to establish goals and prepare a route to achieving those goals. In the case of the organisations shown in Table 3.1 (p. 24) we can see from the size of the capital employed that resource use is extensive. Planning is therefore a crucial part of the activities of these and other public-sector organisations.

The types of thing that need to be planned include:

– the level and type of investment that will be undertaken in the future,

- the policies that will be developed to deal with labour issues,
- the changes that will need to be made to the products/services provided,
- where the organisation will be in five, ten, and twenty years from now.

- *Collect advertisements for the goods/services of the British Gas Corporation and the Electricity Council. Prepare an informal report which shows that there is competition between these two organisations, using these advertisements to substantiate your claim.*

One of the points previously mentioned was the issue of developing a plan in connection with labour. At this point it is enough to say that organisations plan their responses to, for example, labour turnover and replacement, along with creating strategies for personnel development. This is an issue which will be covered in more detail in Chapter 12 under the heading of *manpower planning*. There are other types of plans which organisations will need to consider:

- *corporate plans*, the development of the aims and strategies of all levels of a business and the continual review of those aims and strategies;
- *strategic plans*, short, medium and long-term plans to deploy a company's resources to meet defined business objectives;
- *tactical plans*, after drawing up a strategic plan, the next stage is tactical planning, or how the strategic plan is to be put into action and organisational objectives achieved.

Having considered what types of plans are produced by organisations, let us bring this chapter to an end by considering the stages involved in planning, and then mentioning the impact of change on organisations (see Fig. 3.7).

Over time there will be change facing those who operate both private- and public-sector organisations since factors such as income, taste and population size – the determinants of the demand for their products – will also change over time. Those charged with the responsibility of directing the efforts of the private- and public-sector organisations must be able to respond to these changing situations. We can thus expect to see the contributions of different organisations, that is, what they produce, what they add to the economy, what they add to social welfare, also changing over time. In the next chapter we will consider the factors that cause change, ranging from economic, legal, and

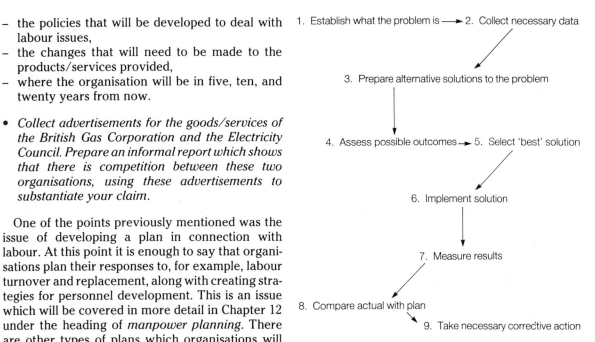

Fig. 3.7 The stages involved in planning

social change to political, demographic, and technological change.

Assignments

Student activity 3.1

This is a group assignment for four to five students. The area surrounding the college is to be divided into segments and each student will be assigned one segment. The objective is for each student to conduct research in the segment allocated and note

a) what organisations exist within that segment,
b) to which sector of the economy each of these organisations belongs.

The group will then collate all of the information obtained by the individuals and prepare a map and/or any other charts/diagrams they feel necessary to show the use to which the land has been put.

Student activity 3.2

This is a group assignment for four to five students. Using the information obtained from Activity 1, produce a leaflet which would be useful to those unfamiliar with the various types of public- and private-sector organisations, which explains what the various organisational types are and the inter-relationships between them.

Student activity 3.3

This is an individual assignment. Select a means by which the information obtained from Activities 1 and 2 can be stored on a computer. Carry out this process.

Student activity 3.4

Working in groups of three, prepare a handbook for prospective businessmen which outlines the sources of funds available to them in setting up a small business. Obtain the necessary information from banks, other financial institutions, magazines, newspapers, and books.

Student activity 3.5

In Switzerland there is a bank run entirely by women. The Eaux-Vives branch of the *Banque Hypothécaire du Canton de Genève* also offers advice on divorce, child-care and further education.

Working in groups of three or four prepare a visual presentation of the kind of business a group of local mothers, each with a child less than three years old, could set up and run in your area. The business can be in any field you think is suitable, must be a practicable venture, and must be the kind of venture which would at least hold the promise of solvency. You must also make recommendations as to the type of business unit to establish.

Student activity 3.6

This is an individual assignment. You may have heard people say they have insurance with Lloyds of London. You will almost certainly have heard of instances where there have been aircraft accidents/terrorist attacks and it has been said that Lloyds will have to pay several millions on insurance claims.

The headquarters of Lloyds (insurance) in London is reputed to be the most expensive new building in London, at a cost of £613 million. Lloyds must, then, be an important institution that can draw on considerable resources.

Prepare an informal report on precisely what kind of organisation Lloyds is, and how it operates.

Student activity 3.7

This is an assignment for students working in pairs. It has been said that, essentially, representative government should be accountable to those whom it claims to represent. The Representation of the People Act 1948 ensured that the principle of 'one man, one vote' was observed. The Act of the same name in 1969 reduced the voting age from 21 to 18. Government is therefore answerable to the people – at least at the time of a general election. The convention of ministerial responsibility has meant that ministers are accountable to Parliament for their departments.

Research the events surrounding the so-called Critchel Down case and prepare a short verbal presentation on the facts surrounding the case and the sequence of events which took place.

Student activity 3.8

This is an individual assignment. Review the newspaper coverage surrounding the resignations of Mr Michael Heseltine MP and Mr Leon Brittan MP in the early part of 1986. Prepare a set of notes based on these two resignations and the notion of ministerial responsibility. Decide whether or not both resignation cases are based on the same kind of issue.

Student activity 3.9

This is a group assignment for groups of four or five students. The idea that all businesses are in competition with each other, since they are all trying to capture a portion of our scarce resources (income) – as mentioned on page 30 – helps to some extent to explain why so much is spent on advertising. Those of you, like me, who like to watch American football probably find yourselves so wrapped up in the game that you do not consider the advertising revenue which is at stake. As an example of the sums spent on television advertising, money so spent on Superbowl XX totalled $36 million – hardly surprising when one considers that a thirty-second advertising slot costs $550,000 and the broadcast (including the game!) lasted for three and a-half hours. Not that advertising is cheap on UK television, at more than £193,000 for thirty seconds of peak weekday evening viewing time.

Prepare a presentation which could be filmed and used on a local network television station which compares the advertising media used and the message and content of two advertisements, one for a video recorder and one for a political party.

Student activity 3.10

Working in teams of four, collect copies of (colour) advertisements which appear in Sunday newspaper magazines, general interest magazines, and specialist magazines. Prepare a presentation which shows how the use of colour/ image/tone/ words/phrases, etc., has been exploited by the advertiser as a means of selling a product. Select those which you feel are successful and those which you feel are unsuccessful, saying why your team felt the way it did about the advertisements.

Skills assessable

Assignment	Skill 1	2	3	4	5	6	7	8
1	1.8	2.4 2.5	3.7 3.9	4.3	5.1	6.1		
2	1.5 1.8	2.2 2.5	3.5 3.6 3.7	4.1 4.3 4.5				
3							7.1 7.2 7.3	
4	1.4 1.5 1.6 1.8 1.9	2.2 2.4 2.5	3.4 3.5 3.6 3.7 3.9	4.3 4.4 4.5 4.6		6.1 6.2 6.3	7.5	
5	1.3 1.5	2.1 2.2 2.4 2.5	3.4 3.5 3.7	4.2 4.3 4.6		6.1 6.2 6.3		
6	1.8	2.2 2.4 2.5		4.3 4.5		6.1 6.3		
7	1.8	2.2 2.5		4.2		6.1		
8	1.8	2.2 2.4 2.5		4.6		6.1 6.3		
9	1.3 1.4 1.6 1.8 1.9	2.4 2.5	3.5 3.6 3.7 3.9 3.11	4.2 4.6		6.1		8.4 8.6
10	1.3 1.6 1.8 1.9 1.10	2.2 2.4 2.5	3.4 3.5 3.6 3.7 3.9 3.11	4.1 4.2 4.10	5.1 5.10	6.1 6.2	7.5	8.3 8.4 8.5 8.6

4
THE MAJOR FORCES CREATING CHANGE

We live in a world which has not only been made smaller by improvements in communication technology but which is constantly being changed by technological developments of all types. Our working and social lives will be so radically different from those of our parents that the change we have to face threatens the mental health of many. The requirement for us to adapt to change and the need to be able to cope with the pressures change brings puts a strain on all which few relish and with which only a minority appear to be able to cope satisfactorily. This chapter considers the causes of change.

Causes of change

All organisations must operate within an *environment* – that is, none operates in isolation. We can refer to this as the *external environment* since it surrounds the organisation. There is little an organisation can do to change this external environment, the best most can do is to *react* to changes that occur here – the better organisations *plan*. As stated in Chapter 2 organisations are *systems* in that they consist of many different parts (sub-systems) such as finance, production, personnel, sales, and so on. Organisations (systems) are said to be *open systems* because they are open to the influence(s) of factors in the external environment which are beyond their control. This external environment consists of many influences (environmental factors) which organisations must cope with. Such environmental factors may be economic, legal, social, political, demographic, and technological. The activities of competitors will be a factor over which organisations may again have little or no control, since such activities are also a part of the external environment. A change in any one of these factors will almost certainly have an impact on an organisation.

• *List five economic events/conditions which you think are likely to influence a small retail organi-sation and say how changes in these economic events/conditions will affect the organisation.*

The six factors listed above are the *major* elements of the environment within which organisations (in both the private- and the public-sector of the economy) must operate. While a change in one factor in isolation will affect various organisations in varying degrees, it is important to note that such a change will almost certainly have a knock-on effect, with other environmental considerations also being affected. For example, a technological change will probably have economic and social implications, while a political change may cause legal and demographic changes. Thus, a seemingly insignificant change in an economic factor may have considerable impact on organisations as a result of a social development initiated by that economic change. These six factors, though of considerable significance, are not the only factors in the external environment. We could also consider other 'general' areas such as the value system within which an organisation operates (see Chapter 3 for an explanation of the term *value system*), the atmosphere or 'culture' predominant in the country where the organisation operates, the general level or standard of education, and the general level of industrialisation.

• *Consider an example of a technological change which occurred within the last year which had a social and economic impact.*

The external environment can be considered from two points of view in relation to organisations: first we may wish to consider those factors listed earlier as, say, the 'general' or 'obvious' environment and, secondly, it may be useful to consider a much more specific external environment – the 'task' environment – so called because it relates to those factors which are relevant to the tasks of an individual organisation. Such 'task' factors include the forces generated by, for example, customers, competitors, and suppliers specific to an organisation.

While organisations have to contend with the rigours of the external environment, they must also control their own *internal environments*. The internal environment of an organisation is the collection of factors which affect the operations of the organisation and over which the organisation *can* exercise control. For example, we could include areas such as labour relations, motivation, the prospects for promotion, training, supervision, social relationships at work, the organisational structure, working conditions, reward systems, and

Fig. 4.1 Can you think of other people who play a part in the external environment of organisations?

the atmosphere or 'culture' *within* the organisation (amongst others) as areas within the internal environment which have an impact on employees. Similarly, we could consider other internal factors which, in this instance, would have an impact on management and management's ability to do its job. The issues here would include: management's ability to manage; control systems in the organisation; leadership styles; forecasting and planning.

Let us now consider, in more detail, the 'general' factors likely to bring about change.

Economic factors

The economic forces which will have an impact on the activities of organisations range from issues which will affect the nation as a whole (the so-called macroeconomic issues), such as unemployment, inflation and the balance of payments, to those factors which may only impinge on one organisation (so-called microeconomic issues), such as demand for the products of a single organisation or the demand for labour exhibited by one organisation (see Chapter 13 for an explanation of the term *demand*).

* *What effect will a change in a macroeconomic factor have on organisations in (a) the private sector of the economy and (b) the public sector of the economy?*

If we take some of these factors and look at them in more detail the effect of changes in them can be shown to be significant. Inflation, the situation of persistent increases in the price level (an erosion in the value of money over time), affects all organisations to varying degrees, depending on what is thought to be the cause of current inflation and the degree to which such a cause affects those organisations. Some argue that inflation is caused by excessive wage demands, which force up an organisation's costs. If this is the case you might be able to see that, should inflation rise, organisations will attempt to raise their prices in an effort to maintain profit margins. Thus, a change in an economic variable has had an effect on organisations. In turn, consumers notice that they are having to pay more for products. Because most consumers are also producers (workers) they simply ask for a pay rise – and we are back at square one with wage demands. It is this circular movement (leading to an upward movement in prices) which is said to be an *inflationary spiral*.

There are others who argue that prices rise not in response to rising costs of production but, rather, as part of a natural process in economies where goods are allocated according to a price system and where there is excess demand. The issue of demand and the workings of a price system are considered in more detail in Chapter 13. However, at this stage let me briefly explain the premise that excess demand causes inflation. The argument is that since there are more people with money (bidding that money for goods which are in short supply) than there are people who are willing to sell goods at prevailing prices, something has to give. What gives is the price. The only way allocation problems like this can be solved in an economy where buyers and sellers are free to operate as they see fit (the capitalist sector of mixed economies – see Chapter 3, *Value systems*) is for prices to rise, thus cutting off some of the demand. This rise may not be sufficient to equate supply with demand, so another price rise takes place. The process will continue until supply equals demand. If this is the cause of inflation then, again, you may be able to see what kind of an impact it will have on organisations.

In general, inflation is bad for most organisations since most will be likely to lose something as a result. If organisations have to spend time and resources trying to combat the effects of inflation they cannot be devoting their all to the aim(s) of the organisation. Only a few, such as those who find their stock, for example, has inflated in price, win anything from inflation. (See Chapter 14 for a discussion of government policy and prices.)

- *If you were in a position to be able to attempt to reduce inflation, what would you do if (a) you felt it was caused by excessive wage demands and (b) you felt it was caused by excess demand?*

Another macroeconomic condition is that of unemployment. The number of people who are willing to work but cannot find employment has increased over the years to such an extent that many now argue we, and other Western countries, will always have a large pool of unemployed. There are a number of educational establishments and private-sector organisations that are gearing themselves up for the full-scale launch of the leisure industry which will, to some extent, be providing facilities for the masses who are out of work or who do not work, say, a forty-hour week.

- *What is the likely impact of mass unemployment among school-leavers on an organisation producing home computers?*
- *Can you think of an activity that may benefit from the fact that there are many people with plenty of free time on their hands as a result of unemployment?*

The condition of the balance of payments (discussed in more detail in Chapter 15) also affects organisations. The balance of payments is always said to balance, as an accounting technique, but will more often than not have a deficit or surplus balancing item. That is, there is never likely to be an exact equality between the value of goods sold overseas and the value of goods bought from foreign suppliers. If we are in the position, as a nation, where we have a surplus balance, then we must have sold more than we bought (from overseas). However, this surplus balance may lead to problems since we have had money flowing into the country (people have earned more) but goods flowing out.

- *There is likely, therefore, to be excess money in the system – could this be inflationary? Explain.*

On the other hand, we may have a deficit balance, which means that the nation must have bought more from overseas producers than we sold to overseas buyers. What we must ask ourselves is: How can we pay for these goods/services? While the flow of goods/services into the country may be beneficial from the point of view of our standard of living (assuming this is related to the number of goods we have), it does create the problem that we have to finance this activity at the end of the day. It may also be the case that people are buying foreign, rather than British, goods, which could lead to unemployment here.

- *How is a surplus on the balance of payments likely to affect organisations in this country?*
  How is a deficit on the balance of payments likely to affect organisations in this country?

We have only considered three of the many economic variables which can affect organisations. A significant point to consider is – what happens when one or more of these variables changes? What impact will the change(s) have on organisations and how well will organisations react to the changes? Furthermore, what happens to those organisations that are not able to respond quickly to changes in economic conditions? All that has been said in connection with macroeconomic issues will also apply to the microeconomic issues, such as the demand for the product of a firm, the impact on local organisations of the need to price labour, the effect of competition on firms, etc.

Any change in an economic variable, whether that variable is a macroeconomic issue or a microeconomic condition, will have an impact on organisations in both the private- and the public-sector of the economy (see page 5). Some organisations, as a result of good planning or good management or luck (or a combination of all three) will survive change – others will suffer. There will, of course, be the instigators of change: those innovative organisations which set things in motion; the creative, far-sighted entrepreneurs who see an opportunity in a market. Not all organisations will suffer from change or have to cope with it; some bring about change for their own sakes. Consider the examples of Stanley Kalms of Dixons who changed people's attitudes and created a demand for pocket calculators in 1972, or Alan Sugar (*Alan Michael Sugar Trading* – AMSTRAD), who in 1985 initiated change in the field of document preparation by showing the man in the street that he could afford to own a personal computer/word processor.

Legal factors

All organisations, from the smallest to the largest, in the public- and in the private-sector of the economy, have to operate within the legal environment created by various Acts of Parliament and case law in this country. The legal environment also comprises rules and regulations made and enforced by government departments through delegated legislation.

- *How does a* Bill *become an* Act *in Parliament?*
- *What is meant by 'case law'?*
- *What does 'delegated legislation' mean, and why does it exist?*

To give an idea of the areas of law with which a business has to contend, consider activities within the business, from the initial setting-up of the organisation through to actual trading. First, an organisation has to be formed. Let's assume we decide to set up a company – the first area of law with which we will come into contact is the *Companies Act 1981* (see Chapter 3 for an explanation of how to set up a company).

Once we have established the legal context within which we will operate we must then obtain resources with which to work; we will need raw materials, property (premises), labour, and capital (in the form of both machines and money). This will take us into further legal fields – for example, as far as raw materials are concerned we will be involved in *contract law*; to obtain premises we will be involved in areas of *land law* such as freehold or leasehold methods of holding property; for labour

we will be involved in regulations contained within successive *Employment Acts* (this area could be further extended by the introduction of regulations relating to the activities of *trade unions* or by the effects of *health and safety* legislation); while the area of obtaining money and machinery brings us around to *contract law* again. So far we have met:

companies legislation
contract law
land law
employment legislation

and we have not yet begun production!

When we eventually begin production we will have to contend with regulations governing the amount of pollution we emit, the noise we make, the nuisances we may create or the products which we may produce negligently.

When we try to sell our products there will be regulations concerning what we can say in advertisements, our trading standards, and the claims we may make for our product. We will also be regulated by the Sale of Goods Act (1979), and by the whole body of contract law.

Since what has been said applies to all private-sector organisations – with the exception of the legislation relating to company establishment, which would not apply to sole traders or partnerships (see pages 19–21) – you should be able to see that such organisations operate within a somewhat restrictive legal environment.

Public-sector organisations have their legal problems and pitfalls, too. They are also bound by contract legislation, employment legislation, land law, health and safety legislation, etc. It is not uncommon for members of the public to take court action against a Government department or Minister of the State for what is considered to be action which is *ultra vires* (beyond their powers).

- *Identify a situation which occurred within the recent past in which a Government department or a Minister was found to have acted* ultra vires *What was the decision of the court concerned?*

Any changes in the law will affect organisations and their activities. Given that some areas of the law (such as employment legislation) are changed with alarming frequency, it is hardly surprising to note that many organisations every year find themselves the victims of legal action. Any change in the law is likely to have wide-ranging implications for both the private- and the public-sector of the economy.

When the Data Protection Act came into effect in May 1986, it was estimated that more than 2000 firms which ought to have registered had failed to do so – the change in the law took them by surprise.

Political factors

The political environment which affects organisations can be viewed from the point of view of the domestic political scene, i.e. what happens within this country in connection with local or central government, or from the point of view of the external (international) political scene. When considering the domestic political environment and change, along with the associated impact on organisations, half a dozen of the more obvious events which spring to mind are:

- the events of 1 April 1986 concerning the abolition of the GLC and other Metropolitan County Councils;
- the issue of ratecapping (see task on page 27);
- local democracy *v* central-government control;
- the emergence of a third force in British politics (the SDP/Liberal Alliance);
- the impact of a Government with an overwhelming Parliamentary majority (Conservative Government after re-election in 1983);
- tighter control of public expenditure.

Each of these events could have initiated a political impact on organisations in this country to such an extent that the resulting change forced private- and public-sector organisations to react. The impact, for example, of the abolition of the GLC was more generally felt by public-sector organisations who had to fill the gap left by the GLC's demise. This change brought about considerable reallocation of resource use in London boroughs. Ratecapping had its advocates and adversaries from both the private- and public-sector of the economy. The private-sector businesses argued, among other things, that without sufficient funding local authorities could not spend on the infrastructure, which adversely affected the opportunities faced by business for making profits. The public sector was concerned about the employment prospects of existing employees (redundancies, promotion, pay and conditions comparable with private-sector employees, etc), and the provision of services.

- *How much money does your local authority spend (per annum) on provision for social services? Construct a chart and a diagram showing how this expenditure has changed over the last five years. What are the implications of*

the changing pattern of expenditure and the actual amounts spent?

The issue of local democracy versus central-government control is one which has been discussed for many years and which has implications for organisations. Essentially, if local government is to be permitted to do the things it was elected to do it needs finance. The major source of this finance would come from the rates system and a major contributor is the industrial and commercial sector. Thus, any change in emphasis in favour of the local democracy issue would be likely to have a considerable impact on the business community.

- *Find out how much is charged in rates to four businesses that are close to your college/place of work. Compare these charges with the amounts charged to the owners of domestic property.*

The emergence of the SDP/Liberal Alliance as a political force to be reckoned with meant the realisation that different economic/political emphasis may be pursued if they either come to power in their own right or hold the balance of power. The implication of this would be the resulting (political) change and its impact on organisations.

- *What are the essential components of the economic policies of:*
  the Conservative Party
  the Labour Party
  the SDP/Liberal Alliance.

The overwhelming majority of seats held/won by the Conservative Government which was re-elected after the 1983 election meant that, in theory, the Government was strong enough to institute policies which may have had enormous impact on the way we do business,. or conduct public-sector organisational activity. In fact, there were a number of occasions when the Government was defeated – as a result of backbench rebellion – thus ensuring that some of the (arguably) more radical proposals were not initiated.

- *What was proposed as a result of the Shops Bill (1986) and why did it face so much opposition during the vote in April 1986?*

The effect of tighter control of public spending was to change some conditions in the public- and private-sector of the economy which would remain in their new, altered, state even if public-expenditure control was relaxed. For example, the *change in attitudes* of parents towards teachers (notably adversely affected by tight control on government expenditure) as a result of arbitrary teacher industrial action in 1985/6; and the *changes among teaching staff*, many of whom left teaching to take up employment in the private sector, which offered better pay and more employment benefits. The field of education also provides another example of how tight control on public spending affected an important and large area of provision in the public sector. Because of poor conditions of employment and the proposed changes in contracts of employment and contractual duties of teachers in 1985/6 there was much disruption in school activities. The consequence of this was the notable increase in attendance at private-sector schools during 1985/6 specifically.

Controls on public spending had an effect on other areas, such as the collection of refuse which, in many areas, was privatised – again, an impact of change felt by a private-sector organisation (the winner of the contract to collect refuse) and a public-sector organisation (redundancies among local-authority dustmen).

An important point to consider is that even if local-government expenditure controls are relaxed, would this change the situation concerning the teachers and their perceived grievance? And would it allow the reintroduction of public-sector refuse collection?

In the area of international politics there are changes being instituted which are of a political nature and which affect organisations in this country. The activities of organisations such as the EEC are further discussed in Chapter 15. The outcome of action of a political nature, generated by this and other similar organisations, could well have considerable impact on domestic organisations, too. Bear in mind that we do not operate in isolation in the UK – we are affected by the actions of others, and our own actions affect the activities of others.

One area where we can concentrate attention is that of *extreme* political activity abroad which affects organisations in this country, such as terrorist action and wars. The activities of terrorists may seem far removed from the realm of business or public-sector organisations but they are, in fact, closer than many of us think. If you consider terrorist activity in various parts of the world, one thing that ought immediately to spring to mind is the *nature* of the activity. If the action taken is indiscriminate bombing, consider the impact on the business community. How can shopkeepers conduct business with any degree of normality when they and customers fear for their lives? What are the implications from the point of view of insurance?

- *What inducements does the British Government offer businessmen to encourage them to establish businesses in Northern Ireland? Why does it offer such inducements?*
- *If the terrorist action is likely to be the kidnapping of prominent businessmen, what precautions are their employers likely to take (a) to lessen the risks faced by their employees and (b) to pay any ransom demanded?*
- *What are the cost implications for the organisation which has to take such precautions? What are the implications from the point of view of competitiveness?*

There was once a time when terrorist activity was directed towards military or diplomatic personnel, but by mid-1986 such attacks on, for example, US businesses outnumbered those on the aforementioned targets. It is now felt that businesses have become an 'easy' target in the sense that, while the terrorists may prefer to kill a prime minister or high ranking diplomatic official, businesses are subject to much less stringent protection. Security surrounding our Prime Minister, for example, is much greater than that associated with all the major banks in the area where you live.

If one considers the available data for the number of recorded worldwide terrorist incidents, and compares that with the number of incidents directed at businesses, it will be seen that the percentage of such attacks to be directed at business targets has increased from 27% in 1983 to 36% only two years later (data from Risks International, an American security consultancy). By 'businesses' do not be misled into thinking solely about permanent structures (buildings) which can be the subject of terrorist attack. In 1985 the world watched in despair as terrorists seized the liner *Achille Lauro*, and in May 1986 police had to step up security around cross-Channel ferries as a result of suspected car-bomb attacks.

However, not all business will suffer from the effects of terrorism – some *make* it their business. The American firm Risks International charge $1500 a day to advise corporations on security. In 1985 Western airlines had to pay $900 million in insurance premiums.

Another factor to consider is the impact on businessmen in this country who trade with others with whom it is felt we ought not to have trade relationships. One example is trade with a country such as Libya, which, during April 1986, was publicly claimed to be a base for the training of terrorists. A similar argument on moral grounds, though not one levelled as a result of terrorist action, was aimed at those who trade with or who have business connections with South Africa. The argument in this instance concerned the ethics of dealing with a country which practised apartheid.

The incidence of war is a major political issue which has implications for organisations, and the final one that we shall consider here. UK organisations will be affected either because of the impact on supply of their raw materials or the impact on a market for their products. The issue of raw materials is significant because it tends to have an immediate effect on producers in other countries. If I cannot get raw materials I cannot manufacture. On the other hand, if the country that I used to export to is experiencing internal unrest or is at war, I *may* be able to find another market. A link with the previous discussion is that terrorism has been likened to 'war on a budget' – a cheap way of forcing readjustment on the part of major powers.

Demographic factors

Demography refers to the *size* and *structure* of population. There are a number of ways in which the impact of change in a demographic factor will be felt by organisations in the private- and public-sectors of the economy. To appreciate the impact of a demographic change one needs to consider areas such as the following:

1. The size of the population and the significance of its size.
2. The structure, in terms of age and sex.
3. The distribution of the population geographically.
4. Occupational distribution within the population.
5. The needs of the population.

It is only when you appreciate the overall concept of demographic changes that you can appreciate the needs of the population and how these needs may change over time.

The *size* of the population is determined by three variables:

a) the number of babies born per year (birth rate);
b) the number of people who die per year (death rate);
c) the net effect of immigration and emigration (migration rate).

• *Obtaining data from the* Annual Abstract of Statistics *produce a chart which shows the size of the UK population for every year since the year you were born. Prepare a short visual presentation to demonstrate the changes.*

The biggest fear concerning population growth is that of insufficient resources. The earliest exponent of this situation was the Reverend Malthus (*Essay on Population*, 1798), who claimed that rate of growth of food supplies could be measured in an arithmetic progression (e.g. 2, 4, 6, 8, 10) but the rate of growth in population size was to be considered from the point of view of a geometric ratio (e.g. 2, 4, 8, 16, 32). The result would be that population growth would outstrip food supply.

• *Malthusian theory has yet to be proved correct. Why do you think population growth has not outstripped food supplies?*

As the size of the population changes so will demand for a multitude of goods/services. Public- and private-sector organisations have to be ready for such a change. One of the implications, for example, of a population which is growing in size is that more people are going to demand medical services – thus the National Health Service in the UK will need more resources.

Of equal significance to the size of the population is the *structure*, especially the *age structure*.

• *From your own research, obtain data showing the age structure of the UK population. Plot the changes using this year and data for 20 years ago for each age group and draw conclusions about the age structure in the form of an informal report.*

The age structure is significant in relation to the type of demand for products/services which confront public- and private-sector organisations. Suppose, for example, that the age structure is such that there are proportionately more younger than older people in the country. The demand in terms of public-sector health-care provision will probably be weighted in favour of maternity and paediatric facilities. The demand in the private sector will be for those things that the younger members of the population want. Take, for example, holidays; the demand may be for adventurous, lively holidays with plenty of facilities for sports and other 'recreational' activities. If, on the other hand, the population is ageing (i.e. there are proportionately more older than younger people), the demand for health-care facilities, for example, will be aimed at geriatric provision, and the demand in the private sector may be for more cheap, winter-sun (OAP) holidays.

Any change in the age structure of the population is likely to set in motion reactions within the public and private sector of the economy. Bear in mind that such reactions in, say, the public sector of the economy are likely to have repercussions within the private sector, too.

The *sex structure* refers to the relationship between the number of males and the number of females in the population.

- *Obtain data showing the breakdown of the population according to age and sex structure. What does this data tell you about the sex structure of the UK population?*
- *What are the implications of the differences in sex structure as per age grouping in the UK population?*

The geographical distribution in the UK, as the term implies, refers to the dispersion of the population between Scotland, Wales, Northern Ireland, and the regions of England.

- *Obtain statistics which show the geographical distribution of the UK population. In groups of four or five discuss the reasons why some regions have a relatively larger population than others. After discussion in small groups each group should elect a spokesperson to put forward the views of his/her group to the rest of the class. General discussion to follow.*
- *Having completed the previous task, discuss the implications for organisations of changes in the geographical distribution of the population.*

Occupational *distribution* refers to the distribution of people among the various occupations which exist. Occupational *mobility* concerns the ease with which people can move from one job to another. In one sense the degree of occupational mobility measures the relative skill transferability of workers. It is the aim of a course such as the BTEC National Diploma to put you in a position whereby you can obtain, practise, and perfect specific business-related skills. In other words, such a course attempts to give students skills which are transferable. The greater *mobility* enjoyed by workers the less likely they are to suffer from unemployment. That is not to say that all unemployment can be cured by increasing the transferable skills of employees – but a measure of unemployment *is* due to relative (occupational) immobility.

- *Give three examples of people from specific occupational areas who have become unemployed in this country because their own organisation has ceased to trade and who are still unemployed even though there are different jobs available in their area.*

When we talk of labour mobility we are, therefore, saying something about the ease with which workers can move from one job to another. Another aspect of this is the geographical mobility demonstrated by employees. This refers to the ease with which unemployed people can move from one area to another to obtain work.

- *What do you think causes relative geographical immobility?*
- *This is a discussion topic which can be dealt with in groups of four or five. Suppose there was a change in educational policy such that more vocationally relevant courses were run in schools – what do you think would be the impact on employers in this country?*

To conclude this section on population and the impact of changes on organisations in that respect, let us finally consider people in terms of their needs. We can consider needs from the point of view of (a) individual needs and (b) collective needs. As an individual I have specific needs which I suspect are not very different from your individual needs. Many people would argue that we need certain commodities to ensure that we sustain an acceptable standard of living. The implication is that standard of living is related to the holding/consumption of goods/services. Now, that may well be true for the majority of people but before we go further it should be emphasised that, as far as a significant minority are concerned, goods/services *alone* do not affect standard of living. I would feel, for example, that I had a very poor standard of living if my life were full of goods but I could not walk in pleasant surroundings and breathe fresh air or surf in the ocean without fear of contracting disease from pollution or being exposed to radiation from atomic waste.

Since it is important that we at least appreciate that others do not always share our beliefs, it is sometimes necessary to remind ourselves that there are various ways of looking at an issue. For simplicity, let us assume that some items of consumption are necessary to sustain an acceptable standard of living. For us in the UK that may mean not only the basic requirements such as warmth, food, clothing, and shelter but also certain consumer items such as a (colour?) television, a washing machine, and a car.

A basic need we all have is for employment of some kind. There may be many among you who perhaps view the prospect of not having to work as desirable. However, many of those who are out of work and who have little prospect of employment will tell you that one of the first things to suffer is one's sense of dignity. A person *needs* gainful employment. It may be that the desire to work stems from the desire we have to obtain the resources which can be used to buy material goods (to improve our standard of living?). Whatever your opinion, opportunities must exist for people to be able to make enough for themselves and their families. Any change in the material needs of individuals will have an impact on organisations in the UK, in both sectors of the economy.

The collective needs mentioned earlier concern society in general. Societies have specific requirements in order for them to operate efficiently and equitably. Such requirements include: the existence of a legal system, coupled with respect for law and order; the existence of good health-care facilities which are open to all; adequate educational facilities; and an effective infrastructure (transport and communications).

The needs of *individuals* and *collective* needs are not unrelated. Suppose, for example, that I and many like me have an individual need for a car. When our needs are fulfilled and the number of cars on the roads increases it will not be long before we (collectively) display a demand for motorways, better accident and breakdown facilities, and more parking spaces. We thus have individual needs which stimulate collective needs.

It could well be that our collective needs, which must be met by producing and distributing goods/services, could not be adequately organised by many small, independent businesses. The larger the size of a population therefore, the more likely it is that a change in the scale of organisations becomes necessary. As population grows, the organisations which once served it (which were themselves probably small) can no longer do all that is required. Organisations which need to expand will often benefit from *economies of scale* in their activities.

- *What is meant by 'economies of scale'?*

It is probable that many functions could not be carried out by small organisations – consider the provision of water or electricity to whole regions of the country, each of which serves millions of people. There would also be problems in other areas of the public sector. Consider the situation which might arise if, in every large city in the country, political organisation was conducted in many small, discrete, elected units – each representing a few streets or a neighbourhood. Since cities have problems which often require concerted action on many fronts, would it not be naive to assume that the existence of neighbourhood elected areas would yield the overall political cohesion necessary?

As the population expands, not only do organisations expand, but they also tend to change their structure (see page 12 for an explanation of organisational structure). Organisations also experience a change in performance, as mentioned earlier, as a result of economies of scale. An interesting issue, from the point of view of the consumer, is that organisations which produce on a large scale, with specialised technology, produce for the mass market. With large markets and large suppliers it is no longer feasible to cater for idiosyncrasies or impulses – standardisation becomes the norm. This means consumers also have to change – they often have to modify their demands.

The impact of changes in population on government is not an area on which many of us tend to dwell. I have spent some time discussing how changes in various aspects of demography have an impact on organisations in the public and private sector but have not yet gone into any detail with regard to what is possibly the most significant of the public-sector organisations – the Government. The influence of the size of the population on the form of government has been an issue which philosophers have discussed since the time of Plato.

Perhaps the most useful contribution was set forth in 1762 by Jean-Jacques Rousseau (in *The Social Contract*) who suggested that every member of society enters into a 'social contract' simply by the act of his being and remaining a member of that society. This contract calls into existence a 'collective moral body' made up of all citizens, who jointly exercise sovereign power. This means that everyone has a dual role in that they are sharers in the sovereignty of the state on the one hand, while being subjects of the state on the other. The significance of this is that sovereignty is viewed as being the will of the people – not the will in terms of a unanimous view but a situation where 'every voice was taken into account': the legitimacy of government rests on its actions being consistent with the will of the people.

It was noted earlier in this chapter that one of the variables which determines the size of the population is the migration rate. Since the percentage of the UK population from an immigrant background (e.g. first and second generation, in particular) has increased, we can expect to see this play an increasingly important role in British politics. We are, for example, beginning to see the emergence (and the recognition of by the major political parties) of the so-called 'black' vote. The Labour Party, in 1985, came close to having an official 'black' section.

The size of the population also has an important effect on government administration, since this is less efficient the larger the size of the population, and the costs of administration increase excessively even with the use of computerisation.

Any change in the composition or size of the population is likely to have an impact on government, and may need to be met by a corresponding change in the *machinery* of government.

Technological factors

We are living in a world of rapid technological change which is affecting all organisations. We could consider technological change from the point of view of new raw materials used; from the point of view of new forms of power used in manufacture; or from the point of view of the machinery and equipment used in both productive and leisure activities. From whichever point we consider the impact of technology it cannot be denied that organisations have been subject to rapid change to an extent that has never before been experienced by either private- or public-sector organisations.

- *List half a dozen raw materials available to today's manufacturer that were not available to manufacturers more than twenty years ago.*
- *As a class, discuss the many ways of generating electricity which have been proposed in the past twenty years. Consider the drawbacks of each form.*
- *What technological changes have you noticed in your home, around the town where you live, and in the place where you work/study?*

The most exciting and potentially powerful technological advance within the past ten years has been the use of *microchips*. With the aid of these components, manufacturers can now produce such powerful computers, word processors, and other electronic equipment that the face of the entire public and private sectors of the economy has been changed. We can now use computers to assist in design and manufacture (CAD/CAM systems); no self-respecting secretarial pool will be without word processors, ultra-modern facsimile (fax) equipment, and space-age telecommunications systems; local authorities have their own computers, with a wide range of applications; colleges and schools use computers: even the once very traditional legal system is now offered a number of computer packages to make life easier.

The significant point is the impact that such technology is having on the working lives of employees. Technological change brings about higher labour productivity – that is, a given volume of output can be produced with less labour.

- *What applications has your college found for computers? Discuss usage with the rest of your class, and try to identify other areas where a computer could be used to help in the running of the organisation.*
- *What applications has your local authority found for computers? Discuss usage with the rest of your class and try to identify other areas where a computer could be used to help in the running of the organisation.*

Technological change has hit the retail industry with force, too. The next time you are shopping consider the use of technologically advanced equipment now at the disposal of retailers: cash tills that can send information to stock control; tills that work out how much change to give so that the correct amount is always given to customers, and organisations can employ less skilled till operators; the use of bar codes on packages so cashiers do not even have to punch in the amount of a transaction; the use of sophisticated stock control techniques, with hand-held devices that can record the quantity of stock on a shelf rapidly, etc.

The many changes in technology that have taken place have occurred with such pace that the legal system has, in many areas, failed to keep abreast. There is no legal limit, for example, on the number of hours one can be asked to work in front of a VDU screen, although manufacturers recommend fairly strict time limits with specific breaks away from the

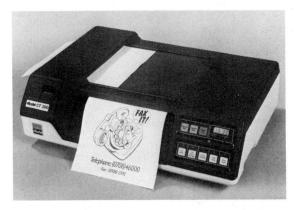

Fig. 4.2 Among the internal environmental factors we can include new technological equipment

screen (employers can and do set their own limits). The law has problems keeping up with technology.

Many years ago, the games children played tended to reflect the type of society they were entering. I particularly remember playing a game where we had to protect a team-member from being hit by a ball while he risked his neck to construct an object before actually being hit. It sounds crazy now, but that game taught us a lot about team activities and comradeship and trust in colleagues. Today, the games young people play, such as space-invader-type games and other computer packages, tend to be individualistic, pitting one person against another or against the machine. Are we preparing people for the future, where manual dexterity and no trace of techno-fear are important? More importantly, are we preparing people for change?

Assignments

Student activity 4.1

This is an individual assignment. From observation of the environment surrounding your college/place of work, consider any possible situations/events which are likely to affect the organisation in question, saying whether they are likely to be

a) economic,
b) political,
c) social,
d) technological, or
e) demographic.

Say how such situations may affect the organisation and what you would do to compensate for the effects (assuming they are thought to be undesirable) if you were in a position to do so.

Student activity 4.2

This assignment is to be completed by working in groups of four or five. Obtain a copy of the *Sunday Times* for 27 April 1986 from your library and review the article in *Business News 2* (page 85) concerning a speech made by Lord Sieff to the Royal Society of Arts.

Lord Sieff mentioned a need for a *change in the attitude* of teachers in *connection with industry*. Prepare a briefing document for the use of your group members in a discussion with the business studies staff at your college (a briefing document is a set of notes for action or notes of your objectives, *plus* anticipated obstacles/reactions, followed by

your response(s) to such obstacles/reactions). This discussion (which you can organise) should consider the issue of change and the attitude/responsiveness of educationists to change. Elect one of your group as a chairperson.

Student activity 4.3

This is an individual assignment. The article shown opposite concerns the effect of change – change in the price of oil and its impact on other variables.

In the form of an informal report consider

a) what kind of changes (e.g. political, economic, etc.) are likely to result from the event which led to the article,
b) who is likely to be affected by the changes you noted in (a) above,
c) the long-term effect on the oil industry of lower oil prices (particularly North Sea oil companies).

Student activity 4.4

This is an individual assignment. Consider a recent change in the area of (a) employment law or (b) consumer legislation. In the form of a short article for a business magazine, show how the change in question affected various sectors of the population. Say what the impact was, and indicate who you think the law affected most.

Student activity 4.5

Work in groups of three or four on this task. Over the years changes in circumstances have resulted in the dereliction and waste seen on many (previously profitable, fully-employed) sites throughout the country. Examples include the giant buildings which lie empty at sites such as the Royal Victoria Docks in London's East End, old textile mills in Lancashire and Yorkshire, disused steel works in Wales, and empty and idle open spaces throughout the country. Change, primarily economic in nature, has left scars on the face of the country.

Your group have to conduct research into the area/site of your choice which will enable you to prepare a display (photographs/articles/ memoirs/anecdotes/notes, etc.) which should show what the area/site looked like at the height of its success and what the area looks like today.

Prepare a group strategy which will rejuvenate the site/area. You may assume that this is merely an exercise in showing what can be done to an area to revitalise it, do not worry about having to obtain

Coal price split widens

NEGOTIATIONS between the National Coal Board and the Central Electricity Generating Board over the price of coal for power stations are 'going very badly', according to close observers of the talks.

The CEGB wants to cut its £3 billion coal bill by £500m this year in the wake of falling oil prices, which have made British coal uneconomic as a source of power.

If the CEGB wins in the negotiations, this will be even more difficult to achieve without widespread cuts in the mining industry. A study by Dr Bill Robinson of the London Business School, to be published this week, suggests that up to 100,000 mining jobs could be lost in the quest for profitability by the Coal Board.

Electricity industry chiefs believe that they have Mrs Thatcher on their side in the battle to cut the price of the 75m tonnes of coal they burn annually, which could ultimately lead to a cut of 6% in the price of electricity.

The energy department is steering clear of the battle between the two nationalised industries. 'It is purely a commercial matter between the two industries,' an energy department official said.

Source: *The Sunday Times* (Business News 2), 27 April 1986

planning permission. Suggest a venture which you think would be welcome in the area.

Your display should take on the appearance of the type of display seen at public demonstrations of proposed planning/development ventures. You may like to invite local industrialists/retailers/dignitaries/residents to your college to view the 'proposals' and comment on your work.

Skills assessable

Assignment	*Skill* 1	2	3	4	5	6	7	8
1	1.8	2.1 2.2 2.4				6.1 6.2 6.3		
2	1.3 1.5 1.8	2.2 2.5	3.2 3.5 3.6 3.7	4.3 4.6 4.10		6.1 6.2		
3	1.3 1.5 1.8 1.10	2.2 2.4 2.5		4.3 4.6				
4	1.3 1.4 1.6 1.8 1.9	2.1 2.2 2.4 2.5		4.3 4.6 4.5 4.6		6.1 6.2 6.3 6.4	7.5	
5	1.3 1.4 1.5 1.6 1.8 1.9 1.10	2.2 2.4 2.5 2.7	3.4 3.5 3.6 3.7 3.9 3.11	4.2 4.3 4.6		6.1 6.2 6.3 6.4 6.6	7.5	8.3 8.4 8.6

5
THE IMPACT OF CHANGE AND RESPONSES TO IT (1)

Change can be initiated by many factors within society and the responses to change are themselves many and varied. Since change is a phenomenon which we all have to face (as consumers, as workers, as employers) it is appropriate at this stage that we consider the nature and extent of the likely impact of it, together with the responses it generates.

Ryuzaburo Kaku, President of the Japanese camera company Canon, has stated that 'society changes and a company must foresee it first'. The implication of this for organisations is there for all to see – if you fail to notice change or fail to respond in time, you do so at your own peril. In Chapter 4 we considered the many ways in which change could be initiated in both the external and the internal environments of organisations. In this chapter I would like to give you a slightly different view by considering *the impact* of such external environmental issues as political and legal change, technological change, and changes in the mode of production. The impact of changes in marketing strategy and the impact of changes in the internal environment (changes in the structure of an organisation) will be considered in Chapter 6.

Political and legal change

Political change

We have already seen that political change can mean change brought about by the domestic political scene or the international political scene. In order to consider the impact and response(s), let us consider change in the domestic political scene first.

- *What do you understand by political change?*

Changes of a political nature – that is, changes concerned with the government of a country – range from extreme or major changes, such as a change of government, to marginal governmental changes, such as minor amendments to government policy at the local level.

In the category of political change, let us first consider what I have referred to above as an *extreme or major* political change and its implications. A change in government always brings with it new brooms, whether that change is a complete change to a new political party, or whether the change is exhibited merely by a re-elected government restructuring itself. If we take the first case of a government after a general election being of a different political persuasion than its predecessor, the resultant change should be quite clear. Although we have seen the emergence of a strong third political force in Britain (SDP/Liberal Alliance) through the latter part of the seventies and into the eighties, the country still has basically a two-party system (Conservative Party and Labour Party). Whenever a complete change of government occurs, for example, as in 1979 when the Labour government lost its position to a Conservative government, we expect to see major changes in relation to the policies pursued by the victors.

- *What is the basic economic policy, industrial policy and foreign policy of the Labour Party?*
- *What is the basic economic policy, industrial policy and foreign policy of the Conservative Party?*

Having considered the basic policy of the two main political parties in this country you should be able to see what the implications would be of a change in government. Perhaps the simplest way to appreciate what such a change would mean is to think of the impact on specific groups within the economy.

- *If after a general election a Conservative government was formed which took the place of what had previously been a Labour government, what do you think would be the effect on*

  a) *economic policy as it affects small businesses (in what way(s) would it be altered?)*
  b) *foreign policy with regard to our relationship with the USA, the USSR and the EEC?*
  c) *policy in connection with the National Health Service and Education. In order to get the most from this task you will need to know what the possible position would have been if there was a Labour Government prior to the change mentioned above. Research this point as necessary.*

In terms of what I earlier referred to as *marginal*

governmental changes, you can assume that what is meant are minor changes in either central government policy or such changes in the second tier of government in this country – local government. Minor changes are more generally those variations which occur from time to time which make policy workable. It may be that the Secretary of State or a Minister has to slightly amend policy in order to win sufficient support from his own backbenchers. It could be that a local council needs to shift its position on a particular issue only very slightly to ensure that it acts within its power.

- *What is the difference between a* Secretary of State *and a* Minister?
- *Who are the* backbenchers? *What role do they perform? What power do they have? Find an example of a successful back-bench rebellion.*

In the previous chapter some examples were given of political events which could have had a considerable impact on organisations in this country (see page 38). In this chapter we are concerned primarily with the impact of change on business organisations, along with the likely responses of those organisations to such change.

If we stay with the polar view of political change it will help to establish some ideas in relation to change and organisations. The 'polar view', as I have termed it, is the observation of political events at the ends of the spectrum – in other words, extreme or major changes at one end of the spectrum and minor or marginal political changes at the other. When we are considering the impact on businesses the first issues have to be 'what and which businesses?' We could consider the impact in a very general sense on businesses in this country, or the impact on areas of business (those in specific fields), or the impact on specific types of business (e.g. sole traders, partnerships or companies – see Chapter 3 for details of the types of business unit in existence).

By way of explanation I will look initially at the impact on an area of business that could be affected by political change. Having shown the way, there will then be no reason why you should not perform a similar operation with respect to other areas of business.

Taking a major political change as the starting point, we could consider the impact on, say, the coal industry of the political decision to divert resources into the development and use of atomic power as a means of generating electricity. The initial impact on the coal industry of such a decision would obviously be a decrease in the demand for the

product of the industry – coal. Such a decrease in demand would be followed by a fall in the profitability of coal and a subsequent decrease in the demand for the services of miners by British Coal. A reduction in the number of miners in employment would have an impact on the businesses in the localities where miners live. If, for example, several miners in a village or town become unemployed, the money they would once have earned and spent is no longer available for spending. Thus, the local retailers who rely on such expenditure for their own income would be hard hit, too. The wholesalers supplying these retailers would be the next to feel the effects, then the producers, and their employees. The impact of a major political decision on a specific area ought now to be appreciated.

- *Using national newspapers reports at the time concerned, research the impact and effect, specifically on local businesses, of the year-long miners' strike which began in March 1984.*
- *Consider the impact on an area of business of your choice of a major political change.*

Bear in mind that the example of redundant miners (above) has not come about entirely because of the decision to use atomic-fired power stations. A general decline in the demand for coal has resulted in the closure of many pits in England, Scotland, and Wales. On the bright side, the Coal Board (now known as British Coal) established National Coal Board Enterprises to help redundant miners to make a new start. Hence, the impact of the change may not be an entirely negative one.

- *Consider the probable impact on one area of business of a relatively minor political change.*

We can now consider the impact of political change on *specific* types of business. One such change that springs to mind is one which was a stated objective of the Conservative Government which came to power in 1979 – that is, the reduction in formalities and 'red-tape' associated with running a small business. (I often find I am asked to define what is meant by a 'small' company or a 'medium-sized' firm. In readiness for your asking this question let me say that, as at May 1986, the Companies Act definition of a small company had been extended to cover companies with an annual turnover of less than £2 million and a balance sheet total of less than £975,000. For medium-sized companies the turnover figure was extended from £5.75 million to £8 million, while the balance sheet total was increased from £2.8 million to £3.9 million.) The requirements concerning the keeping and reporting of information to Government departments/agencies has long been recognised as being counter-productive and extremely costly to small businesses. The change brought about by the desire to free small businesses of this burden will clearly be felt by sole traders and partnerships but, more especially, the small (possibly family-run) companies. In other words, the impact will be limited to just a specific section of businesses in this country – namely, small businesses. The resulting amendment to legislation concerning small companies led to a significant reduction in the accounting burden for 90% of companies in Britain.

- *Consider what type of political change is likely to affect only a specific type of business unit in this country.*
- *What relatively minor political change that has occurred within the last year is likely to have an impact on specific types of business in your locality? What is the nature of the impact likely to be?*

We have seen in Chapter 4 that political change is not confined to this country – in other words, it is not entirely 'domestic' in nature. Some political changes that occur outside the UK's boundary do have an impact on organisations here. We have only to consider the impact on British banks of the political activities in South Africa, or the impact on British chemical manufacturers or producers of baby products of using developing African nations as test-beds for products, to appreciate how political activity can affect their positions.

- *Select an example of an organisation that has recently been affected by a political change which was international in nature. Say how the organisation was affected and why.*

Legal change

As well as political changes that affect business organisations we could also spend time considering the impact of legal changes and the responses of organisations to such change.

Changes in the law occur from time to time because the legal system has to keep up with change itself. For example, legislation concerning companies and their operations, employment conditions, trade unions, the individual and his/her rights, and so on, has been enacted and modified over the years to fit circumstances as best it can today. Very often a change in the law will affect all equally, though from time to time only the law as it relates to particular groups or organisations is changed. For example, the Consumer Credit Act 1974 imposed a liability on those concerned with arranging finance facilities for customers to hold specific licences for such action. The initial impact of this legislation was that retailers which were affected had to find hundreds of pounds to purchase licences to allow them to perform operations which they had been performing for years without such licences. The response of any trader to this type of situation can be predicted – given that businesses could not carry on as usual without a licence, those concerned had to buy one. A case like this, where the law prohibits action until certain requirements have been met, has a clearly predictable outcome since the law must always be obeyed – the consequence of non-compliance is too severe.

Another example of a change in the law which affected many businesses was the introduction of the Data Protection Act 1984. The Act imposed a requirement on organisations (some organisations were exempt) which used computers to store information on people to enrol on a register. Since many organisations had not appreciated the significance and all-embracing nature of the legislation it became apparent in early 1986 that many of them would not, in fact, have registered by the deadline set by the Data Protection Registrar. Strictly speaking, the impact of this change in the law meant that all organisations and individuals who controlled the content and use of a collection of personal data which was processed, or intended to be processed, automatically would be operating outside the law if they failed to register (failure to register being a criminal offence). However, since the Registrar apparently underestimated the number of organisations and individuals who would have to register, leniency in the timing of registration was shown. Nonetheless, there were many organisations that had not appreciated the impact of this change in the law until much too late in the day.

Finally, a political and legal change which had an impact on organisations was the Wages Bill, which became law at the end of July 1986. The impact was felt primarily by the half a million or more young people under 21 – those who lost wage protection. The impact was also felt by the employers, however. The major beneficiaries of the legislation were the hotel and catering industry, employers of one-tenth of the working population.

- *What is meant by the term 'working population'? How many people are there in the UK working population? How many of them are in work?*

It is the fast-food sector of industry which is experiencing the greatest growth, with organisations such as McDonald's hamburger chain employing 18,000 people in Britain, and their competitors, Wimpy, employing 11,000.

- *What is the implication for a fast-food chain, such as Pizzaland, which employs many young people, of the introduction of legislation concerned with removing wage protection?*

Technological change

With the rapid growth and development in technology over the past ten years it is hard to know where to start, what to include, and what to leave out of any discussion on the subject. Although this chapter is concerned with the impact of, and responses to, change in relation to businesses, it would be inappropriate to ignore its impact on households.

- *Consider a business with which you are familiar. Who is the most important person as far as that business is concerned?*

We sometimes forget that the most important person to a business is the customer. It is therefore significant to consider the impact of technological change on businesses, while keeping a close eye on the customer (households). If the customer is not happy with the new technology in your business he or she may go elsewhere.

Technology can be said to be concerned with the practical application in industry of mechanical arts and applied sciences. We can, however, see the increased use of technology in the home (Fig. 5.1, page 50).

- *List ten examples of the use of technology in the home.*

In Chapter 7 you will meet some of the applications to which new technology has been put but, for now, I will merely discuss the impact of technological change on business organisations and their responses to this area of change.

The computer has obviously been the greatest single technological change this century to affect businesses. The use of computers to store data (employee information, wage-rate data, tax information, stores, production, and materials handling data, etc.), to assist in the design and manufacture of products (computer-aided design and computer-aided manufacture) has revolutionised the manufacturing industry. The use of advanced micro-chip technology in word processors, facsimile transmission systems, data storage and retrieval systems, and videotex has transformed offices throughout the country. (A fuller explanation of all the systems mentioned above is given in Chapter 7.)

- *What impact would you say the use of a computer has had on a business with which you are familiar?*

The first two points that need to be raised by a business thinking of buying a computer are 'What type of computer would best serve our needs?' and 'in connection with what aspect of the business?' Not all computers are effective in all situations – each has its own applications. And not all aspects of a business lend themselves to computerisation.

It would be incorrect to conclude that the immediate impact of the use of computers would be job redundancies. Trained staff are needed to operate computerised systems, and, once trained, employees become a valuable resource which employers would prefer to keep – technology is not necessarily synonymous with wide-scale unemployment. The most immediate effect of the introduction of new technology is the need for staff training and development. In response to this we not only see employers providing more in-service training via their own in-house schemes but we also see them making provision for attendance at outside courses when they do not have the facilities or expertise to run such courses themselves. There is a growing awareness of the need for this type of education provision in colleges and schools throughout the country, too.

The Government has also been involved in the world of office automation and development. The Department of Trade and Industry Office Automation Strategy was launched in 1982 as a means to promote the use of new technology in the office. The Strategy aimed to match the suppliers of advanced integrated electronic office systems (such as Hewlett Packard Ltd, Racal Information Systems, IBM (UK) Ltd, Rank Xerox (UK) Ltd, and ICL, among others), and supplied public-sector users (such as BBC Breakfast TV, British Gas, the Central Electricity Generating Board, and the Department of Transport, among others) over a two-year trial period. (See Chapter 1 for an explanation of the public sector, and Chapter 3 for an explanation of public-sector businesses.)

As well as the much greater use of computers we have also seen, particularly since the mid-70s, an explosion in the number of word processors currently used in offices, chemists, hospitals, football clubs, etc., throughout the country.

Fig. 5.1   Even in the home we can see the impact of technological change

- *What would you say has been of major concern to the users of Visual Display Units (one example being word-processor screens)?*

One considerable effect of the use of Visual Display Units (VDUs) has been the fear, on health grounds, of users. It should be emphasised that the greatest risk appears to be for pregnant women who use this equipment. There are opposing views on this subject but it is nevertheless of concern to many. Some argue that the low levels of radiation emitted from the sets can cause foetal damage, while others argue that it is possibly the strain of sitting in front of a screen for long periods plus the likely bad posture adopted which has resulted in the high levels of miscarriage among pregnant women users. Many people who have to use such devices also complain of severe eye strain and migraines. Thus, the health of employees ought to be of major concern to organisations using VDUs.

In response to the impact of change in working conditions brought about by the greater use of VDUs in offices, many employers are now offering staff the use of lead-lined smocks and specially designed screen filters when using VDUs. Employers have also been put into the position of having to negotiate different conditions of employment for such staff. Various manufacturers of VDUs recommend specific limited time periods for the use of the devices, punctuated by breaks away from the machine (of a specific time duration). Unfortunately, not all manufacturers recommend the same length of time for work at the machine and breaks away from the machine, and there is some confusion over exactly what is the maximum period anyone may remain in constant use of such a device without their health suffering. Thus, employers vary considerably in the number and duration of breaks they allow away from VDUs. This is an area for which the Health and Safety at Work Act has no provisions.

The impact of change in the mode of production and on the nature of products

Change in production has come about in a number of ways, for example, as a result of technological change in connection with manufacturing equipment; as a result of changes in the structure and pattern of costs of production; as a result of changes in the capacity of labour to produce; or as a result of changes in materials used. Change in the nature of products has come about as a result of changes in aspirations and tastes of consumers, and changes in marketing strategies.

Changes in the technology of production have a knock-on effect on the mode of production, and sometimes on through to the organisational structure itself. Thus, changes in technology can result in alterations to production processes and methods, as well as to the number of people employed, hence the *mode* of production may be altered; eventually the impact will be felt by the whole organisation.

A very significant change in connection with the mode of production which has already been mentioned (see page 49) is the use of computer-aided manufacture. An explanation of the system appears in Chapter 7. At this stage we are concerned with the impact of using computers in the production process.

- *If you had the opportunity to use a computer to enable you to manufacture, how would you make use of its capabilities?*

An example of the use of computer-aided manufacture is the system used by a number of car manufacturers whereby robotics are incorporated into advanced automated manufacturing systems in areas such as spot welding, machining, and engine assembly.

One of the impacts of such change in production is the greatly increased demand on finance for investment. When the British car manufacturers, Jaguar, initiated their own robotics programme at the end of the 1970s they were part of the BL complex and had suffered from the BL investment freeze of that period. When the Government eventually gave BL £2 billion for investment, Jaguar absorbed £100 million for its robotics programme. Computer-aided manufacture is not an immediately cheap alternative to labour – investment costs are extremely high, though economies are made in the long run.

- *Identify an organisation that is using computer-aided manufacture and find out how much the investment costs of the system were. Identify the benefits of the system and savings to be made.*

A major benefit to Jaguar – and yet another impact brought about by the change in mode of production – was the increase in the quality of production. Jaguar suffered for many years with poor quality control, which was costly and which also led to poor customer relations. Improvements in quality and reliability, brought about by the changes in production techniques, have brought their own rewards in the form of greater sales and profitability.

Extending the notion of production to include many more activities that take place within an organisation, which all play a part in the process of satisfying customer demands, we can consider the example of the Helena Rubinstein cosmetics business and its approach to changes in its organisation. The organisation has installed a Comprehensive Electronic Office (CEO) system at its UK headquarters in West Molesey (Surrey), which is its national UK distribution centre. Products making up more than 500 product lines come into the organisation from France, Germany, and Italy; information about movements of such goods into and out of the warehouse is necessary for effective management control and decision-making. The whole computing package allows for the full integration of information concerning:

stores
movement of goods
processing of inputs
customers' account records
data concerning over 1000 retail outlets served by the company.

The impact of such changes in the total picture of production has been to create a more cost-effective, and thus more efficient, company.

The ability the company now has to produce mailable, enhanced documentation through the word-processing capabilities of the system also helps create an image of high professionalism. The system also permits better decision-making and more effective financial and strategic planning, since directors have access to all information via their own terminals.

Other systems which have an impact on production and which involve change include Manufacturing Automation Protocol (MAP) and Technical Office Protocol (TOP) systems. The ideas behind these systems will be covered in Chapter 7 – suffice to say at this stage that both systems involve rethinking the way production is approached in an organisation. MAP involves setting standards for linking up computer-controlled machines while TOP has been designed as a set of standards to ensure the linking of computers used by draughtsmen, engineers and production managers. The immediate effect of both systems should be the improvement in internal organisational communications brought about by the better flow of data to and from systems on the shop floor.

The challenge for British production is the need to develop new products and processes which require less energy consumption during manufacture. Britain faces this challenge because, before long, producers will be using factories built in the Middle East, which will be using cheap (local) oil. Organisations are now looking to develop new processing techniques in the field of pharmaceuticals, food, paint, plastics and petrochemicals. The impact of this drive has been felt by academic research laboratories as well as the manufacturers themselves. Polytechnics and universities are being encouraged to get more involved with research for businesses. This push towards involving academia in research has not come solely from businesses – London's Imperial College of Science and Technology has found, for example, that it has had to turn to industry for financial assistance in the wake of shrinking government sources of funding. The response of manufacturers faced with the threat of overseas competition has therefore been to try to utilise the resources present in educational establishments as well as the resources of businesses.

One relatively new and very exciting field of production involves the use of *biotechnology*. Put simply, it is possible to transform cells into miniature chemical manufacturing plants via the process of 'recombinant DNA'; it is also possible to create minuscule protein factories using 'cell hybridisation'. The process industries, that is, those concerned with food, chemicals, energy, and waste treatment, could be transformed by such production techniques. The impact of these processes will be felt mostly in the field of medical understanding because the antibodies produced are impossible to obtain in bulk using traditional methods. Thus, prevention and cure in the future should be enhanced. We generally expect the impact of change in the mode of production to affect the organisation, those who work within it, or competitors; in the field of biotechnology, the impact would appear to be felt most heavily in other fields, such as health care.

The response of organisations to such production methods has been somewhat limited since the funds necessary for development in this field are extensive. Large companies such as ICI have been able to invest in biotechnology by using money gained from other areas of their business.

- *What was ICI's pre-tax net profit figure last year? What does this figure represent as a percentage of turnover? Using the ranking of companies by size of profits, calculate average pre-tax net profit as a percentage of turnover for last year's top ten companies. How does this figure compare with the ICI figure?*

Companies that have been involved only in biotechnology have shown very poor financial returns. Organisations, such as the American firms, Cetus (with earnings per share of only $0.02 in 1985), Biogen (with a net loss in the first nine months of 1984 of $10.9 million), and Genentech (with profits of only $3 million on a turnover of $67 million in 1984), have all suffered depressing results in this field. Britain's contributor in this area of production, Slough-based Celltech (which itself showed a loss of £1.9 million in 1984), is hoping for improvement in financial positions when major products come on to the market. Research and development is costly and reasonable rates of return on investment in, for example, the manufacture of chemicals were not expected until 1987 at the earliest – with pessimistic projections suggesting profits could come anywhere between 1987 and 1991.

Design

Design has become an increasingly important part of the production process and many organisations are now prepared to accept that it is the key to success. In fact, many would argue that it is the overall design of the organisation which is significant. In other words, organisations project an image, a corporate identity, and it is this which very often needs designing/redesigning. Design is the important means by which organisations let us (consumers) know of their intentions.

- *Within the last ten years several organisations have broken out of the mould set by their competitors and have projected an image which is quite distinct and which has helped lead to success. Consider the following examples and say how they differ from their competitors:*
  a) Virgin Atlantic
  b) Habitat
  c) McDonald's Hamburgers.

A number of organisations are now using the services of industrial designers to good effect. One of these is the Peterborough-based capital equipment manufacturer Baker Perkins. This organisation produces equipment used in printing, baking, and biscuit-making; its teams with responsibility for new products have a core made up of a senior design engineer, a production engineer, and an industrial designer. The industrial designer at Baker Perkins is seen as the co-ordinator or communi-

cations link between the various departments of the organisation. The designer in this sense can help at various stages in the production process: he can make a contribution to the marketing input; his ability to sketch may be useful in enabling communication (concerning a problem or machine part) to develop within a production team; his ability to conceptualise a problem or component may help in the costing of an item.

We tend to think of the production process in a very limited way, that is, as being solely the processes involved in actually making goods. We should not however ignore the impact of the ancillary activities of, for example, office staff. Effective office operations can lead to benefits for the whole organisation.

- *Imagine you are responsible for the running of a small office with four secretaries and a clerk. There is no hope of promotion for any of these staff members. The office has not been decorated for years. The lighting is poor. Facilities for tea/coffee/snacks do not exist. Equipment is outmoded. You have limited funds available. What are the first three things you would do to improve efficiency?*

The office environment

One area in which organisations have attempted to motivate office staff is through changes in the office environment. This could mean alterations to lighting, office layout, or even hours of work. To use just one example, let us consider alterations to hours of work. While it is the norm in this country to work fixed hours, with starting and finishing times being fixed each day, many organisations are finding that increased efficiency is resulting from the introduction of flexible working hours. One such system, known as *flextime*, has been devised by the Hengstler Corporation. The fixed times of arrival and departure are replaced by a working day which is split into two different types of time:

- core time, the period when employees must be at work.
- flextime, the beginning and end of each day, during which time it is up to individuals when they arrive/leave.

With most systems that are now in operation, flexible hours also exist around lunchtime. Basically, the system works in this way:

a) all employees have a *target time* (given number of hours) for which they are contracted to work;

b) all employees work within an *accounting period*, this is a number of working days which will have a specific target time;
c) the organisation has a *bandwidth*, which is the time between the earliest start time and latest finish time in a day (the time when the doors of the organisation are open);
d) during the day employees are able to start and finish at whatever times they want during *flextime* but they must be in work during *core time*;
e) at the end of the accounting period employees must ensure that they have completed the set number of hours which they are contracted to work. It is at this time that *reconciliation* occurs. In other words, if you have worked less than your contracted hours you have to make up the difference in the next accounting period. If you have worked more than your contracted hours you will be able to take time off in lieu during the following accounting period.

Organisations as diverse as the public sector's British Gas and the private-sector holiday and foreign-exchange company, Thomas Cook (which uses the Hengstler system in its headquarters in Peterborough), have introduced flextime systems for more efficient operations.

The impact of this change is that employees are happier on the whole with the flextime system and the organisation thus benefits from having a motivated and contented workforce. The response to the idea of flextime is that many more organisations are trying to introduce the system, though it is virtually impossible to operate it in an environment where workers depend on other workers being present, as, for example, on a production line.

- *Assume you are considering the introduction of a flextime system into your organisation. What problems do you think you would encounter?*
- *What benefits could you offer employees from a flextime system?*

Change will enter the business arena in many forms. We have already seen how changes in political, legal, and technological circumstances, as well as changes in productive methods, are likely to affect an organisation. In Chapter 6 this theme is continued, with an examination of the effects of changes in marketing and of changes within an organisation.

Assignments

Student activity 5.1

This is an individual assignment. You are a member of your college debating society and the topic under discussion at the next meeting is: 'Britain has the party political system it deserves. It has a two-party system and we will always have a two-party system'. Your opposition to this statement hinges on the effect which you think change can have on a political system,. Your task is to prepare a *five-minute speech* which you will put to the society in the hope that you can convince them of the soundness of your views. You must attempt to show how change has altered our political system, and thus how it can alter it again in the future. Write the speech.

Student activity 5.2

This is a group task which can be undertaken by groups of three or four. Obtain literature from one of the main political parties in Britain which shows what each would do if elected at the next election. You are to assume that you work for a small local newspaper which is about to run a series of features on the political parties and their objectives. Your group must produce a layman's version of the political propaganda which (a) would be suitable (easy to read) and (b) should contain all of the important features of the party under discussion.

Student activity 5.3

This is a group assignment, with four to five students taking the role of union members and four to five students taking the role of management. There is a fear among some VDU operators that the low levels of radiation emitted from these devices can be injurious to health, particularly for pregnant women. Your group is to divide into two sub-groups, one representing the unionised workforce of Secretarial and Administrative Services Limited and the other representing the management of the company. There is to be a joint consultation and negotiation meeting between the two groups to iron out differences of opinion with regard to the use of VDUs, and other associated issues such as possible redundancies caused by their use and the need for adequate training.

The union negotiating position must be established by the relevant group. You can include any number of benefits/concessions which you would like to see from management. Prepare your negotiating position.

The management negotiating position must also be established by the relevant group. You may include any issues which you feel might be raised in such a situation. You may, for example, attempt to reduce the size of the workforce since people will now be much more efficient thanks to the advantages of using VDUs. You may feel that while training is a necessary prerequisite of use, you ought to try to get agreement that such training is conducted in the workers' own time, arguing that this training would make each of them a more efficient and enhanced worker, capable of getting work elsewhere if necessary and at the same time commanding a higher wage.

When both groups have decided on their objectives, the parties must meet and conduct the actual consultation and negotiation exercise.

Student activity 5.4

This task is to be undertaken by groups of three or four. You have decided to go into business for yourselves in a locality within a three-mile radius of your college. Assume that you can obtain finance from a bank and a Government loan, which will be sufficient to buy a lease and prepare your premises for business. Your task is twofold:

1. Investigate the area concerned and decide what type of business you would prefer to establish, given the geography, population make-up, and general spending patterns of your locality.
2. Prepare a short document which specifies what type of image you will attempt to project as an organisation, and what methods you will employ to develop such an image.

Student activity 5.5

This is a group assignment for five to six students. Staff at your college have complained that the majority of students appear very apathetic towards work and generally demotivated. As a consequence, your departmental head has requested that a small group of students establish a working party to consider ways in which students may be motivated. Your terms of reference were kept deliberately wide to allow the group to propose any measures which they felt could help. Such measures do not have to be economically realistic – the head is only concerned at this stage with generating ideas for later consideration.

As the working party, produce a document which carefully outlines the proposals for motivating students.

Student activity 5.6

This assignment concerns the article on defence on page 56 and is an individual assignment. When the article appeared in the press this country had a Conservative government. What does the article tell you about the nature of defence, as seen by the major political parties at the time? What is the nature of the change political parties must face in connection with areas such as defence, education or health-care? How would you say the various political parties have attempted to respond to changes in defence conditions?

Student activity 5.7

This is an individual assignment. With reference to the articles concerning Barclays Bank and South Africa on page 57, what kind of changes do you think must have occurred to encourage Barclays Bank to take the action it did? What was the connection between Barclays Bank trading in South Africa and the National Union of Students in Britain? What does this tell you about pressure being brought to bear on organisations?

Labour defence split revealed

Ministers hit back over the Trident programme

THE Ministry of Defence has committed £3bn to the Trident submarine programme, John Stanley, Minister of State for Defence, said yesterday.

Both Labour and the Alliance are committed to cancelling the programme and there is a suspicion at Westminster that the Government is deliberately escalating its expenditure on the £10bn programme in an attempt to embarrass its opponents.

George Younger, Secretary of State for Defence, attacked Labour's plans as a threat to Britain's defence and to Nato.

He told *The Independent*: 'It removes the shield of the nuclear deterrent which enables us to be certain that a nuclear attack on us will not be contemplated lightly.' He said: 'Mr Kinnock's only response to the deafening outcry against his defence policy is to cover his ears.'

By Anthony Bevins
Political Editor

THE fundamental split between Neil Kinnock and Denis Healey over Labour's non-nuclear defence policy was exposed yesterday when the party launched its foreign and defence policy package, *Modern Britain in a Modern World*.

While Mr Kinnock and the defence paper resisted the idea of protection from the American nuclear umbrella, Mr Healey said in a BBC radio interview: 'The existence of nuclear weapons inside Nato, of which we shall remain a loyal member, will certainly be an effective deterrent against a Soviet first strike on Britain. What we renounce is that we can gain anything by somebody committing a first nuclear strike on our behalf.'

The danger of the rift is that Mr Healey has the backing of many of the shadow cabinet on the issue – and that if Mr Kinnock refuses to defer he will face the prospect of a re-run of the 1983 General Election defence debacle.

The Conservatives and the Alliance were yesterday eager to encourage such conflict, and to play up potential or existing public fears about what is undoubtedly a bold policy; abandoning Polaris, cancelling Trident, diverting resources to conventional defence and getting rid of all American nuclear bases. Mr Healey underlined the threat to Labour unity when he told a press conference: 'We believe that the members of Nato should seek to raise the nuclear threshold in Europe so as to move towards "no first use" of nuclear weapons.

'But we recognise that Nato's strategy in Central Europe must be indivisible and that Britain must accept the agreed strategy of the alliance until it succeeds in changing it.' The document repeatedly questioned the value of the Nato deterrent, asking: 'In the sure knowledge of what it would do to ourselves, and our country for generations, is it reasonable to believe any longer that either we, or the Americans, would launch nuclear weapons to halt a Soviet invasion of Europe?'

It also asked: 'What enemy will believe that the Americans will commit suicide to punish an invader of western Europe?'

As Dr David Owen, the SDP leader, was quick to point out yesterday, Mr Kinnock said on 29 September: 'If we're not prepared to use the weapons system ourselves, we certainly would not be asking anyone else to jeopardise themselves by the use of that nuclear weapon. It would be immoral to do so.'

Although Mr Kinnock told *The Independent* last month that there was no reason why the Americans should 'risk their own necks when the exchange could be limited to Europe', he appeared to concede some ground to Mr Healey yesterday when he said about Nato nuclear cover: 'The whole prospect of giving cover to conventional forces by means of nuclear weapons is somewhat unlikely in the very nature of the weapons themselves.

'We shall of course not be proposing the disintegration of Nato command because we acknowledge our responsibility as allies, and insofar therefore as cover can be said to exist, that cover naturally is maintained.'

But there was no hint of that in the policy paper – or any mention of the additional resources which would be spent on conventional forces, or the timetable for removal of American bases.

Mr Kinnock has said that Britain would be non-nuclear within a year of Labour taking office. He said yesterday: 'It could take a year, perhaps a little more, perhaps a little less, and that refers to the technical requirements.'

Source: *The Independent*, 11 December 1986

Barclays to quit South Africa

From Tony Allen-Mills
in Johannesburg

BARCLAYS Bank will announce today that after years of criticism of its dealings with apartheid it is pulling out South Africa, well-informed sources said in Johannesburg last night.

Sir Timothy Bevan, Barclay's chairman will announce a disinvestment deal at a press conference this morning, they said.

Source: *The Independent*, 24 November 1986

SA fears more may follow Barclays

From David Beresford
in Johannesburg

SOUTH Africa yesterday was putting a brave face on the most sensational anti-apartheid disinvestment move to date – Barclays Bank's sale of its stake in the country after six weeks of secret negotiations.

Source: *Guardian*, 25 November 1986

Others feel chill as Barclays pulls out

AS analysts debated whether Barclays Bank's decision to sell its interests in South Africa was political or commercial, speculation is growing that other British companies may follow suit.

Source: *The Independent*, 25 November 1986

Skills assessable

Assignment	*Skill* 1	2	3	4	5	6	7	8
1	1.8	2.2 2.4 2.8		4.3 4.6 4.10		6.2 6.2 6.3		
2	1.3 1.4 1.5 1.8	2.2 2.5	3.5 3.6 3.7 3.9	4.3 4.6		6.1 6.2		
3	1.3 1.7 1.9	2.4	3.2 3.7	4.3 4.6 4.8 4.10				
4	1.3 1.4 1.6 1.8 1.9	2.2 2.4 2.5	3.6 3.7 3.9	4.3	5.1 5.2 5.5 5.6 5.10	6.1 6.2 6.3 6.4 6.6	7.1 7.2 7.4	8.2 8.3 8.5
5	1.2 1.8	2.2 2.4 2.7	3.4 3.5 3.6 3.7 3.9 3.11	4.3 4.5 4.6 4.10	5.2 5.4	6.1 6.2 6.3 6.4 6.6	7.1 7.2	
6	1.1 1.8	2.1 2.2 2.4 2.5		4.6		6.1 6.2		
7	1.3 1.6	2.2 2.4 2.5		4.6		6.1 6.2 6.3		

6
THE IMPACT OF CHANGE AND RESPONSES TO IT (2)

The marketing aspect of organisations is much wider than most people think. The layman tends to think of marketing as advertising or as selling but, in fact, it encompasses very much more. The marketing department is concerned with developing a marketing plan which specifies:

– what has to be done
– when it is to be done
– who does what
– how it will be done
– what targets are to be achieved
– the expenditure budgets for each activity.

Rather than being viewed as just another function within an organisation, marketing ought to be considered from the point of view that it pervades an organisation. Marketing should be seen as an integrator – a means by which all of the resources of the organisation are directed towards the achievement of an organisational objective.

- *What are argued as being the main organisational objectives?*

A change in marketing strategy could involve any of the features of marketing shown in Fig. 6.1. It may include changes in the way information is obtained; changes in the internal communication processes of organisations; changes in promotional activity; or changes in the method of or approach to after-sales service.

- *How do businesses usually obtain information about customer preferences and dislikes?*
- *What are the major problems in using market research questionnaires?*
- *What methods are there for promoting goods/services?*

We have already seen how politics, the law, technology, and changes in production techniques have affected organisations. In this chapter we will consider not only the impact on organisations of changes *in* marketing strategy but also the impact of changes *on* marketing strategy. The impact of internal organisational change will also be considered.

The impact of change in and on marketing strategy

This is not intended to be a section concerned with marketing per se (see Chapter 13 for an explanation of the term 'marketing mix'). It is, however, necessary to establish a few ground rules before we can proceed – that is, to say a little about the activities marketing is concerned with – although the objectives of this section are to discuss the impact of changes *on* marketing strategy (how change has altered marketing strategy) and the impact of changes *in* marketing strategy (how changes in marketing have affected organisations).

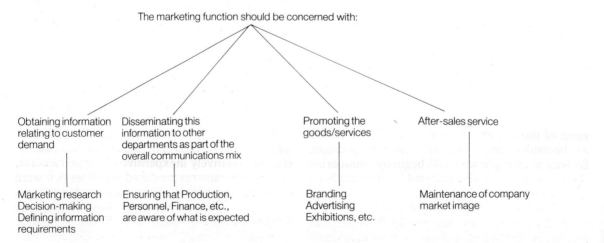

The marketing function should be concerned with:

Obtaining information relating to customer demand	Disseminating this information to other departments as part of the overall communications mix	Promoting the goods/services	After-sales service
Marketing research Decision-making Defining information requirements	Ensuring that Production, Personnel, Finance, etc., are aware of what is expected	Branding Advertising Exhibitions, etc.	Maintenance of company market image

Fig. 6.1

Promoting goods/services includes all the activities which favourably influence the task of selling the product. In this respect the activities which encourage sales can be classified according to whether they stimulate demand in an *indirect* way, such as advertising; whether they stimulate demand in a *direct* way, as with free samples; or whether pressure is brought to bear through personal selling.

To give an idea of some of the methods used, here is a list of the more common techniques:

Advertising, e.g. catalogues.
Competitions – for both trade and/or consumer, e.g. free gifts, leaflets, packaging.
Displays – at the point of sale, e.g. price reductions, special offers.

Fig. 6.2

Changes in the internal communication process will be mentioned in the final section of this chapter. At this stage we can consider promotional activities and after-sales service as a means of considering the impact of changes in and on marketing strategy.

The impact of changes in marketing strategy

Fig. 6.3 'Marketing' can often make us think just about market research questionnaires, but it involves much more than that. Another part of the process may include demonstrations and exhibitions

- *What would you say is currently the most persuasive advertisement on television? Why do you consider it to be so persuasive?*

Promotions involving movie stars, considerable sums of money, and extremely lavish campaigns are becoming the norm rather than the exception. By way of example we could begin by considering the cases of Kodak and Polaroid in the still photography market.

In 1986 Kodak lost a patent-infringement Federal Court case in the USA, brought by Polaroid. This meant that Kodak had to stop selling instant-picture film – thus making all of its instant-picture cameras

around the world redundant – and stop selling the cameras. This obviously produced a gap in its product range and caused a reduction in profits, so Kodak was forced to turn to another area of the still-picture market. Kodak had for some time placed a lot of emphasis on sales of (high margin) consumer film and relatively inexpensive disc-type cameras, but the disc cameras produced negatives that were too small and which consequently yielded pictures which were grainy and unclear. The quality camera market had been neglected by Kodak for a long time and, as a result, Japanese firms had been able to get a foothold in the market for 35 mm cameras – a growth area throughout the 1970s and 1980s. As a result, Kodak's marketing strategy was then turned to the introduction of a new Kodak 35 mm camera (the VR35), with the concurrent introduction in retail stores of 'minilabs' which cut the processing time for films from twenty-four hours to twenty-four minutes. It is argued that Kodak attempted to put forward the image of being 'more like a mover than a victim.' In the USA alone Kodak had to spend $20 million on initial coast-to-coast advertising.

As for Polaroid, who now have the sole right to manufacture and sell instant-picture cameras and film, the future is not at all secure. The increase in consumer interest in 35 mm cameras (beginning in the early 1970s) had a considerable impact on the instant-picture market. The boom had been in sophisticated, easy-to-use 35 mm cameras, not instant-picture cameras. Since 1978 Polaroid has seen sales of the cheaper model in its instant picture range drop from 9.4 million per year to 3.6 million (by 1986). In an attempt to recoup sales, Polaroid launched the 'Spectra' in the USA (to be known as the 'Image' in Europe) which, it was claimed, made use of innovative film chemistry designed to improve the quality of instant pictures to such an extent that they could be favourably compared with those taken using a 35 mm camera. Polaroid also claimed to be using innovative optics and electronics in the new model. As part of the promotion campaign, Polaroid intended to use the services of the actor, Ben Cross (from the Oscar-winning film, *Chariots of Fire*), the services of the studio famous for special effects created in *Star Wars* films, and $40 million.

Marketing, as far as Kodak and Polaroid are concerned, is more than advertising a product; it is about image and about technical expertise for the amateur – quality still photography made easy. It also involves spending a lot of money to inform and persuade.

- *With the current advances in electronic and video photography, permitting instantaneous still pictures to be displayed on television sets do you think there is a future for still photography?*

The use of film stars (as mentioned above) to advertise commodities has long been recognised as being an effective, though costly, means of encouraging consumers to buy. What tends to be happening more frequently now is that products are actually being used in films. For example, Madonna, in the film, *Desperately Seeking Susan*, used a Polaroid camera throughout the film. In the film, *Santa*

Claus – The Movie, scenes were set in a McDonalds hamburger bar. Coca Cola was the drink being consumed in *Ghost Busters*, and it also appeared frequently in a giant 21st Century advertising billboard in the film *Blade Runner*. The movie *Back to the Future* featured JVC equipment and Adidas training shoes. More and more companies are now taking the opportunity to have their products displayed via the movie media either by:

a) *creative placement* – taking advantage of outdoor advertising sites, or the side of, for example, taxis or buses, to display adverts which can be seen as the camera 'pans'; or dressing actors in clothes with particular logos; or using a real TV commercial in scenes which include a TV set; or

b) *on-set placement* – using a product in the film itself, for example particular brands of cereal in breakfast scenes, wines in restaurants or hi-fi in the home.

This means of 'placing' products is not limited to movies, the potential is there for television, too – it is certainly cheaper for the manufacturer than hiring film or TV stars to endorse a product.

Another example of how a change in marketing strategy can bring about the reward of increased sales and profits is the case of Perrier water. The marketers of this product have certainly managed to persuade us that this is more than mere water – how else can we explain that, no matter how much we complain about the price of petrol, we are prepared to spend more per litre to buy Perrier than to buy petrol? The marketing aspect is not only concerned with press and media advertising – the fact that the bottle is a particular shape and is made of glass rather than plastic is significant. The. fact that the permission of the Comité Interprofessional des Vins de Campagne was obtained to call Perrier 'the champagne of table water' is also significant. Even the gas in Perrier is supposedly better than the gas in other bottled water, since it contains traces of rare gases such as krypton, argon, and xenon because of the rock strata which the water passes through. The marketing men have indeed done well to create a 'designer water'!

Another example of how a change in marketing strategy increased sales of a product is the case of Cadbury's creme eggs. The advertising agency, Gold Greenless Trott, created an environment which, in itself, encouraged sales of the confectionery. After research had shown that people in general only tended to demand creme eggs at

Easter time, the advertising agency decided that this would form an important part of their promotion campaign. As a result they produced advertisements telling the public that creme eggs were here but 'they're not here for long!' They also changed the emphasis on eating the creme eggs by asking 'How do you eat yours?' after it was realised that people tend to eat the eggs in a variety of ways. The campaign showed various people eating creme eggs by nibbling them, or biting huge chunks at a time, or even eating them whole. In this way marketing was able to change consumer attitude to the product.

The impact of change on marketing strategy

There are occasions when a marketing strategy has to be changed to reflect changes occurring within society or changes occurring within the population which makes up the consumers of a product. For example, there may be a change in consumer attitude or taste. In the mid-1980s it was realised, for example, that many young (18 to 25 year-old) beer drinkers in Britain were showing a preference for low-gravity lagers. It was considered that this generation, brought up on sweet, carbonated soft-drinks, would hardly acquire a taste for the traditional British heavier, bitter, stronger beers. This meant that a change in marketing was called for.

The American lager, Miller Lite, was launched on the drinking public in 1986 via a £10 million advertising campaign, centring predominantly on press, poster, and television advertising. The basis of the promotional campaign was the comparison between the Miller Lite lager and the traditional, heavier, British beer. One of the more memorable advertisements showed friends searching for not only a lighter beer but also, apparently, a lighter lifestyle. The world was depicted as being grey, and other people in the advertisement were shown as being obese, with men in a pub drinking beer from buckets. The words from the song which accompanied the advert were, 'It's my bevy – it ain't heavy, it's Miller Lite.' The promotion centred around the notion that traditional (British) beer was definitely not 'in' for the young male.

- *Consider a beer or wine advertisement which appeals to you. What is it about the advertisement that you find so appealing?*

Promotion does not only involve advertising in the sense of an advert on the television or a picture in a magazine. The American beer manufacturer Anheuser–Busch, in an attempt to break into the British lager market with its Budweiser brand, established an American Football league in Britain, just at the time when American football had begun to capture everyone's imagination in this country. The establishment of the league was only part of a promotion campaign which cost Anheuser–Busch £8 million. Thus, a change in public attitude (towards American football, in this case) led to a change in the method of promotion of a product.

When an organisation changes its promotion campaign, competitors are forced into action of their own in order to at least remain in a competitive position.

- *Prepare a set of notes enabling you to give a presentation outlining an advertising campaign which you feel was started as a result of the actions of a competing firm.*

It is argued that no amount of marketing can help if a product is poor. The household cleaning appliance manufacturer, Hoover plc, was in considerable financial difficulty in 1981 when it realised that what was needed was a revitalisation of product lines. Along with a tough corporate rationalisation programme the company transformed its product range.

It was not until intense Japanese competition (in the mid-1970s) that Hoover began to lose market share; up to this time the organisation had relied on tried and tested models. The recovery was brought about by the introduction of the Turbo and Sensotronic range of cleaners. The promotion was aimed at making a dull chore (housework) appear to be a fashionable, up-to-date 'experience'. An important change in the product, from the point of view of marketing, was the change in ideas about colour for the cleaners. Out went the boring, sedate colours which had been used in the past, and in came bolder, brighter colours for machines that possessed a number of appealing gadgets to help with the housework. This was a major factor in helping to change the image of the product and the company. Similarly, Hoover washing machines were also updated, with the top of the range model (a computer-controlled automatic) offering sixty speed and temperature combinations. This was a considerable departure from the appliances which had been available before 1970.

- *What do you think are important considerations for someone who is about to buy a vacuum cleaner? What would influence your decision to purchase one?*

Change in the market, as demonstrated by new equipment produced by competitors, forced Hoover to react and change its own product lines. Consumers' preferences were changing, along with changes in technology, which initiated a change in demand in that consumers were not prepared to put up with 'old-style' equipment: consumer demand had changed and manufacturers had to do the same.

Another area where marketing of products has proved problematical is where technological advance has, in a sense, been too rapid. Many consumer durable goods – in the audio and video fields, in particular – become obsolete within twelve months of their launch. Organisations have found that their own research and development has come up with ideas and prototypes which if released on to the market, would create problems for the sales of their existing goods. The introduction of 8 mm video cassettes and digital tape are two examples of developments which caused this sort of anxiety for manufacturers.

When video was first introduced to the consumer market there was rivalry between three formats: Beta, VHS, and Philips V200. The Philips system soon lost ground and the battle between the remaining two was finally won by the VHS format. This left those consumers who had bought a Beta player with the problem of being unable to get a good selection of prerecorded films to watch at home, since most video shops stocked the best choice only in the VHS format. When the new 8 mm video cassette was about to be launched it was feared that consumers would again be confused and would, in all probability, wait for a long time before buying to see which format was going to be successful and whether or not 8 mm would win in the end. Another problem for the 8 mm video cassette was the requirement for buying another video recorder – unless one purchased the JVC version (VHB–C).

The problem facing the manufacturers of Digital Audio Tape (DAT) was that they also produced compact discs (CDs). It was recognised that the quality on DAT was high (comparing favourably with CD), and it had the added advantage over CD in that the latter could not be used for recording. The major problem was that if companies produced and sold DAT this would sabotage the sales of compact discs – of which they still had many, either in stock or sitting on the shelves of shops waiting to be sold.

The increased use of computerisation, in particular, is certainly a powerful weapon of change which has had a marked effect on advertising. The work of the film crews producing advertisements was viewed by many in the past as a career to be relished – jetting around the world to exotic locations, filming beautiful models, and being well paid for the privilege. As you (and perhaps members of the film crews just mentioned) can probably tell, I was never in this line of work, though the impressions I have of the business are shared by many. However, the end is in sight for such film crews. We are now seeing the emergence of production companies which concentrate on special effects or computer-generated images for advertisements, such organisations being based in areas such as London's Covent Garden and Soho. The technology now available to these production companies enables them to get across more information in an advert, more cost effectively. The ad-maker today uses a computer console (such as a CAD terminal – see Chapter 7) just as much as a camera. Computer-designed creations such as the well-known Max Headroom, who even has his own show on TV's Channel Four, will become commonplace on our screens in advertisements. Gone (temporarily?) are the exotic locations and all that goes with them, it seems.

After-sales service is one final area of marketing that needs to be considered. There have been countless organisations that have fallen by the wayside because they did not realise the importance of after-sales service. A good example of this is Sinclair computers, an organisation which produced exactly what people wanted – cheap home computers. Although innovative, the man behind the organisation (Sir Clive Sinclair) was not a businessman. The downfall of the organisation was almost entirely attributable to poor quality control and lack of after-sales service. One only has to compare Sinclair with a close rival, Amstrad, to appreciate the impact that marketing can have, as well as the importance of effective after-sales service. The brains behind Amstrad (Alan Sugar) was a marketing man who exhibited a single-minded dedication to quality control and who paid attention to after-sales service. Anyone who wanted to buy a new model Sinclair faced the prospect of a long wait and, if anything went wrong, an even longer wait. Anyone who wanted to buy an Amstrad could almost invariably find what they wanted in the local computer store; the after-sales service was also quick and efficient.

- *Talk to a selection of people who have recently bought a new car or expensive audio/visual equipment or a consumer durable. Find out whether they considered the after-sales service which was offered when they made their purchase. How important was after-sales service to these purchasers?*

Reliable after-sales service is a crucial part of selling a product. A reputation for servicing and advice is one well worth having. It not only affects sales in general but will also have an impact on the organisation's image – which of itself must be worth a point or two against the opposition.

We can see then that change in one form or another has had an impact *on* marketing strategy, since organisations, in several cases, have had to review the operations of the whole business (not just the advertising media). We can also see that changes in marketing have had an impact on the activities of various organisations.

The impact of internal organisational change

When we talk of organisational change it is generally thought that we are referring to that brought about as a result of a change in organisational *structure* (see pages 12–14). Although this is a common assumption it is not the only means by which change can occur within an organisation, other types of internal change can be concerned with those aspects shown in Fig. 6.4 below.

- *Imagine you have been at work for a couple of years. You enjoy your job and get on very well with your colleagues. On arrival at work this morning you were told the business had been taken over by a bigger firm and there were going to be organisational changes. How do you now feel about this situation? Why do you think you are likely to exhibit the feelings just mentioned?*

In the above task many would say they feel anger. They may feel as though they have been let down. Some would argue they feel a sense of outrage, bitterness or simply depression. For many of us, in situations where we are happy and contented, change would come as an unwelcome surprise. One situation where change is just as unwelcome as it may be in any other area is in employment. We like things to stay the way they have been because that gives us security; we know where we are in relation to everyone else in the organisation; we know where we belong. When something happens to challenge our security – to threaten our 'safety' – we rebel against it. Many people suffer from quite severe depression and anxiety at the thought of fundamental organisational change, not simply because of the upheaval it may cause but because of the displacement one is about to feel. The world which you thought you knew and could rely on is about to be taken apart.

We are continually reminded that change is inevitable, but even so it can still make us feel uneasy. Staff feel bewildered, work is disrupted, clients/customers are often confused and, as a result, likely to be at their most objectionable. In many organisations change seems to take place just for the sake of it and, because of this, we may jump to the conclusion that the planned organisational change we are about to go through is unnecessary. Basically, change is resisted for one or more of three reasons:

a) security/insecurity;
b) economics;
c) sociopsychological.

a) *Security/insecurity*: humans prefer the status quo on the whole – change is viewed as a threat to security (a threat to stability);
b) *Economic*: change is feared since it may lead to loss of employment – machines may be employed to do your job;
c) *Sociopsychological*: (excluding insecurity and economic, mentioned above) this can include such things as what a person's *perception* of the change involves; *emotional* reaction to change which highlights fear and prejudices; the *cultural* values held by those concerned.

On the other hand, if the proposed change does

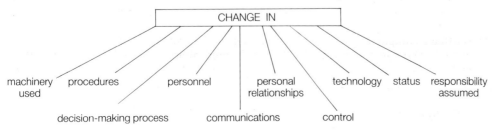

Fig. 6.4

not adversely affect you in any of the above ways (a, b or c) then you will not perceive the change as a threat – you are thus unlikely to resist it. Conceivably, change may be welcomed, particularly if the change is expected to remove a problem or a fear.

- *What changes would you like to see initiated at your place of work/college? Who would feel threatened by your proposal? Why?*

Attitude to change therefore depends on your personal circumstances in relation to the proposed change. On the one hand there will be those who can accept the change as being necessary and willingly adopt it, while at the other extreme there will be those who are so radically opposed to change that they exhibit forceful, positive resistance which may even be exemplified by attempts to destroy or sabotage the proposal. Within these two positions, which can be said to be at either end of the spectrum, we can expect to find a range of possibilities – people who, in given circumstances, will exhibit behaviour typical of a person *coping* with change; those who will sometimes exhibit behaviour typical of passive resistance, such as trying to avoid the proposal; and those individuals who will attempt to ignore any change they do not care for. This can be illustrated as in Table 6.1.

Table 6.1

Does the employee like the proposed change?	Reaction of employee	Demonstrated by
Yes	Willingly accepts it	Adoption of proposal
Possibly	Accepts it	Makes use of the proposal
Indifferent	Accepts it	Makes the most of the situation
Wary/possibly not	Passively Resists	Attempts to avoid or ignore the change
Definitely against	Actively resists	Attempts to destroy proposal

If people are likely to feel threatened by change, the best way forward may be for those responsible for initiating change, or those responsible for relaying information concerning proposed change, to not only inform the staff that it is about to happen but to also tell them *why*. This will be discussed in more detail when we consider organisational development later in this chapter.

- *You own and run a small retail confectionery business. What would prompt you to consider changing, for example, store layout, façade or goods stocked?*

More often than not we find that change is initiated because performance is not what it should be: achievement is below target. Those organisations contemplating change ought to be aware that the best course is to analyse the data at the root of the organisation's performance and then only to bring about change when such data is fully understood. In this way, employees can be informed of the reasons behind proposed manoeuvres and be satisfied that such assumptions that have had to be made have been made rationally.

One or more of the types of changes mentioned on page 63 are very likely to affect all of us at some stage in our careers. Let us very briefly consider them and their possible impact:

Changes in machinery/technology used – a major fear many of us will have is that a machine could take our place at work. Employees, particularly in manufacturing though increasingly in office work, too, now see the loss of employment opportunities and attribute this to developments in machinery. Items discussed in Chapter 7, such as CAD/CAM systems and word processors, pose a considerable threat to the livelihood of many.

- *Who were the Luddites? What were they concerned with?*

Changes in procedures (includes changes in decision-making processes, communications, and control) – changes in the methods used at work sometimes upset those who have become familiar with the traditional processes. The way organisations operate is referred to as the organisation's culture. When we get used to operating in a particular way we are often not at all pleased to be told to do it a different way.

Changes in personnel – this has a surprising demoralising effect on staff. The impact tends to be temporary but is nonetheless real. When you get used to working with particular people who then leave to join other organisations or who are promoted, you have to face the task of initiating someone else into the organisation's culture. It is beneficial to an organisation to have new people with new ideas and enthusiasm but, to those who have to work with the newcomer, the prospect is sometimes unwelcome.

Changes in personal relationships – very similar in impact to the previous type of change. Although it is true that familiarity sometimes breeds contempt, familiarity also gives us security. If personal relationships at work change it is that much more difficult to carry out your job until you know where you stand with colleagues.

- *How would you say the relationship between you and your parents has changed in the last five years? Has this change in relationships brought about any problems? How do you deal with these problems?*

Changes in status and responsibility assumed – one of the problems that comes with promotion is that you are often expected to behave in a different way. It is frowned upon in many organisations if managers, for example, fraternise with staff. As status in the organisation changes so attitudes and relationships change.

Managers have a number of functions, for example, they must

plan
organise
set objectives
administer
manage people
make decisions
achieve objectives

Lists such as this appear in most management texts but, what many students fail to appreciate – and what is very significant from the point of view of change – is how a manager does these things. If change is managed effectively it can lead to organisational success, just as mismanagement of change is almost certain to lead to problems, if not failure.

It has been argued that change is continuous, hence organisations no longer remain organised as such but are rather continually reorganising. In this respect I am painting a picture of what is happening in the largest of our organisations and in the smaller organisations in specific (dynamic) fields, such as computing.

- *Why is computing regarded as a dynamic field? What other types of business can you think of that are as dynamic?*

The management of change is referred to as organisational development as it is concerned with the planned, integrated approach to change which considers the whole of the organisation. In the past,

change tended to be concerned with individual departments within organisations – it was therefore change taking place in isolation. Such changes often cancelled each other out. One of the examples often used is the change that would have taken place in the days before organisational development, such as that associated with improving productivity. Method study would have suggested perhaps deskilling (see Chapter 8) jobs, while personnel were perhaps introducing methods designed to combat absenteeism and reduce labour turnover. Thus, in an attempt to improve the organisation, this type of change tended to have a self-cancelling effect.

The modern approach to organisational change has a number of characteristics:

a) change should be systematically planned;
b) it should be regarded in a comprehensive way by considering the impact on the entire organisation;
c) the process will probably take a considerable period of time;
d) organisational development experts stress the importance of seeking outside, third-party, advice on change; this has the advantage that an outside agent has no vested interest in individual departments (it also ensures that the experts perpetuate their own existence!);
e) emphasis tends to be placed on the importance of work groups.

In this and the previous chapter we have seen how change comes about and have considered the impact such change is likely to have. In the past change tended to be regarded as being a continuous process which was smooth and measurable. We are, however, beginning to see the emergence of change in radical forms – that is, sudden, abrupt change. With the rapid technological developments that have occurred since the late 1960s we, as both employees and consumers, have had to cope with events which have radically altered our lives. So a course such as the BTEC National attempts to prepare young people for an environment where change will be the order of the day; for an environment where change will be sudden; for an environment where prospective employees will need to have freely transferable, business-related skills to ensure any hope of employment.

Assignments

Student activity 6.1

This is a task which can be undertaken by the whole

class/large groups. The objective of this task is to market the BTEC courses for your college. You are to allocate tasks among the class such that the whole group produces various items which will together form a marketing approach for the college. The type of items which could be produced include:

- advertising posters (with an indication of where they would be located for maximum effect);
- leaflets (with an indication of where, when, and how they would be distributed);
- displays (with an indication of where and when such displays could be mounted and viewed by prospective students);
- a one-minute radio commercial (this could be produced on an audio cassette with a view to getting a local radio station to give it air time);
- a video commercial (which could be used by staff and students on open-days and visits to local schools).

A variation on the radio commercial theme would be to encourage the whole group to form a number of small, competitive units each producing a three-minute audio commercial on a cassette. At a pre-arranged time the whole group would then listen to all the tapes and select the best.

Student activity 6.2

Working in groups of three or four you are to conduct research into the use of film stars/film sets as an advertising medium. Select six popular films which have been screened either at cinemas or on televisions in the last year which have made use of brand-named products. Say how the product was 'introduced' to the audience (what made you notice it?) and what perception you formed of that product as a result of seeing it in the film.

Discuss the findings of your group with other groups and subjectively evaluate the efficacy of the *placement* (see page 60) used.

Student activity 6.3

This is an individual assignment. You are to prepare a speech which will be given at the local Chamber of Commerce monthly lunch, addressed to the issue following. In your speech you must cite as many examples as possible of manufacturers' sponsorship of sports events. You are not expected to agree or disagree with the contention, merely to give both sides of the argument. The speech should last for a minimum of five minutes and a maximum of fifteen.

'The sponsorship of sports events should be banned since it distorts the way in which free markets allocate goods. This distortion occurs since the large producers, who have the benefit of extensive resources which can be devoted to sponsorship deals, have an unfair advantage over the smaller (though possibly more efficient) producers, who do not have such funds.'

Student activity 6.4

This is an individual assignment. Recent developments in communication technology are bringing closer the time when many of us will no longer have to travel in to work every day. Within what many expect to be a relatively short time we can expect to be in contact with the office via a communication link which could, on the one hand, involve us confronting a computer terminal every morning or, on the other hand, see us sitting in front of a camera. It is conceivable that we may use a combination of the two. Some organisations are already using interactive videoconferencing (transmission of images in much the same way as television, though not broadcast, along with the advantage of interaction – the ability to freely communicate with the person on the screen) for meetings between people at different sites. It may not be long before we can communicate with the office in the same way.

Given that you may be in this position in a few years, prepare a short report outlining what you consider to be the possible advantages to (a) the employee and (b) the employer of such a system. Note also the possible disadvantages to any parties of the use of such a system.

Student activity 6.5

This is an individual assignment. The so-called 'Big Bang' has been referred to as the most dramatic event in British financial history. By reviewing newspaper reports of the event, such as the *Times* report to be found in the 27 October (1986) issue, produce a brief, interesting, and informative article saying what you think the Big Bang was concerned with; who it affected and how; and what is meant by Stock Exchange Automated Quotation (SEAQ).

Skills assessable

	Skill							
	1	2	3	4	5	6	7	8
Assignment								
1	1.3	2.4	3.4	4.3		6.2		8.2
	1.6		3.5	4.4		6.3		8.3
	1.8		3.6	4.6				8.4
	1.10		3.7					8.5
								8.6
2		2.2	3.4	4.3		6.1		
		2.4	3.5	4.5		6.2		
			3.9	4.6				
			3.11	4.7				
3	1.5	2.2		4.3	5.1	6.1	7.1	8.3
	1.8	2.4		4.6	5.2	6.2	7.2	
		2.5		4.10	5.5	6.3		
4	1.5	2.2		4.3		6.1		
	1.8	2.4		4.6		6.2		
		2.5				6.3		
5	1.8	2.2		4.3		6.1		
	1.9	2.4		4.6		6.2		
		2.5				6.3		
		2.6						

7
TECHNOLOGICAL PROCESSES

Technology and technological change has been subject to almost continuous development throughout history. In order to appreciate the way in which organisations operate, an understanding of technology and an appreciation of its impact is vital.

The nature of technology and technological change

In the simplest sense, technology could be taken to mean mechanical techniques; but, in the wider view, technology could be all of the knowledge possessed by society. Since this is neither the time nor the place to consider the total body of knowledge possessed by society, we will be concerned only with processes and mechanical techniques, plus the knowledge employed by business organisations, as being indicative of technology.

When I discuss technology and the changing world with students I mention conversations I once had with a very elderly neighbour when I was a student in the mid-1970s. I realised one day that she had probably forgotten more about the world as it had been than I would ever know, so when she talked about what life was like when she was a child I listened intently. She had been born in the 1890s, and could remember things about her childhood that really brought home to me how the world had changed. She remembered simple but poignant details such as shopping and having things weighed out and wrapped, like sugar and salt and tea.

There was no electricity; there were no cars; photography was in its infancy. Queen Victoria was on the throne until my friend was about six (in all she has seen two queens (Victoria and Elizabeth II) and four Kings (Edward VII, George V, Edward VIII, and George VI). The Prime Minister was the Marquis of Salisbury, and in her life (she was still alive when Britain's first female Prime Minister was elected) she saw 21 different people become Prime Minister – several of these serving on a number of occasions.

We lived close to a flight path from Heathrow airport, and one day, while sitting in the garden, we watched Concorde fly out of sight. I passed a comment about the speed and beauty of the amazing craft, at which she reminded me that people had not been able to leave the ground via powered flight when she was born. She was about eight when Orville Wright flew under power for the first time (*for a fleeting 12 seconds!*). In her lifetime she saw man fly for the first time and eventually walk on the moon; she saw technological advances in medicine from the early days of very basic medical care to heart, liver, and kidney transplants; she saw the days before radio and then saw not only stereo radio and colour television, but also personal stereo radios, miniature (pocket) televisions, videos, and home computers. Technology in her day was being able to get running water from a tap inside the house; it was being able to use a toilet which flushed into a sewer system; it was about war where men fought on horseback; it was about housework being an arduous task; it was about collecting the harvest by hand using a scythe; and it was about manufacturing textiles using equipment produced during the Industrial Revolution.

- *Talk to the oldest person you can find (if you know an old person but don't know them to talk to, introduce yourself – you will find the experience an education in itself) and find out what life was like when they were your age. You may like to find out:*
  - *how old they were when they left school,*
  - *what type of work they did,*
  - *how much they were paid,*
  - *how much it cost to travel,*
  - *the cost of a meal in a restaurant/café,*
  - *what they did in their spare time.*

It has been argued that education attempts to reflect technological progress, in that what educators do is merely provide employable resources for a technologically advanced world. In other words, they give specific skills designed to enable young people to cope with increased technology. The implication of this strategy for education is that young people may not then have the opportunity to acquire the skills required of members of society, which they would need to be able to handle the increased power greater technology brings.

Technology affects the nature of work. Consider the example of production. Technological developments may require assembly-line operations, with teamwork being the norm. In other situations the technology may require employees working in isolation from each other, demonstrating various degrees of skill. As a result, increases in technology may lead to jobs which become less attractive because of repetition or restriction in the number and type of tasks performed by operatives. The implication of jobs such as this is that employees will soon become dissatisfied at work and therefore less motivated to work hard.

The way that we are, the way we behave towards others, the things that we produce, the type of organisations we create, all say something about the nature of the culture that we live in. The present culture in this country can be differentiated from that of, say, nineteenth-century Britain not only in terms of attitudes and general behaviour but also (perhaps more significantly) in terms of the technology used in organisations.

The development of technological processes

The impact of technology on the design, production, and distribution of products is considerable. Technological change can even dictate an organisation's structure.

The change associated with technology has become more apparent as time has gone on, primarily because the period between one technological breakthrough and another appears to be getting shorter. For example, the early experiments on magnetism were followed by some *two hundred and fifty years* before J.C. Maxwell perfected a general theory of the electromagnetic field in the 1870s. Professor Röntgen discovered X-rays in 1895, but it was only *thirty years* or so later that they were being used. When Hahn and Strassman discovered nuclear fission in uranium in 1939, they only had to wait *eleven years* before the first nuclear pile was created. The pace of technology is quickening with time and we can expect more and more technological breakthroughs per decade than ever before.

- *List what you consider to be six milestones in technological advance throughout history.*

There have undoubtedly been milestones in technological history – for example, the development of the steam engine and the production of electric motors, telephones, and television. In the past, however, an invention was not immediately followed by the introduction of gadgets which made use of that invention – in fact there were often many years between initial experiments and the establishment of a product for commercial use, just as there were often many years between one technological breakthrough and another. However, it seems that today, no sooner do we hear of a technological breakthrough than it appears in our homes in the form of a device designed to make life just that little bit easier, or more relaxed, or prolonged.

As a result of increased technology, communication in general has increased. It is now possible to see what is happening on the other side of the world as it happens; we can hold instantaneous conversation with people on other continents; we can share experiences and events with people practically anywhere in the world. The increased speed of communication saves time in itself; it also saves time and resources by helping to avoid the need for travel to deal with problems. Because increased technology is saving us time (it is taking us less time to do certain things), we have more time available to do other things.

At this stage, let us consider a couple of examples of the increased use of technology in organisations by considering the experiences of the Imperial Group and the Royal Bank of Scotland.

- *List the major activities of The Imperial Group.*

From the above task, you should have found that, among other activities, the Group operates about 4000 public houses around Britain. The significance of this is that it is difficult to obtain up-to-date information on which products are being sold, and in what quantity, when there are so many outlets. Such information as the general consumption pattern for items stocked could be obtained, but, once processed, the information would be historical – in other words, it would not serve a useful purpose because it would be out-of-date. The ideas being generated to solve this problem revolve around the concept of installing automated cash registers and some form of metering or reader on beer pumps which would send information to a personal computer installed in each public house. Thanks to improved telecommunications networks, this information could be sent from each personal computer to a computer at headquarters every evening, where it would be processed and transmitted back out to regional sales managers via their own personal computers.

The situation concerning The Imperial Group is getting close to reality because of the increased use of advanced technology such as, in this case, digital language. Conventionally telephones used wave form or analog language; the use of digital allows greater capacity as well as improved quality. We should therefore see many organisations replacing analog systems (see page 72 for brief explanation) with digital systems as the need for more data communication increases.

It was mentioned previously that increases in communication technology help to avoid the need for travel, and a good example of this is the case of the Royal Bank of Scotland – which uses video-conferencing. The ability to send data, oral transmission, and pictures through a telephone line permits members of conferences to remain at their workstations *and* be in a conference with other employees at the same time. Thus, while communication is quicker, increased technology also provides us with *more* and *better* (more up-to-date) information.

Not everyone would agree that increased technology is necessarily a good thing. Ban The Bomb supporters, the Peace Movement, Greenpeace, and many other ecological and/or anti-war groups would argue against certain aspects of technological development, particularly in the case of nuclear power and arms production, for example.

- *Your group has decided to debate the issue shown below. You are to divide into two factions – some of you have to assume you are against expenditure on arms development and want more spent on social services and education, the rest want to spend on a nuclear deterrent as a means of ensuring peace in the world. The issue is:*

  There has not been a major war in Western Europe for 40 years because countries hold a nuclear deterrent. We have to sacrifice expenditure on education and health-care to enable us to spend more on arms as a means of ensuring peace. More expenditure on education would be worthless if we were to be attacked tomorrow.

Technology usage and the functions of the technological process

- *In sub-groups of three or four spend ten minutes discussing among yourselves what functions you think technology performs. A spokesperson from each sub-group can now present the findings of the three or four to the rest of the class or group. Is there a consensus view in the overall class or group of the function(s) technology performs?*

Questions concerning the purpose of technology are sometimes dealt with as though they were as profound as statements concerned with the meaning of life itself. New technology is not developed as a means of initiating social reform or as a means of providing a more meaningful existence for the working classes, or any other such romantic notion. We have developed technologically advanced states with one overall objective in mind – to allow us to produce more efficiently (to enable a more economic use to be made of scarce resources). It would be worthwhile at this stage to spend time considering examples of the technologically advanced equipment and processes which are available or which are being developed in order to reinforce the point that technology is used to increase output and minimise costs.

Computer-aided design/computer-aided manufacture (CAD/CAM)

Computers have been introduced in the development, design, manufacture, and distribution stages of some industries. Initially, there were distinct areas within organisations that were automated – these tended to be design, analysis, documentation, and production. In the design stage the application of computer technology was initially very limited; it was the managerial functions that tended to exploit the use of computerisation. For example, in analysis (computers could aid analysis by rapidly transforming data into recognisable forms such as charts, diagrams, accounts, and tables of statistical data). Other managerial functions such as production control could be performed with the use of computers and it was not long before these machines could be used on the factory floor. Certainly the initial use was limited, but with the introduction of robotics computers found a wider application.

The secretarial services of many industries were among the early departments to recognise the potential savings to be made from the use of machines such as word processors, and from the use of the capacity of a computer to store information and allow its easy and quick retrieval. Now it is becoming unusual to find these distinct areas of automated work in action since such processes can be integrated into *single systems*.

As far as CAD/CAM is concerned, its initial application is in the field of design. Take, for example, the problem of designing a new car. In the past designers would spend months at a drawing board, following this with further months preparing and testing scale models before spending more time and money building prototypes which, if all went well, were put into production. It was hoped that enough would be sold to give a viable return on the investment. With the use of CAD a computer can be used to:

- visualise the product via three-dimensional 'models';
- calculate costs of production;
- perform design changes without re-doing drawings and calculations;
- test designs and evaluate performance such that possible manufacturing problems are uncovered before expensive prototypes are built.

The impact of being able to 'test' concepts before prototypes have been built is probably best appreciated when one considers that engineers can now even test components to see how they will respond to various conditions, such as changes in stress, load, heat, pressure, etc. Components can be divided into small parts by the computer and the reaction of each part to a change in a variable can be calculated. This is called finite element analysis (FEA).

As a result of using a CAD system to design a product manufacturers also find that much of the useful information gathered at this stage can be taken out of the computer in hard copies, which will form the basis of maintenance and training manuals.

As far as *manufacture* is concerned (CAM) it is noticeable that more and more processes in factories are being done by computer. When manufacture is a continuous process there needs to be an element of control – man can now not only direct a machine to get on with a task, but he can also programme the machine to control processes, produce feedback, and react to avoid waste and errors in production. Robots, as mentioned earlier, are used to conduct repetitive tasks quickly – without tea-breaks, and without asking for a pay rise.

Partly finished and completed jobs are moved around factory spaces by automatic guided vehicles (AGVs) and, taking the example of car production again, if the manufacturer is really up-to-date all the operations involved in design and manufacture will be amalgamated into one computer-controlled process referred to as computer-integrated manufacture (CIM).

Suggesting a vital change to the chassis of a car in production, to incorporate a new safety feature, would not involve an upheaval on the production line because of the following points:

1. All the information concerning the existing design is already stored within the computer – this can be easily and quickly retrieved.

2. The modifications can be quickly drawn up via the CAD system.

3. Necessary calculations concerning load bearing, stress capabilities, increases in cost, etc., can be done by the computer.

4. The revised design can then be tested by computer simulation.

5. Plans showing dimensions can be produced by the computer and this information can be transferred into instructions for the manufacturing machines. The system adopted will probably be computer numerical control (CNC), whereby a machine can be programmed to perform a sequence of operations.

6. Since all the information is available to all those concerned, not just the production team (because we are employing a computer integrated manufacturing system), managers from various departments can access data. This means personnel, for example, can estimate manpower requirements (see Chapter 12); stores will be able to estimate raw materials requirements; marketing know what is being produced and so can plan marketing strategy accordingly. All of the components within an organisation can operate more efficiently because they are *integrated* in their actions.

- *What would you say were the implications for the following groups of people of the introduction of CAD/CAM into their organisation:*
  a) management,
  b) production line employees,
  c) shareholders?

Word processors

I expect most of you will have at least seen a word processor even if you have not had an opportunity to use one. Many home computers can be used as word processors, while at the sophisticated (and expensive) end of the market we have 'dedicated' word processors.

- *What is meant by the term 'dedicated' word processor?*

The market for word processors is a strange one, showing fairly modest growth (3½% p.a. projected to 1989) but with falling costs in the bottom end of the market.

- *What is meant by the bottom end of the market'?*

Sales for all dedicated text-processing systems – that is, electronic typewriters and all types of word processor – in volume terms (by number of keyboards) was 217,000 in 1983 and is expected to be in the region of 284,000 by 1988, though the market is expected to decline after 1988.

One of the problems faced by manufacturers of dedicated word processors has been the competition from microcomputers. Although micros have a reputation for word processing software (a programme package which tells the machine it is a word processor) which is not user-friendly (intimidates user when mistakes are made/does not assist when errors occur) and which also may be limited and subject to a number of program 'bugs', they have done slightly better in terms of sales because they are more versatile. The manufacturers of dedicated systems have recognised this threat and been forced to compete by producing packages of their own which enable the word processor to deal with accountancy packages (software), BASIC (a computer language) and other useful office facilities such as data retrieval.

Word processors allow you to produce 'perfect' copy all the time. Errors can be eliminated via correction on the visual display unit (VDU)/visual display terminal (VDT) before asking the machine for a 'hard copy' – that is, a typed/printed copy on a sheet of paper. Only basic keyboard skills and a short course in the capabilities of your particular machine would be required. Operating a word processor therefore becomes a job which many can do almost on leaving school.

- *Obtain literature concerning the application and attributes of a selection of word processors. Produce a chart/diagram which shows the features these machines possess.*

Facsimile transmission

Facsimile transmission is a form of electronic mail which is often referred to simply as 'fax'. Before 1980 the transmission of pictures/documents via this medium was not particularly successful since the quality was often very poor. From 1981 onwards fax had become much more acceptable as a method of transmitting vital charts, documents, photographs, etc. The reason for the apparently sudden improvement in quality associated with fax systems comes from the Japanese. In 1980 the Japanese launched a *digital* fax standard (digital transmission has improved quality over its forerunner, analog – as mentioned on page 69) as a means of transmitting data and information since other methods, such as telex, were not suitable for the transmission of their written material (bear in mind that their written language appears as a considerable mixture of characters).

- *What other countries can you think of where fax would be an ideal method of electronic communication transmission but where telex would not? Why have you made the suggestion(s) you just noted down?*

The images to be transmitted are converted into electrical impulses by scanning with light and converted into either (a) an analog signal (older machines) or (b) a digital signal (machines manufactured since international standards were agreed in 1981). (Analog systems use the public telephone network. Messages are sent in the form of sound waves and often pick up interference, such as noise on a line, which distorts the signal. Digital systems use a modem, which converts the analog signal into a pulse which is sent down the telephone line. The pulse can be regenerated along the line – as opposed to amplified, which would also merely amplify any distortion – and, when it reaches its destination, is then converted back into an analog signal. The result is that digital greatly improves quality of messages received and therefore quality of images for fax systems.)

These analog or digital signals are then converted back to an identical image by a remote machine. Each fax machine is thus capable of both sending and receiving images. For this reason they are often referred to as *transceivers*.

- *Visit a local office suppliers and find out which fax machines are most in demand in your area. What type of organisations appear to be using such devices?*

Videotex

The first thing to note is that one of the types of videotex is called *teletext* and this is not to be confused with the electronic messaging service operated on a word processor-to-word processor basis (very much like telex), referred to as *teletex*.

Videotex is a generic term for two services, viewdata and teletext, as shown in Fig. 7.1.

Prestel links the technologies of television and telephone and, although videotex is restricted to the number of characters which can be displayed on a screen (thus limiting the amount of alphanumeric text which can be displayed), it compensates for this loss by using colour and graphics in presentation. Graphics are displayed in alphamosaic form – that is, images are composed of rectangular grids; more advanced systems have the capacity to build images

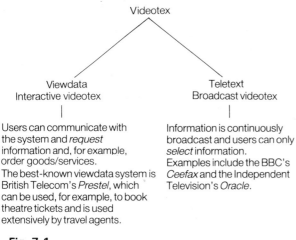

Users can communicate with the system and *request* information and, for example, order goods/services.
The best-known viewdata system is British Telecom's *Prestel*, which can be used, for example, to book theatre tickets and is used extensively by travel agents.

Information is continuously broadcast and users can only *select* information.
Examples include the BBC's *Ceefax* and the Independent Television's *Oracle*.

Fig. 7.1

from lines, circles, and squares (alphageometric).

Information is selected via a menu. This routes the user through the information available from an index or a summary. The information is stored on 'pages' (which is a block of stored information) and each page can be made up of a number of frames (that which is displayed on the screen at any given time).

Advanced videotex systems of the interactive type are being developed with a number of features which would help considerably in an office environment. The introduction of *light pens*, which can be used to annotate frames on the screen, either by directly 'writing' on to the screen or by using the pen on a desk-top graphics tablet, permits wider use since advanced keyboard skills are not required. The development of techniques which permit systems to access other compatible videotex systems increases the use to which such devices can be put in businesses. The ability to communicate directly between two or more terminals is being researched since it could present a number of advantages to business communications in general.

The latest development in the teletext arena is the possibility of satellite teletext, which opens up the likelihood of worldwide teletext. To give an idea of one implication of this, we could consider the experiences of Scandinavia. Because the Finns, Danes, and Swedes move around in each other's countries on business and pleasure to a large extent (and to cater for a number of, say, Finnish-speaking nationals who reside in Sweden and vice versa), the countries swap pages from their own national networks. Thus, a Swedish visitor to Finland can locate pages of news in Swedish on Finnish teletext;

just as a Dane visiting Sweden could find Danish teletext on the Swedish network.

- *If international teletext becomes a reality between, say, countries in the EEC, what type of information do you think would be broadcast?*

The above has been just a sample of the technological advances that have been made which have helped to increase knowledge and efficiency while also helping to minimise costs. However, this is not the end of the story as far as technology is concerned. In Chapter 5 the systems of Manufacturing Automation Protocol (MAP) and Technical Office Protocol (TOP) were mentioned as means by which the approach to production, design, and control have been altered as a result of technological developments. Since these systems affect the way the technological process functions they will be dealt with here.

Manufacturing Automation Protocol

One of the problems with development in production automation has been the incompatibility between computer systems, which has led to difficulties in integrating manufacturing processes.

The US manufacturers General Motors began work on MAP in 1979, since they had 40,000 systems controlling equipment in their factories, but only one in seven were capable of passing data to machines outside the process they happened to be involved with. Manufacturing processes were thus difficult to integrate. As a direct result of the lack of technical standards it was also the case that an organisation could not buy equipment from a number of manufacturers (which may have been advantageous cost-wise), since such equipment could not be mixed – that is, it was incompatible.

Technical Office Protocol

This system, originated by the US Boeing organisation, was designed with two objectives in mind:

1. To enable the computers used by draughtsmen, engineers and the production managers to be linked and
2. To enable a link-up with MAP so data could flow between the draughtsmen's offices, the offices of the engineers and the production manager, and the shop floor.

New technology can thus be used in the production process either directly (by performing productive operations) or indirectly (by controlling processes). New technology also plays an increasingly important part in a vital area of businesses, that of information processing, storage and retrieval. Several years ago the computer tended to be used for limited activities – accounts, for example – but as time has marched on and technological developments have taken place, the activities where a computer can be employed and the situations in which a computer is being used have increased. Organisations have realised that computers are not only useful for handling numeric data by performing accounting activities (number-crunching) but are also useful in bringing together sets of data, analysing them and then enabling executives to forecast on the basis of the information available.

In the past businessmen considered using computers; as time progressed consideration revolved around *which* computers; today they are considering the implementation of networked systems.

- *What type of operations could be performed by staff using a personal computer (a PC)?*

PCs are thought to be so important to organisations that 95% of large companies in the UK are now using them to a greater or lesser extent. Latest developments in this field suggest that organisations will now be trying to take PCs out of the field of *personal* devices and instead linking them together (into a *network*), so that information can be shared. Networking has a number of advantages for businesses. For example, those organisations with limited resources and, say, only two or three printers but possibly half a dozen PCs could find that employees on one floor could be composing material which could be printed on another floor where there is a printer not currently being used. Employees at various stations around the organisations could all 'plug-in' to information or software packages at the same time if the system was networked, allowing a number of employees to work on the same file, for example.

- *List and discuss other examples of organisations where you think a network would confer benefits.*

One final example of the use of new technology and its impact involves car manufacturers and the enormous costs incurred as a result of operating distribution networks. To give an idea of just how much money is involved, it is estimated that it costs

British Leyland £10 to handle a trade document; French manufacturers Peugeot Talbot receive approximately 15,000 invoices each month and send out 1200 payment advices.

- *What level of costs would you think are involved in the Peugeot case?*

To save time and money in the processing of documents – putting them into envelopes; sealing, stamping and posting them; having the receiver open them, reply to them and file them – Europe's motor manufacturers and suppliers have established the Organisation for Data Exchange by Tele-transmission in Europe (Odette). Manufacturers such as Ford, Peugeot, Austin Rover, Fiat, etc., and suppliers such as Lucas, GKN, Philips, and SKF have agreed to replace trade documents concerned with every part that goes into a car with electronic messages exchanged by computer. It is thought that Europe's car manufacturers and suppliers will save £2 billion a year when the scheme is operational, provided the tens of thousands of small suppliers presently at work in the industry spend large sums each and join in the scheme, and provided manufacturers can forget petty national rivalries.

In Chapter 8 we will be concerned with the problems of cost associated with new technology and the impact of de-skilling, plus the impact of technology on the environment. One final issue to consider in this chapter, concerned as it has been with technology usage and the functions of technology, is the implication of technological change which has resulted in changing patterns of work.

We tend to consider new technology for its own sake – that is, we often reflect on the technical developments that have been made and consider also the type of machinery that we now have available. What we do not hear a great deal about is the impact of technological change on the way in which we do our jobs.

- *Given the opportunity, would you be prepared to work at home – that is, would you carry out the job you do now, or would hope to do on leaving college, at home? Assuming such a proposal is realistic, what do you feel would be the advantages/disadvantages of working at home and being linked to the office via a computer?*

Working at home is something that does concern many people – a situation which you may find yourselves in at some stage of your career. For many years there has been a myth propagated that to do well in your career you not only have to work hard but also have to devote much of your own time to the organisation. Over the years this has been taken further and further, and now many people find that they are spending almost as long working at home as they are at their desks – all goaded by the thought of promotion. The peculiar thing is that once promotion has been won, the same process starts over again. One has to work that much harder than rivals to ensure promotion, good career development, etc. In other words, there are many people throughout the country who actually do a lot more than they are specifically paid to do; there are many who go home after a hard day's work merely to start again.

- *Your organisation is trying to introduce working at home for its executives. It is planned that each executive will have a personal computer, a personal copier, and a desk-top facsimile machine. The entire telephone bill for each executive will be paid for by the company. Your task is to prepare an argument which will convince the executives that this would be a good move.*

The fear of managers is that working at home almost permanently, favoured as being a method by which travel time is cut and the office distractions are avoided, will lead to even more pressure to devote more of your own time to the organisation. Technological developments have made it possible for staff to function on a regular basis in an organisation while being remote from it – that is, employees could be at work (though perhaps not continuously) from home (or, in fact, anywhere outside their actual office).

It is now possible to participate in activities at work, communicate information and data to your place of work, and use work-based support to enable you to perform your job without being at the office. Working from home might also mean that the organisation is able to reduce its office space and, possibly, reduce the number of support personnel. On the other hand, when one does not work in the office one loses the motivational contact of belonging to a work group. It may also be harder to discipline oneself to working, particularly when there are home distractions.

- *Do you find it easier to complete assignments at home or on college premises? What reason(s) do you have for your answer?*

It is interesting to note that employment in manufacturing originated in so-called 'cottage' industries but, with the onset of the Industrial Revolution and greater use of mechanisation, it became impractical

to permit work at home. There was then an upheaval as people had to adjust to working in factories. It now seems that the Electronic Revolution is likely to do much to encourage more work at home, a move away from large premises which house many dozens of employees and towards the acceptance of work from your own residence. This move is only likely to affect executives in the near future rather than the manufacturing industry but, with the cost of personal computers being rapidly reduced in real terms over time and improved tele-communication links via optic fibres, it is not inconceivable that supportive functions such as secretarial and clerical operations could take on the same character.

Assignments

Student activity 7.1

This assignment has been designed for students working in groups of three or four. Each group is to arrange a visit to at least one local business with the objective during the visit of obtaining sufficient information to allow you to complete the task outlined below.

After sufficient time for research and preparation of a group presentation, each group is to report back to the large group/class of which it is a part. This plenary session will be concerned with what your small group has been able to discover first-hand about the *impact of the so-called Technological/Electronic Revolution*. Particular attention should be paid to the way in which operations are conducted compared with, say, ten years ago; the feelings of the staff towards their work today, compared with pre-high tech days; and the impact that the technological changes have had on the management of the business.

Student activity 7.2

This is an individual assignment. Referring to the article on page 76, prepare a briefing document for your training officer on what you consider to be the possible uses, from a training point of view, for interactive (satellite-based) videoconferencing (see Student activity 6.4 for a brief explanation of this term).

Student activity 7.3

This is an assignment for the whole group (class). For this task your group is to assume it is a debating

For many US companies, school is up. Satellite networks beam corporate training programmes coast to coast and beyond. It isn't cheap but the benefits are enormous – and competition is the spur. Why pi in the sky isn't pie in the sky.

Satellites beam the corporate image

Billinman

THE professor looks a touch frumpy. He sports a crooked bow tie and dusts chalk from his threadbare suit as he inscribes a line of abstruse formulae on a blackboard. The image may appear familiar. Don't be fooled. This is no ordinary classroom.

The instructor is a world authority on 16-bit microcomputers. He is imparting his latest experimental findings to students sitting in electronic cubicles thousands of miles away. His voice and image, captured in a Southern California studio, are being instantly compressed, digitised and transmitted via satellite to a dozen remote locations across North America.

Midway through the lecture, a New England engineer-trainee – this lecture is for IBM – presses a button near his outsized video screen to register a question. At a convenient moment, the professor touches the face of a computer monitor at his elbow, opening a closed-circuit microphone linking him with the trainee. Within seconds, he answers the question. Other questions pour in from Michigan, Texas and other points.

A bit Orwellian? Perhaps. But this is not fiction. Big Brother technology has arrived, and it is being put to work in the training centres and lecture halls of some of the US's largest corporations. Training courses distributed via satellite, almost unheard of a few years ago, are becoming commonplace as the cost of satellite time decreases, the range of technology expands and corporations move increasingly into the international arena.

However, 'a satellite network makes no sense for a company with fewer than 20 offices', says Jeff Charles, a research fellow for the Institute for the Future, a Menlo Park, California, think tank. Per location, the price of a satellite dish – not including installation, wiring, and related costs – is about $4,000. To receive specialist broadcasts from outside organisations, corporations must pay an hourly rate plus a one-off subscription fee, sometimes as high as $200,000. The Institute of Electrical and Electronic Engineers, a New York-based university consortium, charges $3,500 to view a satellite broadcast of one of its five-hour courses.

Cost has not inhibited the boom in corporate satellite networks. 'There were less than five networks just four years ago,' says Charles. 'Today there are probably 30, and more are going up each year.' For multinationals, in particular, in-house satellite networks have proved invaluable. 'Point-to-multipoint broadcasting makes a lot of sense when your company has hundreds of offices around the globe, and news must be communicated quickly,' Charles says.

Satellite networks, although primarily designed for worker training, have a number of side benefits. Hewlett-Packard recently briefed its entire worldwide sales force, including salesmen at offices in France, West Germany and the UK, on a new product. 'We were able to have our chief product developers, the chief of our R&D unit, and our chief executive officer, John Young,

speak and answer questions from 82 sites around the world,' says Alfred Moye, Hewlett-Packard's manager of continuing education. The company's latest earth station is in Bristol in west England.

'We're obviously sold on satellites – they provide fast and accurate information over great distances,' says a spokesman for Motorola. Last year, Motorola spent $40 million and delivered more than one million hours of satellite-transmitted training to its workers around the world. 'We offer sales courses, software training, stress management – the whole ball of wax.' Although Honeywell, Hewlett-Packard, IBM and Motorola are leaders in the field, a number of companies – not all multinationals – are rapidly grasping the benefits of satellite training. These include J.C. Penney, Merrill Lynch, Eastman Kodak, Citibank and small but widely scattered retail chains such as Computerland and Micro-Age.

Metropolitan Life Insurance recently spent $1 million to prepare its New York headquarters, eight territorial offices and various regional offices – 80 locations in all – for satellite transmissions. 'Eventually, we hope to expand the network to connect every one of our 1,200 branch offices,' says a spokesman. 'Computer-satellite link-ups can eliminate whole layers of bureaucracy that impede rapid communications.'

Source: *Business Magazine*, September 1986

society formed to consider the possible impact and short- to medium-term consequences of the introduction of new technology in the business studies section of your college. Consider the impact on teaching staff, administrative staff, catering and ancillary staff, students, and the providers of finance (local authority, central government and the Manpower Services Commission). There is no reason why this task should not be used as the basis for an open meeting, with people from outside the college (e.g. local union representatives, businessmen, councillors, etc.) being invited. If so, then part of the task would be to select and invite people from outside the college to attend.

Student activity 7.4

This assignment has been designed for groups of four or five. Your local education authority and British Telecom have jointly decided to introduce a videoconferencing network in your college. The academic staff see potential gains for education and cost savings from the use of the system, and BT hope it will provide them with a working test-bed and advertising forum. It is anticipated that lectures will be broadcast to selected rooms around the college (thus saving on the cost of lecturing staff) on an interactive basis – that is, anyone in any of the other rooms will be able to ask questions and respond to the lecturer. Your group has been asked to consider the proposal and make recommendations either in favour of or against the introduction of the system, from the point of view of students. Your task is to make an oral presentation, as a group, on the views your group holds in connection with the proposal (you must attempt to justify the views you hold).

Student activity 7.5

This assignment has been designed for three students working together. As a new employee of the National Midland Bank (Marketing Section) you are undergoing initiative tests and training with the Bank's education service. As part of the training programme you have been given responsibility for a part of an overall marketing strategy designed to encourage more people to become customers of the bank. You are expected to work with two other inexperienced members of the Section (trainees like yourself) in producing a pamphlet which will show customers what being a bank customer is likely to be like in the year 2001).

Essentially, the bank is concerned that potential customers are not made to feel that new technology will result in a more impersonal service. The pamphlet must therefore give the impression that new technology usage in banking is a good thing, and that such facilities as you can imagine might be used would be advantageous to all.

An imaginative and amusing pamphlet would rank highly with those in authority.

Student activity 7.6

This is an individual assignment. Consider the content of the articles on page 78. Visit a local shopping area and note the variety and extent of use of equipment which you would use as examples of how technology has changed shopping in the last five years. Prepare a short article on this theme.

Interview parents/older relatives/friends, to obtain comments and anecdotes of what they remember about shopping thirty years ago.

Comparing the view of shopping thirty years ago with your view of the process today, say what part technological processes have played in the change. From your study, say what else has changed shopping, other than technological changes associated with it.

Skills assessable

Assignment	*Skill* 1	2	3	4	5	6	7	8
1	1.8 1.9	2.1 2.2 2.7	3.2 3.5 3.6 3.9	4.2 4.3 4.6 4.7		6.1 6.2 6.6		
2	1.6 1.8	2.2 2.5		4.3 4.5 4.6		6.1 6.2 6.3		
3	1.6 1.8		3.2 3.5 3.10 3.11	4.3 4.6 4.8 4.10		6.1		
4	1.3 1.5 1.6 1.8 1.9	2.2 2.4	3.5 3.7 3.9 3.11	4.3 4.8 4.10		6.1 6.2 6.3		
5	1.3 1.5 1.6 1.8	2.2 2.4 2.7	3.4 3.5 3.6 3.7 3.9 3.11	4.3 4.4 4.6 4.9	5.1 5.2 5.10	6.1 6.2 6.3 6.4		8.4 8.5 8.6

High Street visions set tills ringing

A Brunel University professor has turned an old Victorian stage trick into a high street advertising device which he hopes will make shoppers momentarily doubt their sanity. The adverts will float in mid-air.

The technique has been devised by Paul Cook, Brunel's British Aerospace professor of laser technology, to help market another of his inventions, a laser-based eye testing device called Laserspec.

He remembered an old trick used by Victorian magicians to create realistic ghosts on stage using an invisible sheet of plate glass. An actor off stage is illuminated by a bright light and his image is projected onto the glass creating the so-called 'Pepper's Ghost' which seems to float up on the stage.

Using modern lighting and reflecting materials, Cook has taken this idea to produce the Holospacegram, a portable ghost-making machine for shop windows.

A transparent strip carrying a message passes in front of two fluorescent lights. The image then hits a specially-textured reflector which acts as both a mirror and a lens. Bounced off this, the message passes through the glass plate at the front, and the moving words appear suspended about a foot in front of the device.

Estate agents and insurance brokers are said to be particularly keen to use the technique.

Source: *The Sunday Times*, 14 December 1986

Psst! Walls have mouths

WHEN was the last time a poster spoke to you? Or sang? In recent weeks shoppers in the Stratford Arndale Centre near Manchester have been accosted by one.

It could be the first of 200 that London & Provincial Posters will set up at handpicked sites where they will grab the ear of passing shoppers. Market researchers will first decide if they annoy or amuse the public.

Talking posters have been made possible by the solid state recorder. This is much the same as a tape recorder, but it synthesises – rather than records – music, jingles and voices. It has a chip and no moving parts. Chips are tougher than components used in tape recorders, and do not mind wet winters and long hot summers, which makes them better suited to the rigours of a poster's life.

Solid-state recorders have been slipping into public places gradually over the last two years, sounding warnings about pumps on petrol station forecourts and detailing the private lives of tigers at zoos.

Michael Wood, a management consultant working for Creative Planners, has taken the UK marketing rights to an American recorder called the Digitalker.

'Posters are just the gimmicky end of the spectrum,' he says. They could prove useful in any situation where you want to be sure that people get the message even if they cannot be bothered to read it – vending machines and talking fire alarms, for instance, that tell the public what to do in an emergency.'

Source: *The Sunday Times*, 30 November 1986

8

THE IMPACT AND IMPLICATIONS OF TECHNOLOGICAL PROCESSES

The increased use of technology, while having many advocates, is being ignored by a significant minority because of the costs involved and/or the changes which would be required to organisational systems. The likely impact of taking such steps acts as a brake on the rapid introduction of new technology. Another deterrent has been the limited application of available technology. Organisations wait to buy equipment in the expectation that something better or more suitable will come along soon rather than investing now in the current field of either cheap though limited equipment or expensive, omnipotent systems. Many of those who admire the technology and would wish to employ it in their own organisations simply cannot sustain the costs involved.

When we speak of new technology we often do so without appreciating everything that it entails. Indeed, new technology can be thought of as three particular technologies. These are:

> computing,
> microelectronics,
> telecommunications.

When we use the term *information technology*, we are considering the interrelated features of these new technologies.

Cost implications and technological processes

The costs involved in introducing new technological processes ought not to be viewed solely in financial terms. The costs met by users (in terms of health considerations), the very high opportunity costs of investment in new technology, along with the costs of social responsibility faced by employers (who may find that technology reduces the demand for labour) are all areas which we could consider under the heading of 'cost implications'.

- What is meant by:
  a) *financial cost,*
  b) *opportunity cost,*
  c) *social cost*?

The financial costs of new technology can be considerable to the small or medium-sized business, which may find it difficult to absorb the expenditure required. Although the larger firms also have to spend proportionately large sums they can at least afford to finance such activity (or generate sufficient borrowing capacity to do so) to enable them to obtain the technology required.

It may be the case that organisations have very good, positive reasons (as opposed to 'negative' reasons, e.g. they cannot afford it) for not purchasing new technology. It may seem strange that someone would turn down the opportunity to purchase equipment which is thought to be of such great benefit to organisations. Perhaps an analogy will help to explain. Suppose you entered a wildly eccentric local authority lottery and won; the prize is an expenses-paid trip to the USA. Would you take the trip? Can you say categorically that you would *always* take such a trip?

- *There may be many people who would refuse to go on the trip mentioned above. Can you think of four situations that would prevent you from going, supposing you won such a prize?*

You have probably realised that you, along with many other people, may refuse to go if it is to your advantage to remain at home. For example, I would refuse to go at this instant because I want to finish this book and meet my publishing deadline – something I could not do if I were to go to the USA right now. It may be that, given my luck, I would have to go at a time of the year either when I could not get the time off work or when I had something else arranged. For example, one activity which interests me and which involves me in regular practice and training is windsurfing. If I happened to have a particular race opportunity and I felt that this time I could win, I may not go on the trip, since this may be my opportunity to do well – my training would have been in vain if I took the trip. I can go to the USA at any time, but may never have such a good opportunity of winning a windsurfing race again, since competition is fierce and we all get older and slower.

Another situation in which the response would be the same as mine above would be that of the entrepreneur who could possibly lose a good business deal if he were to go away today – a deal which may perhaps yield enough profit to enable him to travel to the USA a dozen times. In these circumstances he would be rash to go on the prize trip.

It should now be apparent to you that all choices involve opportunities or alternative courses of action. No matter which option we choose, we have to forfeit something to get something. As some of my tutors used to say, 'there ain't no such thing as a free lunch' (taken from the title of the book *TANSTAAFL* by E. Dolan). Whenever we choose to have one thing, we have to do so at the expense of not having something else. If we decide to allocate our resources (e.g. spend our hard-earned money) on consumption (purchase) of one product or service, we cannot allocate those resources (spend that particular sum of money) on other goods/ services. How many times have you heard that you cannot have your cake and eat it?

- *What was the financial cost of your going to college/work today?*
  What was the opportunity cost involved?

Some organisations may feel that they would, in fact, be able to operate more efficiently *without* employing new technology. By way of illustration consider the situation I found myself in a couple of years ago. I decided to keep student records (administrative details including grades, names and addresses, references, etc.) on a computer disc for reasons of efficiency. I had a software package which allowed me to input the names on a 'card system', which the computer then sorted alphabetically. All seemed to be going well until I had to retrieve some details a few days after entering all the information. By the time I had accessed a computer, turned it on, loaded the program, loaded the data disc, and requested the machine to sort the information and come up with the details I had requested, it would have been ten times quicker had I kept the information on a manual card index system in a box on my desk. Technology is not always faster – one needs to consider carefully the use to which the hardware and software will be put and the speed of packages used.

It is therefore not always advisable to rush in where new technology is concerned – better to consider the problem rationally and try to devise an effective and cheap method of solving it, than to spend several hundreds of pounds on equipment which may never be fully utilised or which may never do exactly what you want it to do.

Resources (primarily money) can be used on a multitude of investment opportunities. It is this choice (where to devote resources) that concerns

Fig. 8.1   There are opportunity and social costs associated with these, as well as financial costs

businesses which want the best return possible from their investment.

Social responsibility

Having considered the fact that businessmen, just like you and I, have limited resources and must decide where to allocate them to get the best return, we can now move on to consider the social responsibility which organisations may face.

Changes in social values have important implications for organisations simply because all organisations have a 'people input'. Changes in attitudes of customers, along with changes in values, often lead to the development of new products, the introduction of new techniques, the establishment of new distribution networks and so on. It should not require too much imagination to see that changes in values and attitudes can also change organisations. The response of organisations to, for example, the actions of those experiencing the change in values/attitudes (employees) is worthy of consideration.

Changes in attitude have fostered the view that organisations need to exercise much more care over their treatment of employees. For example, it has been considered improper that organisations strive to make profits at the expense of exploitation of workers and/or customers. Such change has meant that new standards of behaviour are expected of organisations – we now look to organisations to express a desire to be 'socially responsible'. We regularly see organisations trying to project an image of caring – a corporate identity which depicts 'social responsibility'.

- *What do you understand by the term 'social responsibility'?*

Always define the terms used in a question – it not only helps to keep your train of thoughts moving but also enables you to deal with all of the areas which require consideration, since you have already specified what needs to be covered. Social responsibility is generally thought to be all of the obligations people or groups of people (organisations) have towards society. In this sense, having social responsibility implies that you respect the values generated by the society you live in, obey laws, and do not interfere with the rights of others.

Management, it is argued, should possess social responsibility – which ought to be considered when the organisation is likely to affect the environment. My actions as a manager, for example, will affect not only my employees but also the shareholders of my organisation, the organisation's customers, society, and the environment. I cannot please everyone, as any manager knows; I have to respond to various pressures and produce solutions which are sure to irritate some of those concerned. The trick is to give the impression of accommodating the conflicting agencies that exist, to make way for the conflicting forces which coerce us into situations or decisions, while at the same time convincing the competing groups that the best is being done for (each of) them.

Most commentators would argue that organisations have a responsibility to society in general. For example, there are efforts to coerce organisations into, among other things, preventing pollution. Since the Chernobyl nuclear power station disaster in the USSR in 1986 many people now recognise that a country (or, in this case, a union of several republics) owes a duty to other countries to prevent pollution.

- *Research the events which took place in the Chernobyl disaster. Prepare a short oral presentation explaining the background to the situation and what the implications of the event were thought to be at the time.*

Social costs are those which organisations impose on others and for which they cannot be made to pay (compensate victims). A particular instance which is frequently cited as a social cost is that of atmospheric pollution caused by road vehicles. Road

users, in fact, impose social costs on the rest of society in a number of ways, as follows:

1. Government tax revenue has to be diverted into road building (away from some other expenditure, such as schools/hospitals/parks, etc.). This is a cost which society finances (though it is true that not all of the money collected as vehicle excise duty is devoted to road provision/maintenance).
2. Because there are many road users, and because some are not as proficient as others, there are many accidents. The cost of this is a very heavy burden on the National Health Service – this money could be spent on other areas (even within the NHS money spent on casualties resulting from road accidents could be diverted into paediatrics, geriatric or mental health-care).
3. More money has to be devoted to police activities designed to ensure that we all drive safely and within the law. Again, this is money which the police could be devoting to other activities, such as apprehending drug traffickers, rapists, and murders.
4. Dangerous fumes are emitted into the atmosphere from vehicle exhausts which, it is suggested, could cause brain damage in children. Though lead-free petrol is becoming available in the UK (this should ease the problem), many people have already been affected by lead poisoning. Thus, whenever you drive a vehicle, someone, somewhere, is suffering some of the costs of that activity.

- *List all the financial costs involved in being a motorist. Give examples of the opportunity costs of being a motorist. List four social costs which motorists impose on the rest of society (do not include those mentioned above).*

Organisations (it is argued) also have a responsibility towards their employees over and above that laid down in employment and health and safety legislation. An example of this responsibility is the moral obligation employers feel not to make employees redundant, if at all avoidable. Certainly in times of very high unemployment, with little prospect of employment being held by many of those out of work, employers must think long and hard before forcing out more people – on to the unemployment register.

- *Consider the background to the Wapping dispute of 1986. On what basis were the printers sacked? Do you think there was a moral obligation on the part of the employer not to sack the workers concerned? What would you have done if you were the employer?*

The changes in social values that have occurred in the past forty or fifty years or so have, to a large extent, come about as a result of changes in the *quality* of secondary-level education, and also as a result of changes in the *quantity* of such education in the UK over this time. The quality of education has improved because knowledge in general has increased; because the approach to teacher training has become more scientific and professional; and because the resources available to teachers and pupils have improved. The quantity of education has also increased – one only has to compare the average age of school-leavers in 1940 with that of the mid-1980s to see that pupils are at school for longer now than forty to fifty years ago, even when taking into account the fact that lessons appear to finish earlier than they used to.

- *What would you say is the objective of schooling?*
- *What should schools do for us as pupils?*

Schooling was always thought to prepare us for life – it was considered that education gave us the knowledge necessary to succeed.

- *What did you honestly think of your five or more years in secondary-level education? Did it help to prepare you for life after school? How many times did you find you had to do something because it was in the curriculum, yet it did not seem to be relevant to your needs?*

There is a view that education no longer prepares us for the kind of life that we can expect when we leave school. This view says that our education system, designed some time ago, may have served well those it was designed for but it cannot, in its present form, serve the young people of today in the way it should. It does not claim that teachers are inadequate, but that educational philosophy may be outmoded. It claims that education is only now beginning to move in the direction in which salvation may be found – that is, towards vocational courses.

The education 'system' developed in an haphazard way; it was the result of a number of events over time which tended to force educational thinking and educational planning in a particular direction.

- *Hazard a guess at the answer to the following question: 'Why were schools established?'*

Charles Handy (in *The Future of Work*, Blackwell,

1984) suggests that schools, and the requirement that children attend, arose out of the evils of child labour during the Industrial Revolution. More could be done to cater for the welfare of children if they attended school rather than worked in a factory or a mine. School was used as a means of keeping children from employment – it was not, as Handy emphasises, designed to prepare them for work. Children at school were not taught the rudiments of coal-mining or the finer art of sweeping a factory floor; schools were used as a means of preventing children from being exploited and subjected to hard, dangerous, and distasteful employment. The idea was a simple one – if a child has to be in school, he or she cannot also be at work.

Another valid question raised by Handy is whether or not schools best serve the young of today, especially in connection with our means of evaluating a person's performance. We tend to evaluate performance at school by reference to success in examinations, though many people who have employed school-leavers will argue that they have had to spend considerable time, effort, and money in teaching them how to be effective employees. In fact, the number of, say, GCSEs a prospective employee has will often say little about the value that that person may possesss as an employee. However, this is little more than one ought to expect, since such qualifications were not designed to say anything about the employability of young people. When universities were given the responsibility for administering school-leaving examinations they based them on what they were familiar with, which happened to be what university applicants had to demonstrate – knowledge and analysis. Thus, GCSE and 'A' level qualifications are fine for university entrance requirements but of little value to prospective employers. Unfortunately most prospective employers do not appreciate this state of affairs and tend to seek candidates with these qualifications, even though in doing so they may well be passing over a suitable applicant who does not possess GCSEs or 'A' levels.

- *How could schools best prepare young people for the future? What would be the most beneficial provision that could be made available?*

What colleges attempt to do on BTEC courses is to provide students with the skills and knowledge which they feel are necessary for prospective entrants to the business world. Such skill and knowledge input is probably best given via role-play and case-study material which permits people to experience the type of situation(s) they may one day find themselves in. People need to be aware of how work is conducted, what relationships are likely to exist in organisations, what can go wrong, and what happens if it does. Education of this type recognises that change is an important phenomenon and is something with which we all have to contend.

Costs to health

At the outset I said we ought not to consider costs solely from the point of view of financial costs and mentioned the costs met by the users of technology. These so-called 'end-users' are the operators of new technology, such as word processor operators and employees who find themselves tied to a personal computer all of their working days. The impact on health of prolonged exposure to low levels of radiation (which are emitted from visual display units) is an obvious cause for concern among health conscious staff. The risks to women operators who are pregnant were discussed in Chapter 5.

- *You have the opportunity to take up the offer of a job which pays a better salary than any other position currently offered to you. The drawback is that you will have to operate a personal computer (and will therefore be sitting in front of the screen) for at least six hours of each working day. Would you take the job? Give reasons for your answer.*

Another cost met by end-users is the strain of having to keep up with a machine. Since technologically advanced equipment tends to operate, or can be operated, very quickly this increases the demands made upon staff for extra concentration and increased manual dexterity. A consequence of the use of word processors, which has led to considerable increases in the speed of typists, is that a number of operators (specifically those who type at very great speed) now suffer from a condition which affects the joints in the hands in much the same way as arthritis.

One of the results of using very fast, technologically advanced (and sometimes potentially dangerous) machinery is the requirement for greater care and attention on the part of operators, in order to avoid accidents. The effect on the eyes is another consequence which ought to be considered for employees constantly using visual display screens, or those who are tied to equipment which has extremely fast operating speeds.

Employment costs

The costs of unemployment in terms of the effects on the individual and on his or her family, on the resources of the State, and on lost man-hours which could be used in productive enterprises, etc., all mount up over time. A major implication of technological advance is the fact that resources in the form of labour (often skilled labour) will become redundant. For example, the introduction of computer-controlled information systems and mechanisation of loader equipment in mining can bring about a reduction in the number of shift workers required by approximately 30 per cent per shift. In the textile industry manufacturers are using computer-aided design (see page 70) and computer-aided pattern cutting (computer-aided manufacture), along with the use of computerisation in quality control – all of which will reduce the numbers in employment.

- *In what ways has the introduction of technology affected employment opportunities in banks? What aspects of banking have been affected by technology in the last ten years?*

Less than 50 per cent of the UK population use banks. It is expected, therefore, that although banking staffs have been cut as a result of automation the effects of this in terms of job cuts may be offset by the effect of more people in the population opening bank accounts and requiring banking services.

Increased technology has tended to make tasks at work easier to perform, thus reducing the need for highly qualified, skilled employees. However, the unskilled are also likely to suffer from the changing nature of work in that they have no (transferable) skills which they can rely on for employment. We only have to look around us to see that, while there are record levels of unemployment, there are also many vacancies waiting to be filled. The essence of the problem lies in the fact that the vacancies are for people with specific skills and the unemployed do not possess these skills. What is needed from education (and this is one of the objectives of a BTEC course) is a base of transferable skills which students will have on completion of courses, thus increasing their job mobility by facilitating movement within a constantly changing employment environment. As some skills/tasks become obsolete because machines take over, other (different) skills/tasks are needed.

Financial costs

Finally, let us now consider the financial costs of technology. The amount spent on new technology will be a function of the perceived need for it, the actual cost of the equipment, the budget available, and the desire of owners to invest in such capital equipment.

- *What is meant by the following terms:*
  - *a) variable cost,*
  - *b) fixed cost,*
  - *c) marginal cost?*

What is the connection between these various elements of cost?

New technology does not come cheap, but then investment in the future has always been expensive.

- *What is the total cost (equipment plus likely training costs) of a new top-of-the-range personal computer?*

A major consideration in terms of the financial costs of technology is the rapid rate of technological change. The existence of considerable competition between manufacturers forces each to invest heavily in the development of the current range of equipment, while at the same time trying to finance the next generation of machines. Another problem lies in the fact that the development costs of the next generation of machines always seems twice that of previous ones. In order to succeed, having spent so much on development, all manufacturers must aim to satisfy a very large market. Because of this, it is becoming more acceptable and more common for collaboration to exist between producers. Collaboration is becoming a very efficient, cost-effective way of manufacturing.

- *Prepare a short case which illustrates an area of collaboration in research and/or development and/or manufacture between two or more organisations within the EEC.*

De-skilling and retraining

Years ago, workers placed much emphasis on 'learning a trade' – that is, following an apprenticeship. People saw a need to be skilled at a particular trade – to be a craftsman. 'Having a trade behind you' practically guaranteed job security/employment, since employers were always willing to hire a 'craftsman'. Improved technology and the increasing use of technology has made many of the old craft skills redundant; we no longer require people who are skilled in every aspect of a trade but rather people who can perform a relatively simple or basic operation on a machine. It is from this that

the term 'de-skilling' comes. For example, one skill for which the British were famous in the past was tool-making, but gone are the days when the tool-maker could command a premium wage. Organisations now find it cheaper to import imperfectly made tools or 'seconds' from abroad and employ tool-makers to correct them in order to convert them into superior grade tools. To some extent the skill of the tool-maker is still being used, though only in a very limited way.

- *Give examples of six trades which once thrived in Britain but which no longer appear to be so important.*

One school of thought suggests that as technology becomes more automated, this will allow people much more control at work, which will in turn give more purpose and meaning to their work. On the other hand, however, there is the view that the entrepreneurs who own the capital, and who thus direct its use, use their resources to increase automation because it is cheaper than using more labour and because it gives them more control over work processes. The introduction of automation allows entrepreneurs (whether they are individuals in business for themselves or the owners of multinational organisations who employ managers as their entrepreneurial representatives) to hire unskilled labour to operate equipment. The act of breaking down component tasks in production – into operations which can be handled with ease by a technologically advanced machine and an unskilled operator – enables management to exercise much greater control over work processes. The extent of this control is further increased when there is severe unemployment within the economy – since this acts to exert downward pressure on wage demands and decreases the power of all employees, skilled workers included. When unemployment is high management control over the activities of employees is greatly enhanced, since most employees view the prospect of joining the ranks of the unemployed as bleak indeed.

- *What is the current level of unemployment? What effect do you think this has on the attitudes of those who are employed with respect to changing jobs or asking for better pay/conditions at work?*

As work becomes more fragmented with the introduction of technology and the greater application of the principles of division of labour, the skilled worker may find that his worth decreases.

With new technology unskilled labour will have the capability to perform operations which were previously carried out by skilled workers, particularly where jobs/tasks can be broken down (fragmented) further and further into component operations, and as equipment is introduced which can handle various aspects of production. This fragmentation of work allows management not just to reduce the skill requirements of labour, but also to reduce job-learning times, to increase control by standardising procedures, and to reduce the dependence organisations would normally have on the ability, availability, and motivation of individuals. All-round ability is not necessary since jobs are fragmented and workers have the use of technologically advanced equipment; availability of skilled labour is no longer a problem since employers do not have to search for (and possibly have to outbid each other for) skilled labour when unskilled labour is plentiful; motivation may not be a problem for management since employees have their own motivator – fear of unemployment/economic necessity (there is also the consideration that many employees may not be career-oriented and would thus not need motivating, since it would be just as easy for them to leave and work elsewhere if they were dissatisfied with their present job).

- *What did Adam Smith have to say about the division of labour?*

It is worthy of consideration that by de-skilling a job/task, management is at the same time exerting more control. In the past, craftsmen would have been employed and they would have decided issues such as which methods to adopt for solving a problem/dealing with a job; they would decide issues such as the selection of tools and, in many cases, the selection of materials used. The control that skilled workers would have exercised at one time over their work has been lost to automated processes and computer-controlled machinery which is capable of correcting its own errors, if they occur.

We now see more and more job advertisements along the lines of 'No formal qualifications required – manual dexterity and good eyesight essential'. Is this a reflection of the increased demand for unskilled workers? A good example of the process of replacing skilled with unskilled workers appears in *Working The System*, by P. Thompson and E. Bannon and is reproduced below.

'Yesterday I did a job. It took me an hour to pump it in on the computer. The same job once upon a time would have taken four weeks. The company will soon click that a young girl doing the pumping in will be cheaper than a qualified engineer, so ultimately they will get shot of the likes of me. Eventually they will take someone straight from school, show her how to look the number up in the book and type it in.'

This is where the skilled workers of yesterday are losing to the unskilled of today. In Chapter 5 it was noted that large numbers of young people are entering the relatively well paid, though career-stifling, vacancies in fast-food organisations such as McDonald's hamburger bars. For a very small minority who may be fortunate enough to progress to managerial posts within the organisation the position may be desirable but, for the great majority of employees, future prospects are extremely limited. Very little skill is required and training is basic, thus little opportunity exists for future career growth. People who are skilled in all aspects of a particular job are no longer needed.

The impact of de-skilling falls heavily on the workers, since it is they who have to face tasks which become more and more mundane; it is they who have to work with more advanced technology which takes the skill out of a job; it is they who are losing what little control they may have once had over their working lives, and it is they who will be bored by reduced job demands.

- *You are a member of the union which represents 70 per cent of the workforce where you are employed. Management is currently investigating the possibility of installing more technology. Prepare the case which you would put to management which highlights the fears that your members have about de-skilling.*

However, the future is not completely bleak for workers who find they face de-skilling. Although new technology may fragment jobs and automation of tasks may reduce the range of skills a worker uses, this does not mean an end to all skill development – some of the skills required may be enhanced. A good example of this situation is the clerk or typist, faced with new technology and finding that he or she now has a word processor. This employee would clearly find the skill element of the job of typing enhanced because he or she would have a more complex array of keys to deal with. Many of the traditional aspects (skills) of being a clerk or typist may be lost – no filing for example, since all data can be kept on and sorted by a computer – though the clerk or typist would be skilled in another area.

- *Consider an occupation which you feel has been radically altered as a result of the introduction of new technology. In what way(s) would you say the employee(s) concerned has/have benefited (career-wise) from the new technology?*

Another effect of new technology has been to reorganise large chunks of the workforce to such an extent that social life is very different from that of only fifty years ago. In fact, our social lives are being transformed almost daily as a result of new technology.

Environmental implications of technological change

The environment will be affected in a number of ways by changes in, and the use of, new technology. You may have been told that some industries are located in specific parts of the country thanks to the location of sources of raw materials or sources of power (fast-flowing streams for water power, or coal for steam power, for example) or because of the existence of a ready market for the produce of the organisation. These quaint, though only historical, factors concerned with the location of enterprises have given way to new determinants of the location of organisations.

- *What types of organisation tend to dominate the area where you live/work/attend college? Why do you think such organisations have developed in that area?*

For many years the government has intervened in the location of firms in an attempt to alleviate high unemployment in particular areas of the country. However, the one factor which has probably done more to influence the location of both private- and public-sector organisations than any other is new technology.

- *Why is London more important as a commercial centre than Liverpool or Manchester?*

With the advances in communication technology and the introduction of relatively small, light and compact micro-chip-technology machinery, businesses and government-operated organisations can locate wherever they wish – subject, of course, to the usual rules governing business development, such as planning regulations.

- *Why do you think that oil refining is located in areas such as Milford Haven, the Thames Estuary, and Southampton Water?*

- *For what reason(s) do you think the Driver and Vehicle Licensing Centre (DVLC) is in Swansea and the Central Headquarters for the Department of Health and Social Security (DHSS) is in Newcastle?*

A major determinant for organisations which are on the move or for those looking for an initial site is the *infrastructure* of an area. When we speak of infrastructure we are considering the communication links such as roads, railways, etc.

- *The National Exhibition Centre is located at Bickenhill, near Birmingham. Assume you are trying to promote the centre. Outline the particular advantages of the location from the point of view of transport links with the North East, North West, South East, South West and North Wales.*

Successive governments have tried to influence location decisions in an attempt to move organisations to areas where unemployment is particularly high. As part of this process, enticements (such as grants, reduced rates, etc.) and prohibitive action (refusal to grant planning permission or award an Industrial Development Certificate) have been used to influence organisational location.

- *What is an 'Enterprise Zone' and what advantages would a business gain by locating in such a zone?*
- *Name at least one type of business which is located in a particular region of the country because of each of the following:*
  a) proximity to raw materials,
  b) proximity to labour supply,
  c) proximity to the market for the good/service,
  d) proximity to a source of power.
  If you were locating these organisations today, where would you site them and why?

A number of organisations find that their activities have to be conducted some distance from large centres of population. The impact of safety-conscious, protesting inhabitants may be just sufficient to tip the scales against an organisation wishing to locate in a particular area. Clearly there are some industries, e.g. those making explosives and those concerned with nuclear energy, that must be located away from centres of population – for obvious safety reasons.

Consideration of nuclear energy raises the problem of the pollution which could be caused in the event of an accident, such as occurred in Chernobyl in the USSR in 1986 (see page 81). Additionally, there is the pollution problem arising from the radioactive waste produced after processing.

Fig. 8.2 Property and infrastructure can be improved, with the necessary resources and determination. Technological advance does not have to mean the death of an area

New technology may lead to new sources of energy being developed but nuclear power is currently our fastest growing source of power – though it is one which has more objectors than any other source.

It may, in fact, be argued that production in this technologically advanced age is not affected by the same degree of pollution as it was fifty years ago. In the 1930s there was considerably more smoke produced by the manufacturing industry, for example, but since the clean air legislation this is no longer a problem. Atomic energy is a 'clean' source of power, provided we do not allow it to contaminate the environment in any way. There is also today

a greater public awareness of the dangers of pollution and the risks to health of polluting our planet. Even so, there are still many examples of the way in which we pollute the earth. Examples in this country of poor waste disposal are to be found in the report of the Hazardous Waste Inspectorate, published in July 1986, which noted instances of, for example, inadequately fenced refuse sites, the dumping of toxic chemicals, and false economies in terms of non-compliance with safety guidelines by disposal contractors out to reduce their costs. An indication of the extent of the problem of disposal of all types of refuse is the very existence of the Inspectorate, which was established as an advisory body with the aim of encouraging adequate and uniform national standards in the management of hazardous waste. One instance of the problem which can result from production is that of the dumping of toxic waste. In 1986 it was reported that a firm had been pouring millions of gallons of toxic waste into a dump opposite a holiday camp for twelve years. The waste was finding its way through the ground, towards the sea, and although experts disagreed over the time it would take to reach the sea, and whether or not it would still be toxic on arrival, the fear presented a headache to many people using the beach.

The impact of technological change will be felt by workers, entrepreneurs, customers, and society in general. The implications will attach to various groups, for example, the implication for job security will be felt initially by the workers but then by the State (since it is the State who will be responsible for maintaining living standards of the unemployed); the implication of new technology and its effect on employees will be felt not only by those employees but also by those responsible for industrial relations at the various organisations which are considering the employment of new technology. The implication for you and I is a world of constant change, a world which will be as different in ten years' time as were the worlds of my father and his father – a world which technology has affected in such a way that we no longer wonder what is possible but *when* it will be possible.

Assignments

Student activity 8.1

This is a group assignment designed for the whole group (class). Increased demands by a well-informed public, with the buying power (cash and credit) to match, have meant that the world of production and distribution have become transformed over the past twenty years. This transformation has led to even greater demands being placed on the services of producers and distributors to such an extent that now some of those processes and distribution routes lead at best to inconvenience and at worst to practices and usage which can in some cases totally disrupt family life.

The siting of factories on land which has long been regarded as open space, designated for use by the general public; the proposal to build hypermarkets on land also designated as public open space; the building of an infrastructure which has resulted in the demolition of homes and of buildings which are of historical interest – those are all examples of the loss faced by communities as a result of the growth in some types of production and the resultant developments which are needed in the infrastructure.

Your task is to research a local planning issue and prepare for a public meeting which will hear both sides of the argument. Different members of your group are to role-play local planning officers, prospective designers and builders, members of the local domestic community, and members of local businesses. All are to prepare their own case for or against the proposed development and to attend the open meeting. The outcome (i.e. to permit development or prohibit it) will be decided in a free vote by all members of the group.

Student activity 8.2

This is a group assignment designed for the whole group (class). The local area health authority has approached your college with the suggestion that students should be actively involved in a campaign designed to reduce tobacco consumption. The head of your business studies department has turned the problem over to your group with the following instructions:

> The group is to be divided into four smaller groups and each will work on a project to prepare a poster campaign which will illustrate the financial, social, and opportunity costs of smokers' actions to individuals and the community.

Student activity 8.3

This is an individual assignment. It has been said that organisations ought to exhibit responsibility towards their employees, over and above that required by health and safety legislation. One of the

early proponents of such measures was the Quaker, Seebohm Rowntree. As part of an overall project being prepared by your group on the development of management thought, prepare a brief and concise article on this man and his philosophy regarding the management of workers.

Student activity 8.4

This is an individual assignment. There is a view that the process of education, in the UK in particular, with its emphasis on encouraging young children to make choices throughout their life at school, produces people who find it extremely difficult to fit into a work environment where there is little possibility of exercising choice. The move from school to work is much more of a culture shock than it might have been in our parents' day. Better education raises our level of expectations and we all require better opportunities for the exercise of the skills which school and college have taught us. It is therefore unsurprising to find that many employees feel alienated by the work process.

Produce a set of guidelines which illustrate the processes and practices which you think would make work environments a better place to be and which would thus motivate people to work harder.

Student activity 8.5

This is an individual assignment. There is a view that advanced technology will result in fewer people travelling to work by the turn of the century. Many employees will be working at home, linked to their employing organisation via a computer. Such workers may be thought to be in an attractive position since they no longer have the expense or inconvenience of having to travel to work daily. The employer benefits by having employees who are less stressed when they start work as well as having the advantage of not needing to provide large suites of offices, thus saving on increasingly high payments for rent and rates. However, many people are concerned that such home-workers will no longer reap some of the social benefits of attending work, such as the social interaction with colleagues, the sharing of experiences with work-mates, and the support of colleagues in times of pressure or trouble.

Assume that you will be one of the workers just described. Your working day will involve you in logging into your organisation's computer via your console at home and dealing with issues throughout the day using this medium. Briefly outline what you think would be the benefits (a) to yourself and (b) to your employer of you conducting your work at home. Briefly outline what you think would be the disadvantages (a) to yourself and (b) to your employer of you conducting your work at home.

Skills assessable

	Skill 1	2	3	4	5	6	7	8
Assignment								
1	1.5	2.2	3.2	4.2	5.1	6.1		
	1.8		3.5	4.3	5.2	6.2		
			3.7	4.6	5.4	6.3		
			3.9	4.7				
				4.8				
2	1.5	2.4	3.4	4.3	5.1			8.3
	1.8	2.5	3.5	4.4	5.2			8.4
	1.10		3.6	4.6				8.5
			3.7					
			3.9					
			3.11					
3	1.6	2.1		4.3		6.1		
	1.8	2.2				6.2		
		2.5				6.3		
		2.7						
		2.8						
4	1.1	2.2		4.3		6.1		
	1.2	2.4		4.5		6.2		
	1.5	2.5				6.3		
	1.6							
	1.8							
5	1.1	2.2		4.3		6.1	7.2	8.5
	1.2	2.4				6.2	7.5	
	1.5	2.5				6.3		
	1.8					6.4		

9
DECISION-MAKING IN ORGANISATIONS

Organisations have objectives and, to enable them to achieve these objectives, they need to acquire, use, and dispose of resources – all of these activities involve making decisions. What will concern us throughout this chapter are: the type of decisions that are made; how decisions are made; consensus and conflict; and dealing with conflict.

Decision-making processes

Before beginning a consideration of decision-making processes it is first necessary to say something about what those decisions are going to be concerned with. Decisions may be vital or trivial; they may be routine or unique; the impact of decisions may be immediate or may be delayed. Since decisions pervade the whole of business activity we need to say something about the type of decisions made and the ways in which they can be made. As far as management is concerned there are three principal decision areas – **strategic**, **operating**, and **administrative** (Fig. 9.1).

In general we can say that the decisions of organisations are concerned with *resource use*, whether such organisations are in the private or public sector (see p. 5 and Fig. 1.5), and regardless of their objectives (see Chapter 2).

The resources that are used by organisations are often referred to as the *factors of production*.

- *What are the factors of production?*

It is usual to discuss resources under four headings – *land*, *labour*, *capital*, and *enterprise*.

- *What is meant by the business use of the term 'entrepreneur'?*

During the process of production (creation of goods/services which satisfy wants) the factors of land, labour, and capital will be organised by a person or group of people (referred to as entrepreneurs) in such a way as to attempt to maximise an objective(s) of the organisation. The process of production is shown in Fig. 9.2.

STRATEGIC   OPERATING   ADMINISTRATIVE

Such decisions will be long term in nature and are basic to the organisation since they establish the relationship the organisation will have with its environment (such decisions will concern the goals and objectives of the organisation). These decisions will be non-routine and non-repetitive in nature as well as being relatively complex, due to the number of variables affected.

These are concerned with the structure of the organisation – in other words, the administrative process which enables the organisation to achieve its objectives. Such decisions will concern the effective co-ordination of activities within the organisation to ensure objectives are met.

These will be short term and will concern areas such as pricing and output levels. Since these decisions are short term, that is, since they will be made quite frequently, they take on the appearance of being routine and repetitive in nature.

Fig. 9.1

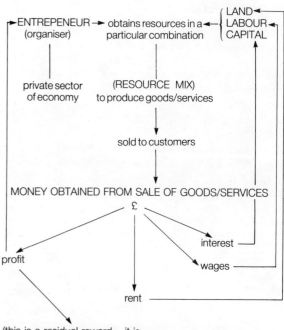

(this is a residual reward – it is only available if any money remains after rent, wages, and interest have been paid. It could be negative, i.e. a loss)

Fig. 9.2

- *What does an economist mean by the following terms:*
  land,
  labour,
  and capital?

It is the task of the entrepreneur to combine resources in the most efficient way (the best *resource mix*) to enable production of a good/service which consumers are prepared to buy at a price which yields a favourable return on investment.

- *What is meant by (a) primary production, (b) secondary production, and (c) tertiary production? Give examples of occupations within each type of venture.*

The making of decisions thus concerns the use of resources. Entrepreneurs must continually decide between a particular 'mix' of resources – more capital and less labour, or vice versa. To a certain extent the use of capital, substituted as it can be for labour, is determined by the opportunity cost of using labour (see pages 79–80).

Making decisions

Decision-making, in connection with organisations, concerns the making of a *conscious* choice between alternatives, unlike many decisions made by individuals (whose choices will not always be consciously considered – some decisions are made via reflex action). Although organisations will always make conscious choices, such choices may sometimes be repetitive and routine in nature and thus take on the appearance of a reflex action. There are many occasions where *individuals* will select a pattern of behaviour by rule of thumb or make choices in an habitual manner. Many small businesses are, in fact, run by people who make decisions concerning the business in this way. When asked on what basis a decision was made, they will usually reply that it was something like experience or 'know-how' that helped them make the decision. This may work well in the small-business environment where decisions may be easily reversed before consequences take hold. In the context of a larger organisation, however, where changes in technology and competitor action occur frequently, a much more scientific means of making decisions is required (see Fig. 9.3).

Stages involved in decision-making

1. *objectives are set and defined* – we must have targets (see Chapter 2).
2. *relevant data likely to affect objectives is collected.*
3. *data analysed* – this will often involve a measure, qualitative or quantitative, of performance or expected returns (see Chapter 11).
4. *a number of solutions will be proposed.*
5. *most appropriate solution is selected.*
6. *decision implemented.*
7. *result(s) evaluated.*

Rational decision-making

The ideal method to employ in decision-making is argued to be one where the approach is completely logical and based only on *fact*; the process of making decisions does, however, often involve more than a rational analysis of facts. Many decision-makers argue that subjective judgement and intuition still play an important part.

- *On what basis do you decide how to spend your free time?*

Problems do not exist in isolation and so, necessarily, the process of making decisions is complex. What you may want to do with your time often has to be fitted in with what everyone else wants to do with theirs. As individuals we often face these apparently competing demands on our time;

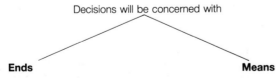

Decisions will be concerned with

Ends
These concern the objectives of the organisation and will involve value judgements concerning what the organisation should be trying to achieve

Means
These decisions are basically rational and will be concerned with how the objectives of the organisation are going to be reached

Fig. 9.3

making decisions in business is also about reconciling what often appear to be competing demands. Making the decision, for example, to increase sales may not leave you with the option of reducing prices when you have also made the decision to maximise profit margins.

- *Find out what is understood by* **price elasticity of demand**. *What is the significance of this principle to businessmen?*

When we talk about rationality in decision-making we generally refer to a situation where appropriate means are chosen to reach desired ends – in other words, decisions are said to be made *rationally*. However, this simplistic notion of decision rationality does not necessarily serve us well. For example, it is often difficult to separate means from ends. What may appear to be an end may, in fact, turn out to be only the means for an end in the future. In other words we could be locked into a *means-ends chain* or *hierarchy*. In many cases the connection between the activities of an organisation and its objectives may well be obscured, or there may be contradictions among alternative objectives, or the means selected to attain those objectives. Situations may arise where non-rational results accrue from seemingly rational decision-making. A good example of this would be decisions made in connection with the running of the economy. Those responsible for making decisions attempt to make them rationally and in doing so adjust variables within the economy to achieve desired ends. However, such movements often produce undesirable, unanticipated results.

- *Give an example of a recent Government economic decision which you feel had undesirable aspects associated with its implementation. What were those undesirable aspects? Do you think they· could have been avoided? If so, how?*

Consensus

One way to consider the consensus perspective of decision-making is via the political meaning of the term. In this sense the consensus perspective is a view of the way in which things work, or ought to work; the view is influenced by political ideals. Those on the right and in the centre of the political spectrum argue that the most appropriate mechanism for solving (production and allocation) problems is the existence of a *free market mechanism*.

- *What is understood by the term 'free market mechanism'? How does such a system solve the allocation problem in terms of employment, and demand for and supply of goods/services?*

One (extreme) assumption is that free market bargaining will allow us to deal with competing claims and permit effective decision-making. What we tend to do in many situations where decisions have to be made among competing groups is to *vote* on the decision to be taken.

- *What are the drawbacks of 'voting' as a means of decision-making?*

When it is not possible to obtain a unanimous decision about a project, a new product, or another line of business, the best alternative may be to go for a *compromise* which is workable. This view – a workable compromise – is another way of considering what has come to be known as a *consensus* view.

Taking decisions by majority rule means that some of the people concerned will have lost when it came to a vote and that there will thus be a minority of people opposed to the decision. The implication of this is that unresolved differences may continue to exist for some time between group members. This is an undesirable situation which may lead to animosity in the future. However, taking a consensus view (a workable compromise) ensures that all parties to the decision will have at least had the opportunity to bargain over the outcome – a situation thus where all can feel satisfied that they took part in the decision-making process.

If there was no such process as decision-making, the implication would be that there were no conflicting objectives (we would therefore not have to make decisions). Similarly, if we suggested there was no conflict, the implication would be that everyone was always in complete agreement over objectives. We know, however, that the world is made up of people with many differences of opinion, values, and priorities; such people will themselves have differing talents and personalities.

It is the task of the manager to consensus-build in situations where decisions have to be taken which will affect a number of people in an organisation. No manager will survive for long in a situation where subordinates continually oppose decisions and where there is in-fighting; what the manager has to do in these circumstances is to bring together the various factions (and talents) of his subordinates in such a way as to get the best from them in a spirit of co-operation. All decision-making and resulting action is a process of conflict followed by a building

Fig. 9.4 Consensus among voters

of consensus which leads to agreement over a decision.

It has been said that the best decisions are produced from disagreement. Once we have managed to overcome such disagreement we can get down to the task of decision-making. The advantage of hearing a conflicting view is that it often gives an insight into potential problems and helps to widen the perspective of those responsible for making decisions.

Conflict

- *'Conflict is likely to generate good ideas'. What would you say is the reasoning behind this statement?*

One way to consider the conflict perspective is via the political meaning of the term, as we did with the consensus view. In this sense the conflict perspective is the view ascribed to by supporters of the Left who argue that economic, social, and political institutions do not work in the interests of the majority of the members of society but, rather, work to perpetuate the existing inequalities between 'the classes'. The view is that there will always be a fundamental conflict of interest in society when economic and political power are concentrated in the hands of a supposedly unrepresentative minority; the deprived majority would thus feel opposition to the existing structure of society.

If our views of society, the economy, organi-

sations, and our fellow man are going to be coloured by our political views and our perception of the way things are, and the way we think they ought to be, then any condition of conflict is likely to contain these prejudices.

The problem we have is how to make decisions concerning the allocation of resources in order to attain particular objectives. There will be those who will argue for the maintenance of the status quo, while others will argue for a revolution which will turn economic, social, and political institutions into forms which they find acceptable.

We can consider conflict from a number of perspectives:

a) individual conflict
b) role conflict
c) intra-group conflict
d) inter-group conflict
e) organisational conflict.

Individual conflict

We find ourselves in this situation when we are confronted with a number of equally acceptable, though mutually exclusive, alternatives. This may be a simple case, e.g. deciding where to go on holiday, or a more complex case, e.g. deciding how to invest millions of pounds. In most instances we are able to *resolve* the conflict and make a decision; in some cases we find it possible to *avoid* conflict (some of the supposed options may not be realistically attainable, after all); finally, we may find that we can *adapt* to the conflict situation. Many of you will be aware of this situation, not so much because the conflict has arisen, but because you can probably remember the process of trying to resolve, avoid, or adapt to the situation. In many cases the conflict situation may not actually be unpleasant but the *frustration* associated with not being able to resolve conflict *is*.

People have differing abilities to resolve conflict and to tolerate situations which cannot be resolved. I am often amazed at the tolerance exhibited by mothers who are trying to hold conversations with other mothers when their children are with them. Children will eventually get to the stage where they pester their mothers, pulling at clothes, shouting, screaming, kicking, and so on, yet some mothers seem able to adapt to that situation for an almost unlimited amount of time. If you get the opportunity to watch parents in such situations, e.g. outside a local school at 3 o'clock in the afternoon, you will witness a good demonstration of the ability to adapt to such a situation of conflict. You may also witness a demonstration of someone's *inability* to adapt to this situation!

- *Watch your colleagues in stress situations. How do they cope? What methods do they employ to enable them to cope?*

You will probably notice that some colleagues cope very well with the stress of conflict – while others do not.

Individual conflict can be caused by dissatisfaction with a job, variance between your (individual) goals and the goals of an organisation, or disagreements with colleagues/subordinates/superiors.

While we experience inner conflict as individuals we can also experience conflict *between* ourselves and other individuals. This is of much significance in organisational settings, particularly when those affected by the conflict are in positions of authority.

- *How do you think you would feel if your manager could not cope with stress?*
- *If this is a situation you had to face, what would you do about it? Does it affect your work rate?*

Role conflict

Roles at work can be regarded as the rights and duties you have and will include privileges, authority, and the use of power. Role conflict arises when there is an imbalance between the role the individual is expected to assume in an organisation and his own personal values, attitudes, or beliefs. This type of inconsistency often leads to stress and, since such states are psychologically unpleasant, people attempt to reduce them to tolerable levels.

- *Interview a dozen people who work in organisations and try to discover what they think their role is, and where they fit in their organisation. Ask if they are happy at work. Consider the data obtained and say whether or not you think effective role assumption at work enables a person to perform his/her tasks happily. Give a presentation of your findings.*

When there is an imbalance between attitudes and expected behaviour most people will modify attitudes (though some may find it possible to modify behaviour only) to increase compatibility with expected patterns of behaviour. For example, assume a person in a posiiton of authority has to behave in a particular way, although this could be inconsistent with that person's attitudes towards, for example, dress in the office or association with staff members. In order that employment continues, it is often the case that behaviour will be modified to such an extent that subordinates are treated according to the accepted norms of behaviour for that firm.

Intra-group conflict

Many groups are established at work; some will be formed by the organisation to carry out particular tasks (formal groups), while others will comprise individuals who have, or who appear to have, common interests (informal groups).

- *Do you belong to an informal group at work/college (i.e. it is not shown on the organisation chart)? What do the group members have in common? What does this tell you about informal groups?*

Informal groups may simply be people who have lunch together, or who play in the company football team, or who, in some way, associate outside the normal boundaries of groups established for work purposes. Conflict within a group can occur as a result of competing sub-groups within the group (these will have been established in part by the organisational structure). It is often argued that conflict is part of the normal internal process of development within a group; it is further argued that this is likely to recur when the members of the group compete for resources or prestige or if the group is affected by change, such as someone leaving.

Inter-group conflict

The solidarity of a group, and the pride one feels from belonging to it, have often been considered to be the positive elements of social behaviour which groups help to develop. These aspects can, however, be the basis for conflict *between* groups – often represented by the 'them' and 'us' syndrome, which itself leads to hostility and conflict.

Conflict is bound to exist between groups since each group has its own identity and goals, and these may not be compatible with other (possibly competing) groups, with which it has to associate. Even if the goals of groups are identical there is normally some conflict, e.g. that between groups within the same organisation, which grows out of the natural competitive spirit of group members.

- *If you belong to a sporting team, how do you view your competitors? Is there any rivalry between your group and other groups? What is the nature of this rivalry?*

It is a natural human instinct to want to belong to groups and, on the whole, we like to think that our group is better than any other. It is in this sense that group rivalry is established; and it is this group rivalry which very often leads to conflict.

Organisational conflict

Any of the previously mentioned types of conflict can, and almost certainly will, exist within an organisation. Conflict will arise between management and shop-floor workers, between different management groups (e.g. marketing v. production), and between management and the unions (e.g. demarcation disputes), and between various unions.

- *Consider a recent example of conflict between management and the relevant union which was well reported in the national press. What do you think caused the conflict? Would you have handled things any differently if (a) you were representing the management, or (b) you were representing the unions involved? How?*

There are thus a number of different types of conflict which may exist (side by side) within an organisation. As students of organisations we need a firm idea of what can cause conflict and the methods people may adopt to deal with it.

The causes of conflict

There will be a number of possible causes of conflict and one's belief as to the cause of any conflict will be based on one of three views – **unitary view**, **pluralist view**, and **systems view**.

Unitary view

In the past management consideration of conflict tended to be based on this view. It rests on the notion that everyone within the organisation has the same objective(s). Thus, members of an organisation will all work together (as a team) and will respect the authority of the organisation and those within it. Any activity likely to interfere with the objectives of the organisation was regarded as 'bad' and dealt with according to a set of rules/procedures/conventions adopted by the organisation. The management view of what caused conflict was thus very narrow, the assumption being that if anything went wrong (if there was conflict) it was because the subordinates adopted 'bad' behaviour, that is did something which was contrary to the objectives(s) of the

organisation. This is not to say that such a view no longer persists.

- *Do you have experience of managers who adopt such a narrow view of conflict? How did you feel in this situation? What impact did this have on your work?*

(If you have no direct experience of the above situation, imagine how you would feel if you were subjected to just such an environment).

The unitary view does not allow for the possibility that there may be other causes of the present conflict, such as a simple misunderstanding. When management adopts a unitary view, the cause of conflict is thought to be a breakdown of authority. Thus, the fact that there may be many causes of conflict is ignored. The competence of management to deal with conflict would thus be severely limited by the application of the unitary view.

Pluralist view

Organisations comprise many groups, the most prevalent among these being the informal groups mentioned earlier in this chapter; each will have its own objectives, value systems, and power structures. It is the recognition of this situation that distinguishes the pluralist from the unitarist, because the pluralist recognises the legitimacy of all groups. Problems of conflict are often recognised as being problems that exist between groups. Solutions to problems are often found by negotiation, the effect of which is that all or most groups will achieve a measure of success. Conflict is thus viewed as a natural outcome of the existence of many groups (possibly in competition) within organisations and not as a result of a breakdown in authority.

- *Consider a recent case of industrial conflict which was publicised in the national press. List as many of the possible causes of the conflict as you can think of, however improbable. Compare your list with that of a colleague. Are there any similarities? Discuss the differences.*

Systems view

This is the widest view of conflict since it takes into account the environment and, in particular, the economic and social conditions within the environment. The view recognises that the organisation does not operate in isolation and thus that issues and problems which appear to be coming from within the organisation (and appearing as conflict) may, in fact, be the outcome of frustration with society itself.

- On page 95 it was stated that your belief as to the cause of a conflict situation would be based on one of three views. Consider a conflict situation you are familiar with and note what you think the cause(s) to be. Consider whether you have viewed the conflict from a unitary, pluralist, or systems point of view.

Resolving conflict

The process adopted for dealing with conflict will depend on the *nature* of the conflict. Ways of dealing with conflict include: avoidance, policies and rules, smoothing, dominance, appeal to higher authority, removal, and group confrontation.

Avoidance – used when an issue does not appear to be important. The problem will be avoided and usually solved indirectly, though there is the risk that the delay caused by avoiding the issue may create further problems.

Policies and rules – by using policies and rules to control the behaviour of people at work the degree of uncertainty in relationships is minimised, thus the prospect for conflict should also be minimised. Some conflict will be unavoidable since we cannot foresee every possible situation and provide a policy to deal with it.

Smoothing – those concerned to end a conflict will attempt to minimise differences between parties and avoid possible problems. This does not always provide a lasting solution, however, and frustration may result from conflict which is merely postponed; 'pouring oil on water' does not get to the root of a problem.

Dominance – those responsible for dealing with conflict merely *order* a settlement. This will inevitably lead to discontent because there will be winners and *losers*. The method can be effective however when time is short and decisions have to be made.

Appeal to higher authority – similar to dominance as a method for dealing with conflict. It has the advantage that the problem is dealt with by someone who can probably see the whole picture objectively. The drawback with this method is the same as for dominance – there are winners *and* losers.

Removal – conflict very often comes about when particular people have to work together, thus a solution may be to change jobs around so that certain people do not meet.

Group confrontation – competing groups meet to thrash out problems and arrive at solutions. On the one hand, there is the advantage that the process can eradicate emotion from a conflict but, on the other hand, such confrontation may escalate the situation.

- Role-play a situation of conflict which may be taken from a recent organisational news article or which may be a recent sociological problem involving conflict. During the role-play adopt each of the seven methods for resolving conflict.

Decisions and the environment

We have already seen that organisational decisions will tend to fall into one of three groups – strategic, operational, and administrative. When we are considering the relationship between decisions and the environment we are primarily concerned with the first two, strategic and operational. What we want to achieve as an organisation and the way(s) in which we intend to go about achieving those objectives will have a direct influence on the external environment. There may be some form of control over the activities we perform or the methods we use, but we will still be using valuable (scarce) resources; we may be disturbing the appearance of a site; we may affect an area with pollution and waste disposal. Any strategic decision made by an organisation may have an impact on the environment, just as any operational decision will. In Chapter 10 we will consider the aspects of scarce resources and legal liability in connection with resource use.

Assignments

Student activity 9.1

This assignment is intended for groups of three or four. On pages 98 and 99 are three articles, all printed in *The Independent* on the same day. Each item is concerned with decision-making processes.

Using the information contained in *one* of the three articles, and any other information relating to the chosen article that you may discover, prepare a brief, informal report stating what you think was involved in the decision process. It will no doubt be worthwhile to consider what you think may have been involved, in relation to the stages involved in decision-making, as given on page 91.

Student activity 9.2

This is an assignment for the whole group or class. The group is to be divided into two sub-groups; one sub-group will deal with the decision-making problem, while the other observes and notes the processes involved.

During the observation period, the observing group is to note the following:

i) what processes were involved in the decision-making activity?

ii) was there a leader? If so, how was the leader elected? If not elected, how did he or she come to be the leader?

iii) how did the group react under the pressure of a time constraint?

iv) was a decision reached?

v) are there any recommendations which could be made for the improvement of the decision-making process in situations such as this?

The group involved in making a decision are to deal with the following task:

Your college authorities have decided that, since the demand for physicists has increased, while that for business studies students has not risen appreciably, the college will be devoting more resources in future to the study of physics.

The direct result of this decision will be a fall in resources made available for business studies students, beginning next term.

Your group have to devise a means by which influence can be brought to bear on the authorities, from a number of sources, in the hope that they will change their decision.

Student activity 9.3

This is a group exercise, suitable for groups of between three and six. The process known as 'brainstorming' was developed by Alex F. Osborn in *Applied Imagination* (Charles Scriber's Sons, New York, 1953) as a tool to help trigger creative ideas among advertisers. The process involves a group in reaching a decision in a particular way and can be used by any type of group, that is, it is not restricted to advertisers.

The process revolves around certain principles:

1. There should be no criticism of ideas until the end of the process.

2. People are encouraged to think freely and creatively – in fact, it is often suggested that wild ideas are the best – it being easy to reform them later. I often impress on students that apparently crazy notions are generally the ones which are most creative and thus most helpful.

3. Do not be concerned with quality of ideas initially, go for quantity on the basis that the greater the number of ideas generated, the greater the likelihood that a sound and advantageous idea is produced.

4. Try to combine ideas suggested within the group and to improve ideas – whether they were your own or not is not significant. What *is* important is that the group cooperate in producing good ideas.

Your task is to spend fifteen minutes considering a problem which is discussed on the front page of a national newspaper today. The group must attempt to 'brainstorm' a solution for the problem you have decided to work on. One member of each group is to unobtrusively record the series of events which takes place and the type of ideas suggested during the meeting. The recorder must take care not to disrupt the flow of the meeting but should attempt to note as many ideas as possible. The final solution is also to be noted.

At a plenary session later, those responsible for recording the information concerning their own groups are to make a presentation to the whole group (class), indicating what happened in the meeting and stating the group solution to the problem.

The whole group is to decide on the 'best' solution.

Student activity 9.4

This is a group exercise for groups of three to four. The speed with which information travels through an organisation and the associated speed wtih which decisions are made is generally a reflection of the organisational structure.

Construct a chart illustrating the organisational structure of your college or place of work (if the members of your group work for different organisations, select only one of these) and produce a short document indicating how decisions are generally made. Reconstruct the organisation chart in such a way that information travels through the organisation with greater speed. Suggest a way in which decisions could be made by maximising the use of the potential and knowledge of more members of staff than is presently the case.

Student activity 9.5

This is a group assignment for groups of about eight

Head teachers ready to accept latest pay offer

By David Felton
Labour Correspondent

HEAD teachers look set to accept the Government's pay offer to teachers although at a meeting today one of their unions will warn Kenneth Baker, the Secretary of State for Education, against imposition of a deal without union agreement.

After a meeting of the National Association of Head Teachers national council David Hart, the general secretary, said Mr Baker's 16.4 per cent two-year offer was better for his members than the provisional deal agreed between the teachers' unions and employers in July.

He said that if next weekend's negotiations at Nottingham did not improve on Mr Baker's offer his union would not sign a Nottingham agreement.

Peter Snape, leader of the other head teachers' union, the Secon-

dary Heads Association, went further and welcomed Mr Baker's involvement in the pay dispute.

Mr Snape said that unless Mr Baker imposed a deal 'the situation is so confused, with both sides split among themselves, there will never be an agreement.'

The second-largest teachers' union, the National Association of Schoolteachers/Union of Women Teachers, yesterday held the third in its series of week-long half day strikes which, according to the union, involved more than 15,000 of its members and affected almost 250,000 pupils.

Letters from Mr Baker to head teachers of all 25,000 primary and secondary schools in England and Wales started arriving yesterday with the request that they post details of the Government's pay offer in staff rooms. The letter said

Mr Baker believed it was most important that teaching staff should have direct access to details of the offer.

Meanwhile John Pearman, leaders of the Labour-controlled employers' body, accused the Government of adopting double standards in its approach to public sector pay.

'The comments made by Environment Secretary Nicholas Ridley about councils opting out of national pay deals are a marked contrast to those being made by Kenneth Baker.

'On the one hand we have the Government telling us that we must comply with centrally-imposed national pay deals, when a few days later we are told we can tear up national agreements on pay and conditions when it suits,' he said.

University rejects study loans

By Ngaio Crequer
Education Correspondent

THE senate of London University voted by an overwhelming majority last night against the introduction of a student loans scheme on the grounds that it would restrict access to higher education.

The senate voted by 64 votes to 7 in favour of a motion put by Jane Cannon, president of the students' union, and Dr William Stephenson, lecturer in mathematics at University College, that a loans scheme would undermine the university's policy of widening access, and the need to secure financial support for students and adults in continuing education.

Ms Cannon quoted the document drawn up by the National Union of Students which concluded from a survey of student financial support systems in the

United States, Canada, Denmark and Sweden, that any student loans scheme would have a seriously detrimental effect on access, particularly for mature students and those from disadvantaged backgrounds.

Dr Geoffrey Alderman, a lecturer in politics said: 'I know there is a body of opinion in this university that says, "If we kiss the Government's backside hard enough, we shall be loved." Of course, it is a wonderful thing to be loved. But we shan't be loved, you see; we shall merely be despised.'

An alternative motion, which derided the current level of financial support for students but which failed to take a view on loans versus grants was dismissed. One speaker said that although this

motion was not a fudge, it would nevertheless send the message that London was tacitly supporting loans.

London University's decision will have enormous influence in the world of higher education because of the growing and vocal opposition to student loans.

■The Church of England said yesterday that it was opposed to student loans because 'they will further inhibit access to higher education for some groups of people, will place a burden of debt on young graduates and will in the short term offer no savings to Government.'

Source: *The Independent*, 6 November 1986

British Telecom engineers reject offer

By Donald Macintyre
Labour Editor

THE threat of industrial action by British Telecom engineers increased sharply yesterday when their main union announced a ballot result in which a decisive majority rejected a pay offer worth between 5 and 5.8 per cent.

BT is expected to hold talks with the National Communications Union next week over its offer, rejected by 53,010 to 16,497 of the union's engineering group. The union's clerical group, due to announce its result on Monday, is widely expected to have voted in favour of industrial action.

But BT extended little immediate hope of an increase in the current offer yesterday, saying only that if the result led to industrial action, BT 'would do everything in our power to ensure that service to our customers continue'.

The offer which is attached to productivity strings, including a widening of job descriptions, adds staged increases to current basic rates, which the union says are £147 per week for craftsmen and £171 for technical officers.

Last night Dave Morris, chairman of NCU engineering group's pay committee said: 'BT challenged us to put this offer to the membership. We did that, and now they have to come up with a better offer.'

The Society of Telecom Executives which represents senior managers and engineers is watching developments closely after itself rejecting outright a slightly lower offer in percentage terms.

The engineering group will almost certainly ballot on industrial action if the offer is not improved.
■Preliminary New Earnings Survey figures from the Department of Employment suggests firemen could receive a 7 per cent rise.

students. More and more decisions relating to conditions at work are being made via a process of collective bargaining. Collective bargaining is a term used to embrace negotiation activity relating to employment.

Your task is to scan the national newspapers for a recent industrial dispute between a trade union and an employer. The group is then to be divided into union representatives and employer representatives and to enter into negotiations with the aim of settling the dispute.

It will be interesting to see if the negotiated settlement agreed by the students is similar to that agreed by the parties in the original dispute.

Skills assessable

	Skill							
	1	2	3	4	5	6	7	8
Assignment								
1	1.8	2.1	3.4	4.2		6.1		
		2.2	3.5	4.3		6.2		
			3.7	4.6		6.3		
			3.9	4.7				
2	1.5	2.5	3.2	4.2	5.1			
	1.6		3.5					
	1.7		3.7					
			3.10					
			3.11					
3	1.2		3.5	4.2				
	1.5		3.7	4.3				
			3.10	4.6				
4	1.8	2.2	3.5	4.2				
		2.4	3.11	4.3				
		2.5		4.6				
				4.10				
5	1.1	2.2	3.2	4.6				
	1.8	2.4	3.5	4.10				
		2.5	3.10					

10
RESOURCE DECISIONS AND ORGANISATIONS

This chapter will consider the issues which result from the scale of operations undertaken by an organisation; scarcity and resources, and the need for organisations to make a profit; those aspects of legal liability and accountability which face organisations; and the disposal of resources.

Scale of operations

One of the major decisions of those responsible for the development of an organisation concerns size – whether to aim for growth, remain at present levels of output, or possibly sell off part of the organisation in a bid to increase efficiency. However, increasing the size of an organisation very often confers with it particular benefits associated with what economists refer to as 'economies of scale'.

- *What is meant by economies of scale?*
- *List four each of both **internal** and **external** economies of scale, and give a brief explanation of each.*

If you have properly appreciated the significance of economies of scale you will have noted that organisations benefit from the impact of falling average costs when their output increases. There does come a time, however, when all this must stop – when a situation is reached where average costs begin to rise as output increases. This is known as 'diseconomies of scale'.

Growth in the size of an organisation may mean that it grows beyond its 'optimum size'.

- *What is meant by 'optimum size'?*
- *What may give rise to inefficiencies as an organisation increases in size?*

There is the additional problem that an expanding organisation not only attracts those eager to make takeover bids but also those keen to regulate organisations, such as the Monopolies and Mergers Commission.

- *What is the Monopolies and Mergers Commission concerned with? From where does it derive its powers? What is the extent of those powers?*

Resource decisions will vary according to whether the organisation is going for growth or whether it is operating during a period of restraint (and thus working conservatively). Those organisations going for growth often do so by expanding output, and thus using more resources. This is not the only way that growth can be achieved, however. Consider some recent examples of mergers and takeovers – these are other factors affecting the size of an organisation.

- *Consider a recent example of a takeover in this country. What will be the financial implication in terms of projected turnover or profit for the newly formed organisation? How do the projected turnover and profit compare with that before the takeover?*

When markets are buoyant and customer demand is high, more and more resources will be devoted to the production of the goods/services which consumers wish to buy, regardless of the size of organisations. Size is important in connection with the use of resources and the destruction of, for example, areas of natural beauty. The larger the organisation involved in this field, the greater the financial muscle it is able to apply. We thus see on a number of occasions large organisations developing parts of the countryside or extracting minerals, etc. from areas which we may need to consider preserving. One often thinks that if the organisation concerned were smaller, the chances of their obtaining the necessary permission to develop or otherwise use a piece of land would be greatly reduced.

It is interesting to note that in any industry there are organisations which vary greatly in size and level of output. An example is the manufacture of motor cars. The giant General Motors (GM) is so large, and has such a volume of output, that its unit costs are very low. Smaller organisations such as American Motors Corporation (AMC), even with a very successful model in their four-wheel-drive 'Jeep', lost $125 million on sales of $4 billion in 1985, primarily because they produce at *low volume* (in relation to GM). In the UK the low volume manufacturers of motor cars specialise and aim at a particular market segment to ensure survival. For example, Caterham Cars, manufacturers of Lotus Super Sevens, build cars in two very small buildings in Caterham, Surrey; other examples include AC Cars at Hampton and Panther at Weybridge. All are manufacturers of specialised vehicles with a devoted and loyal following of *enthusiasts*. Size does not necessarily breed success, though it is true that manufacture in this case is aimed at a specific and small market segment.

There are industries, like the clothing industry, where low costs of production are achieved (economies of scale are made) at fairly modest levels of production. The small producer can do well in an industry such as this where large size is not necessary for survival. As in the motor car industry, there will be specialists, such as those manufacturers who offer hand-made clothes, at a price.

An organisation may increase its scale of operations by aiming for *market expansion*, which means enlarging the area in which it does business.

- *In what way(s) have the following organisations enlarged their area of business in the last five years:*
  a) one of the high street banks
  b) W.H. Smith
  c) Habitat
  d) a major building society?

There are organisations that expand by adding to their list of products, in an attempt to offer customers a wider range and thereby increase the possibility that consumers will buy their products rather than the products of a competitor.

- *What is the newest confectionery to come on to the market? Who manufactures this product? Was their product range previously quite extensive? Why do you think confectionery producers in general introduce new products fairly regularly?*

Resource scarcity and profitability

If you ask an economist what economics is about you will be told something about scarcity and the way in which resources are allocated. If a product or resource is scarce, the implication is that, at the price being asked, there is not enough to satisfy demand. The key is the notion of *price*. Taken to its limit, if we were to increase the price of an item significantly, so that consumers could not afford to buy it, then that item would never be scarce – there would be supplies that consumers simply could not afford to buy. When the price of a commodity is low, the demand generated could be so great that a

Fig. 10.1   Familiar faces of 2 high-street retailers, although the areas into which they have expanded in the last 5 years may not be so well-known. Do you know what other business ventures each organisation also operates?

position of scarcity in supply may soon be reached.

In the early 1970s the price of oil increased dramatically, with the result that consumption of oil (and petrol) was reduced, which relieved the pressure on this planet's finite supply of oil. The fall in oil prices during 1986 saw a decrease in the price of petrol, with a consequent increase in consumption – a situation which increased the consumption of a finite (fossil fuel) resource which man cannot replace.

The one fact from which we cannot escape in connection with resources is that supply is finite. In

1972 E. F. Schumacher wrote, 'If we are now using something like 7000 million tons of coal equivalent, the need in 28 years' time will be three times as large – around 20,000 million tons! What are 28 years? Looking backwards takes us roughly to the end of World War II, and, of course, since then fuel consumption has trebled; but the trebling involved an increased of less than 5000 million tons of coal equivalent. Now we are calmly talking about an increase three times as large.' (*Small is Beautiful*, Abacus, 1974.)

- *What is the significance of the statement above attributed to Schumacher?*
- *What has man tended to do to compensate for the depletion of fossil fuel, while continuing to maintain consumption of electricity, i.e. how can we continue to manufacture sufficient supplies of electricity?*

If we assume that firms continue to try to grow (in order to guarantee their own existence), that is, they will adopt a 'business-as-usual' philosophy about the future and resource use, clearly the world will run out of those resources. We will be driven to using newer sources of energy, such as nuclear power, with all of its problems.

- *Prepare a speech in which you put forward the notion that, in the interest of mankind's survival, we should not use nuclear power.*
- *Prepare a speech in which you put forward the notion that, given the rate of depletion of fossil fuels, we must turn to alternative sources of energy in order to maintain current production levels.*

Coal and oil are clearly not the only resources which we must use conservatively, since all resources are, by definition, scarce. There is one resource with the peculiar characteristic of being scarce in some parts of the world, yet abundant in others – *food*. In the West we try to encourage people to eat too much and to eat luxuriously by constantly bombarding them with advertisements for fast food, cream cakes, ice cream, confectionery, carbonated drinks, and so on. In many African nations we have witnessed the deaths of thousands by famine. Not only do we in the West produce more food than we can eat (note the various food 'mountains' and wine 'lakes' in the EEC) but we also do so very inefficiently. It has been estimated that primitive farmers, fertilising with manure and cultivating by hand, produce 5–50 calories worth of food for every calorie they expend, while the industrialised systems of the West use 5–10 calories,

primarily of fossil fuel, to obtain one food calorie. (Colin Tudge, *The Famine Business*, Pelican, 1977.)

- *Prepare a short discussion document which explains why it is that the EEC has such stockpiles of excess produce from member nations.*
- *Obtain data which illustrates the extent of current stockpiles of food, vegetable oil and wine held within the EEC. What is the current cost of maintaining such stocks? Who buys some of these surpluses and what prices are charged? What would* **you** *do with these stockpiles?*

When we talk of profitability we are concerned with the relationship between a firm's costs and its revenue. To put it simply, if we sell an item for what it cost us to purchase it, we would be breaking even as far as an accountant is concerned. On the other hand, if we are looking at this situation from the point of view of an economist, break-even is a situation where 'normal profit' is made.

- *What is meant by 'normal profit'?*

Since an economist views profit as a cost of the business, when he adds up all of the fixed costs (such as rent and rates) and the variable costs (such as labour and materials) he adds in a figure for profit on the basis that the owners of the business are only taking on the risk of running it with the aim of making a profit. Thus the business owes a return (profit) to the entrepreneur; profit does not belong to a business, it belongs to the owners of that business. Thus, if:

$$\text{REVENUE} - \text{Fixed Costs} - \text{Variable Cost} - \text{Profit} = \text{break-even}$$

then a normal profit has been made.

Many organisations spend surprisingly large amounts on encouraging/enticing people to buy (see Chapter 13 The marketing mix), rather than devoting the resources to the search for more efficient means of production. Resources thus appear to be used in a less-than-efficient way.

- *Find the current cost of a half-page advertisement in a national daily newspaper and show which type of manufacturer (e.g. food, retailer of white goods, like washing machines and refrigerators, retailer of brown goods, like televisions, motor manufacturer, etc.) uses this medium the most in any given week. Say how effective you think this manufacturer's advertisements are, and why.*
- *Find the cost of advertising on network commercial television for one minute. On any one evening, make a note of the time bought by*

advertisers featured and cost this time. Say whether or not you think the advertisements were effective, giving reasons.

The private sector of the economy is not geared such that organisations have a preference for conservation *per se*. Organisations would only adopt such activity if it were to their economic advantage, for example, as part of a public relations exercise. The only instance of organisations in general actively seeking to conserve is that resulting from various 'save it' and 'monergy' programmes designed to encourage fuel savings in the 70s and 80s.

- *What incentive is there for organisations to use power conservatively?*

Organisations in the private sector of the economy are under an obligation (to their share-holders) to produce an acceptable rate of return on investment; as far as shareholders are concerned, this means a decent dividend on shares. There will come a time, however, when the organisation may be fated with the problem of either satisfying the desires of shareholders or working for the benefit of society at large/not working to the detriment of society. Since organisations have to operate within an environment consisting of many constituent parts, only a relatively few members of which will be shareholders, they must consider their future and the impact that their actions will have. It would be commercial suicide for organisations to follow strategies aimed at maximising short-term gains, but which at the same time would be liable to turn public opinion against them.

Profitability is not the only consideration for organisations. Indeed, many often find themselves aiming simply for survival as a short-term goal. While profit is the prime mover in the private sector of the economy it is important to remember that organisations have many liabilities with which to contend. Very often organisations are forced to operate in a particular way because of the pressures put upon them by groups in society to which they (the organisations) are liable.

Considerations of liability

The way in which an organisation uses resources such as labour, materials, and property to produce an output may have serious implications, particular-ly for those of us who may be adversely affected by such action. When we talk of an organisation's liability we are referring not only to a manu-facturer's liability towards the users of his products but also to the liability employers must face in respect of working conditions and injuries which employees may sustain at work; entrepreneurs also have to accept liability for, say, pollution and its effect on the inhabitants of an area.

Before we can proceed with an examination of liability it is necessary to appreciate that it means we have responsibility by law; it is likely that legal action would be taken against anyone who failed to exercise such responsibility. It is also necessary to differentiate between *criminal* and *civil* liability.

Criminal liability

Criminal law concerns wrongs done against society; the objective is to *punish an offender*. The state *prosecutes* and exacts punishment when guilt is established. Criminal law is created to ensure society is properly organised; murder is a crime, along with activities such as stealing and fraud. Such an act will put us in a position where we must accept liability of a criminal nature.

Civil liability

Civil law concerns wrongs done against individuals, the objective being to *compensate the victim*. We can each of us take civil action against another by obtaining a *writ* or by *suing*. Certain actions we undertake may therefore lead to our having to accept liability in civil law.

Liability and land

We can consider the raw materials used in production as well as locations when we deal with the resource of land. Beginning with raw materials, the first legal issue we come up against deals with their purchase. One enters the realm of contract law when undertaking bargains concerning the purchase of raw materials; liability being on both sides of the contract, that is, the seller and the buyer are both liable – one for producing goods and the other for payment.

- *What is meant by 'offer' and 'acceptance' in contract law?*

Non-completion of contractual undertakings will result in action being brought for *breach of contract*.

- *What is understood by 'consideration' in contract law?*

Raw materials will also be the subject of law and liability in connection with descriptions applied to them – such liability is criminal, under the *Trade Descriptions Acts 1968 and 1972*. If, however, there is a mere misrepresentation (a statement of fact made during negotiations with a view to inducing the other party to enter into and conclude the contract), the remedy would lie in civil action.

Land as a site brings with it particular legal problems for organisations. Entrepreneurs who occupy and control premises (not necessarily the owners) have a duty of care to all lawful visitors to the property. Even a person who is not a lawful visitor, for example, a trespasser, can legally expect that the occupier acts reasonably and in a civilised manner towards him. It is not permissable, for example, to inflict intentional harm on a trespasser – thus we, as (domestic and business) occupiers of property, are under a legal liability to ensure trespassers are not harmed.

Finally, in connection with premises, organisations must ensure that their property is a safe and healthy environment for employees, as specified under Health and Safety legislation.

- *What is the legal minimum office space in which employees can be expected to work? Which organisations are exempt from the legal requirements?*

Liability and labour
An employer is liable for the conditions under which employees have to work and is also legally bound by agreements entered into in the contract of employment. Employees are afforded the protection of law in a number of areas (see Chapter 12 on employment law). Legal liability with respect to this resource rests mainly on the use to which labour can be put and the conditions under which work is carried out.

Liability and capital
In general terms we often think of capital as money, though we ought to be considering it from the point of view of machinery (technically, it is wealth set aside for the creation of future wealth).

Liability here is primarily concerned with the protection of and the use of the factor of production (capital). In terms of use the liability will extend from the right of use being affected by restriction, such as planning law and the tort (a civil wrong) of nuisance, to prohibitions outlined in copyright and patents.

- *What is the difference between a copyright and a patent?*

My right as an entrepreneur to use my machinery is restricted in a number of ways:

a) I may not have the necessary planning permission;
b) I may be guilty of preventing neighbours from enjoying their own land by creating a noise (nuisance) or producing pollution or vibrations (see the legal case of *Sturges* v *Bridgman*);
c) I may infringe a copyright or patent by using machinery in a particular way.

The protection aspect involves the rights of owners to take ownership (possession) and to use in a particular (acceptable) way, to the exclusion of others. Others can therefore be held liable for the improper use of a firm's capital.

Liability and the entrepreneur
In those cases where the owner is legally liable for business debts (sole trader and partnership, see Chapter 3) one can easily see how the use of resources may lead to an action for breach of a legal liability. When the business cannot meet its financial commitments it is up to the owners to settle out of their own (private) resources. Since the sole trader and partnership form of organisation do not have a separate legal identity from that of the owners, the owner(s) would also be liable as a property occupier. He or she would be liable, too, for the use of labour and, still in his or her private capacity, would be liable under contract law.

The use of a resource carries with it the risk that an action for a breach of a legal liability is always possible, thus *reasonable care* must be taken to avoid such a breach.

Products and liability
Whenever goods are sold the seller has to accept liability for any defects; it is as well to know this from the point of view of being a consumer because we often hear of friends and relatives being told by retailers that they cannot get refunds for defective goods, and have to take such goods back to the manufacturer. The important thing to remember is that a consumer's contract is with the retailer, not the manufacturer.

- *What is meant by Privity of Contract?*

As well as being subject to the normal rules concerning contract law, retailers are liable for the goods they sell under the *Sale of Goods Act 1979*, which has clauses dealing with the aspects of description of the goods, quality (as in merchantable quality and fitness for purpose), samples, and deliveries. Retailers who are in breach of a condition under the Sale of Goods Act can be sued and have to pay damages to the buyer, or the buyer can reject the goods and repudiate the contract.

- *What is meant by 'repudiation of a contract'?*

Manufacturers and liability

There are certain circumstances where a consumer can take legal action against a manufacturer (and thereby hold him liable) for the supply of defective goods. There are a few situations where action would be brought against a manufacturer rather than a retailer:

1. The person who has and uses the goods may not be the one who purchased them, thus there is no contract with the seller and no breach can therefore have taken place (see the case of *Donoghue* v. *Stevenson (1932)*).
2. It might be the case that a manufacturer could afford to pay much more in the way of compensation, thus an action against him rather than a retailer would make a lot of sense.
3. The defect in the goods supplied may be very serious and thus have consequences for many other prospective purchasers. Action against the manufacturer would thus have far greater impact – for the benefit of society as a whole.

When can a manufacturer be held liable?

1. Under a manufacturer's guarantee. Such promises as may be made in this document are in addition to rights buyers have under the previously mentioned *Sale of Goods Act 1979*.
2. Under the tort of negligence. A civil wrong – the plaintiff (person bringing the charge) must establish that the manufacturer (who would then be referred to as the defendant):

   a) owed a *duty of care*, and
   b) *broke this duty of care by not acting reasonably*, in the circumstances, and
   c) as a result, *caused the plaintiff injury or damage.*

The case widely cited to illustrate this point has already been mentioned – it is *Donoghue* v. *Stevenson (1932)*.

The action mentioned above is of a civil nature, though there are times (if specific standards are not maintained) when the actions of a manufacturer are thought to be so serious that criminal liability is imposed. For example, the *Consumer Safety Act 1978* regulates the activities of manufacturers in respect of standards to be maintained on products as diverse as toys, electric blankets, and oil-fired heaters. Manufacturers of food products are regulated by the *Food and Drugs Act 1955*, which places similar restrictions in regard to the standards of these producers; food sold which is then found to be unfit for human consumption or which was prepared unhygienically leaves the manufacturer criminally liable.

Neighbourbood liability

Producers do not operate in isolation; their actions are likely to have an impact on those inhabitants (neighbours) in the locality. This type of 'interference' ranges from the smells emanating from the local brewery to the noise of an airport. Those of you who have flown abroad on holiday will have noticed the impact of the noise. Some of you may live near an airport and therefore know first-hand the hardship caused.

- *Do you live near either an airport or a brewery (or know someone who does)? In what way(s) do the organisation's activities affect you? What reasonable constructive remedy can you think of to help alleviate the problem?*

Many people are often heard to say that it would be nice to get away from the grime and the smells of the city and live in the country. Those of you who do live in the country would no doubt have a few things to say about the so-called environmentally clean surroundings you have of silage, manure and their effects. The point is, we all have to put up with a certain amount of inconvenience no matter where we live. Exactly what is the extent of the liability which producers have to face with respect to their neighbours?

In the previous section on manufacturer's liability the case which had to be proved to establish *negligence* was outlined and one of the components was a duty of care. A legal duty of care is recognised in many situations, for example, the duty we have as road users towards other road users, the duty an employer has towards the safety and health of his employees. In the Donoghue case one of the judges (Lord Atkin) outlined the so-called 'neighbourhood principle' when discussing the extent of a duty of care. It would seem from Lord Atkin's statement that we (both as private individuals and as organisations) must take reasonable care to avoid acts or omissions which ought reasonably to be seen as likely to injure a neighbour. Neighbours appear to be those who are so close and directly affected that we ought to realise they would be so affected when the act was undertaken.

- *Review the case of* Hedley Byrne *v.* Heller and Partners *(1964) and say how this case may affect the actions of professional people.*

Negligence is not the only tort which affects the legal liability relationship we may have with regard to our neighbours. Another is nuisance. A private nuisance arises where there is an unreasonable interference with a person's use or enjoyment of his land.

- *After reviewing the case of* Sturges *v.* Bridgman *(1879), say how the events in this case may affect the relationship between manufacturers and their 'neighbours'.*

Liability in respect of nuisance can be criminal because there is an offence of public nuisance, which is an unlawful annoyance or harm which affects the general public. Those responsible can be prosecuted (criminal action), although if a private individual can show that he suffered damage over and above that suffered by others he can sue (take civil-action).

- *Review the case of* Castle *v.* St. Augustine's Links *(1922), which is an example of a public nuisance case.*

We thus, as individuals and as organisations, must accept legal liability for torts. The law recognises and protects personal and property rights by compelling the wrongdoer to pay damages to the victim. In some cases the liability is said to be *strict*, which indicates that a person will have to compensate for injury caused, irrespective of whether or not the plaintiff (the person who accuses) can prove the defendant (the person answering the charge) is to blame.

- *Review the case of* Rylands *v.* Fletcher *(1868) and note the implication of the findings in the case with regard to proving blame.*

In some situations a person can be held liable for the torts of others. Such action is known as *vicarious liability*. This position is one which partners must face in a partnership (one partner may be liable for the torts of another partner in connection with the partnership business); it is also the situation faced by principals who can be held liable for the torts of their agents.

- *See the case of* Lloyd *v.* Grace Smith & Co. *(1912) for an illustration of the aspect of vicarious liability*

Accountability (see also Chapter 3)

Resource decisions in organisations are often made by management, unless the organisation is small and such decisions are made by the owners of the business. In making these decisions managers thus assume a measure of responsibility for ensuring that the decisions lead to profitable outcomes rather than losses. It is argued that no executive should be held accountable for events and activities over which he or she cannot exercise control. Accountability is thus synonymous with responsibility.

A major resource of organisations is finance, the allocation of which will be subject to accountability, just as with any other actions undertaken in an organisation. In the financial area we have tools such as responsibility accounting, which is concerned with matching the accounting function with the responsibilities of specific managers to enable organisations to exercise control. The objective of such a technique, linked as it is to accounting records and reports being adapted to different areas of responsibility, is to ensure that each manager sees the accounting analysis which relates to his specific responsibilities. Such a concept has important implications for the organisational control function.

Another important area of accountability is that already touched upon in this chapter – accountability with regard to the environment. Organisations often find that they are the subject of an attack by environmental pressure groups as a result of activities they are undertaking which, it is argued, are adversely affecting the local environment.

- *Choose a site where what you consider to be an undesirable activity is being carried out (this could be, for example, a noisy factory, an organisation which pollutes the environment, or one which is depleting mineral resources) and say:*
  1. *Why you think the activity is undesirable.*
  2. *How you could exert sufficient pressure to stop the activity.*
  3. *What the effect on the locality would be of a cessation of activities.*

The bad publicity generated by pressure groups involved in such areas as environmental protection is certainly not conducive to profitable enterprise.

All organisations are accountable to specific groups in connection with their resource decisions. They all make decisions concerning the number of people they will employ/make redundant and are thus involved with employees (as a resource) and are accountable to those still in employment to the extent that they are under a moral responsibility to inform them of potential problems concerning the security of their tenure. Those organisations in the private sector of the economy that have raised money to establish the organisation by the sale of shares have a responsibility to their shareholders to return a decent dividend on their investment.

Two other groups to which organisations are accountable are creditors and consumers. Creditors are the people who have lent money or who have supplied goods and not yet received full payment; such people will clearly be concerned with the way the organisation conducts its affairs since they will be looking to get interest on their investment (if they lent money) plus the return of the principal (the sum originally lent). Those creditors who have supplied goods and not received full payment will be hoping to get paid. The consumers are the final group to which the organisation is accountable; as purchasers of goods/services it is they who supply the lifeblood of the business. Organisations are accountable for the quality and suitability of products, as well as the aspects of supply and delivery.

- *Many consumers today take advantage of credit facilities when buying goods. The Consumer Credit Act 1974 stipulates that consumers must be able to see how much they will pay in interest charges. Most traders will quote an APR (Annual Percentage Rate) but few understand what this means. Prepare a short note explaining what an APR is and calculate the APR on a £900 loan to be repaid in 52 monthly instalments of £30.*

It can thus be seen that organisations can be held to be liable for a number of acts or omissions, many of which leave them open to civil action in the courts and a few of which leave them open to (criminal) prosecution. There are therefore many considerations to be taken into account in connection with resource usage. The ones considered here have been:

a) the size an organisation ought to be for maximum efficiency;
b) the use of scarce resources in a bid to make profits;
c) liability and accountability.

Resource disposal

There are two extreme situations concerning the use of resources with which to conclude this chapter

and both deal with the way in which resources are disposed of. The first item will be the way in which labour is dismissed via termination of employment and the second item will concern the issue of what happens to resources (property) when a business goes into liquidation or is declared bankrupt.

Termination of employment

Employment legislation (see Chapter 12) is an area of the law subject to frequent changes. Thus, anything written about what the law is today could well be out of date in a year's time. However, one ought to appreciate the basic principles which appear to run through various areas of law. We have seen, for example, that the objective of criminal law is to punish offenders, while the objective of civil law is to compensate victims. In the area of employment law we are concerned in essence with the regulation of practices between employees and employers.

When introducing the *Employment Act 1982* the then Secretary of State for Employment, Norman Tebbit, said, 'This Act is about fair play at work – fair play for the employee and the employer, for the trade unionist and the non-trade unionist alike'. We therefore have to ask ourselves how the law regulates relations between employers and employees. One of the areas in which the law has affected the relationship between employers and employees is that of dismissal.

- *When is a dismissal said to be 'unfair'?*

Dismissal is one form of termination of contract, since an employment contract can also be terminated by the employee wishing to leave employment or by the period of the contract ending. Our greatest concern, however, is dismissal, primarily because of the implications of this action.

When we enter employment we do so on the basis of a contract which gives benefits and imposes obligations on both parties; we will concentrate at this stage on dismissal from that contract. Employment legislation requires that there be a minimum amount of notice given to employees who have worked for a specific period of time.

- *What periods of time must be given as notice of dismissal and what are the requiremens that must be satisfied before notice is given?*

Although regulations have been created which stipulate minimum periods of notice that must be given to staff, many employers give longer periods, particularly to senior staff. Any employee guilty of gross misconduct can, however, be dismissed summarily.

As an indication of the extent of the law, the *Employment Act 1982* gave rights to employees in connection with dismissal and membership of unions. For example:

1. The right not to be unfairly dismissed in a closed shop which has not been approved by a secret ballot in the preceding 5 years.
2. The right not to be unfairly dismissed in a closed shop if they have been unreasonably excluded or expelled from a trade union.
3. The right not to be unfairly dismissed in a closed shop if there is a conflict between the membership of a trade union and their professional code of ethics.
4. The right not to be selected for redundancy on the grounds of non-membership of a union.
5. The right to have their contract of employment preserved until a tribunal hearing if they claim to have been unfairly dismissed for non-membership of a union.

Those employees who feel they have been unfairly dismissed can present their case before an industrial tribunal within a specific period of time.

- *What is the time limit for bringing an action in an industrial tribunal?*

The law provides for an order to be produced providing for reinstatement or re-engagement in some situations, as well as compensation; in other cases, where no reinstatement or re-engagement is ordered, compensation would normally be paid provided the tribunal agreed that the dismissal was unfair. Industrial tribunals also offer protection to those people who feel they have been dismissed on the grounds of racial or sexual discrimination.

Employment is now being terminated, due to redundancy, with alarming frequency in the UK and in other countries, as a result of the general economic situation. An employee can be made redundant if the dismissal is attributable wholly or mainly to the following:

1. The employer ceasing or intending to cease business for which the employee was hired, or moving from the premises presently occupied.
2. The need for employees of a particular kind, performing duties of a particular kind, has ended or diminished.

- *Obtain a copy of the leaflet, 'The Redundancy Payments Scheme', from the Department of Employment. Estimate the number of weeks' pay which would be awarded to three people you know who are currently in employment if they were declared redundant today.*

Bankruptcy and liquidation

The main distinction between bankruptcy and liquidation lies in the limited liability (see Chapter 3) accorded to members of a company. When an organisation finds it is no longer making profits and eventually can no longer trade, it faces the prospect of *insolvency*. Being insolvent means that a company is:

a) unable to meet current liabilities, and
b) cannot persuade creditors to wait any longer for payment.

Those who are sole traders or members of a partnership (both having unlimited liability) will be declared bankrupt, all proceedings being conducted by a Trustee in Bankruptcy.

Companies that are insolvent go into liquidation. The person who deals with the arrangements is a *liquidator*. The process may be a voluntary one.

- *Research the financial press for an example of either a voluntary or involuntary liquidation. What were the implications of the event for the customers and creditors?*

Before an individual can be declared bankrupt he must have committed an Act of Bankruptcy, which is one of the following:

a) he disappears with the intent of defeating or delaying his creditors,
b) he files a declaration of his inability to pay debts in the County Court or presents a bankruptcy petition against himself,
c) he gives notice to any creditors that he is suspending payment of debts.

The court makes a *receiving order*, which has the effect of protecting the debtor from proceedings brought by his creditors and placing his assets in the control of the Official Receiver. The process now involves the debtor setting out his assets and liabilities; he may have to attend a public examination in court as to the conduct of his business affairs and the circumstances of the bankruptcy; his creditors will seek an Order of Adjudication if arrangements cannot be made to settle debts. If an Order of Adjudication is made the debtor's property will be vested in the Official Receiver, who will then act as a Trustee in

Bankruptcy; his job will be to gather all the assets and distribute them to the creditors.

- *What is meant by 'discharge' in relation to bankruptcy?*

The problem in connection with asset disposal as a result of insolvency is that the creditors will almost certainly not receive all of the money they are owed. The granting of credit (finance) as a resource is therefore restricted to 'creditworthy' (those who appear to be able to pay back) organisations and individuals; time and money has to be spent in checking credentials, and insurance premiums may have to be paid to offset the costs of default, which all adds to the cost and inconvenience of trade.

Assignments

Student activity 10.1

This is an individual assignment. Consider the story in the article on this page. Write an article to be published in the local newspaper, saying why you think Great Britain is about to see an explosion in the growth of shopping and leisure facilities on the fringe of conurbations. Point out what problems are likely to emerge from such development.

When producing the report take care to ensure that the nature and language of the article are suitable for the type of publication you are writing for.

Student activity 10.2

This is a group assignment intended for groups of three or four. After many years of industrial pollution, countries throughout Europe attempted to curb the problem with statutes aimed at limitation. The Clean Air Acts in Britain paved the way for times free of the notorious 'pea-souper' fogs so common in the 1940s and 1950s in parts of the UK.

From the articles (p. 110, left) you will see, however, that we have been generating other pollutants over the years. Your task is to prepare a discussion document which sets out your suggestions for controlling pollution generated in one country which also affects other nations, as well as pollution generated in one country which affects its own inhabitants.

Your document must also contain a discussion of what you expect to be the opposition to your ideas and your counter measures against this opposition.

Megastore age reaches Britain

By Richard North
Environment Correspondent

THE vast shopping and leisure complex on the fringe of a conurbation is coming to Britain in a big way. Planning applications are in for 28 million square feet of developments of more than 400,000 square feet each.

Councillors and planning officials will meet in closed session tomorrow night to consider a huge scheme they fear will come to the fringe of Southampton. They hope to fend it off – until, that is, they hear that some nearby burghers are attracting it to their own town.

Then, says Dave Bull, chairman of the city's planning and transport committee, 'we will have to try to get it for ourselves'.

Source: *The Independent*, 6 November 1986

Student activity 10.3

This assignment is suitable for groups of four or five. Consider the article on p. 110, top right. Research the events surrounding the rise to fame and later failure of Sir Clive Sinclair and produce a 15-minute script for a radio programme about the successes and failures of the businessman.

Student activity 10.4

This assignment involves a fair measure of research and thus may best be tackled by small groups, though students could work on this individually if they have sufficient time.

The article on p. 110 (bottom right) suggests that the existence of the colour tabloid newspaper *Today* helped to change the national newspaper industry. Research the background to the introduction of *Today* and, in a format that you consider suitable, show how its existence changed the newspaper industry. (Give examples of the changes which you feel occurred as a result of the introduction of *Today*.)

Britain can clean up on acid rain

by Ian Williams

IT was not just environmentalists who took a keen interest last week when EEC ministers discussed the problem of acid rain. Britain's leading engineering groups are lining up for what they believe will be a multi-billion pound business – cleaning up power stations.

Last week's meeting ended in acrimony. Emissions of sulphur dioxide from power stations are widely blamed for causing acid rain, but a British compromise plan to cut these emissions by 45% over 20 years was rejected by West Germany, Holland and Denmark because they felt it left too many loopholes.

Source: *The Sunday Times*, 30 November 1986

Farm pollution 'may be health risk'

by Andrew Gowers

WATER pollution caused by intensive use of fertilisers on farms is expected in the next few years to become an acute environmental threat, which might cause unacceptable health hazards if not brought under control.

That warning comes in a report published by the Organisation for Economic Cooperation and Development, the Paris-based grouping of 24 industrial countries.

Source: *Financial Times*, 25 November 1986

SIR Clive Sinclair seemed in June 1983 to be the very epitome of the New Elizabethan Technologist – innovative, buccaneering and successful.

Knighted by an admiring Mrs Thatcher, he was also named 'Young businessman of the year,' his profits guaranteed that the City was happy to indulge this Midas of the microchip. He had been right about calculators and computers. Perhaps he was also right about pocket television, wristwatch radios and electric cars.

He seemed to many to herald a renaissance for a UK industry in decline powered by the union of traditional British inventiveness with the new information technology. Within three years, however, that silicon vision had crumbled into worthless sand.

An advanced home computer took an interminable time to reach the market. The pocket television failed to excite. And the electric car emerged as a somewhat ridiculous battery operated trike, sowing powerful doubts about Sinclair's competence in his investors' minds.

Finally, overwhelmed by debt and unsold stock, he was forced to sell his computers, patents and even his birthright, the Sinclair name. Mr Alan Sugar's Amstrad scooped the lot for a mere £5m.

Source: *Financial Times*, 25 November 1986

EDDY Shah is going back to his roots. He is set to bow out of Today, the new national colour tabloid he launched last March, and return to the north of England to concentrate on expanding his provincial newspaper empire.

It is a sad move for Shah, whose new paper has taken very few sales away from the established dailies but whose very existence helped spark off a revolution in Fleet Street which is changing the face of the national newspaper industry.

Source: *The Sunday Times*, 3 August 1986

Student activity 10.5

This is an individual assignment. Read the article below. Your task is to assume the role of consultant to the local council at Galmoy, charged with the responsibility of assisting the council in planning for the possibility that commercial quantities of zinc could be found to exist in the area. You have to prepare a formal report for the Chief Executive of the council which deals with the following:

a) the impact on the farming community of the discovery of zinc,
b) the implications for the infrastructure of the area,
c) the economic implications for the area and the likely impact of the increased incomes which will result,
d) the possible effect on house prices, and
e) the long-term implications for the environment and the community.

In each of the above areas you must give reasons for your views. The report must contain recommendations for:

a) the granting or withholding of planning permission to excavate, and
b) necessary action to be taken by the council if they decide to grant planning permission.

Skills assessable

Skill	1	2	3	4	5	6	7	8
Assignment 1	1.8 1.10	2.2 2.4		4.3 4.6 4.10		6.1		
2	1.3 1.5 1.6	2.2 2.5		4.3 4.4 4.5 4.6 4.10	5.1 5.2 5.4 5.10	6.1 6.2 6.3		
3	1.6 1.7 1.8	2.1 2.2 2.4 2.5	3.4 3.5 3.6 3.7	4.2 4.3 4.6	5.2 5.5 5.10	6.1 6.2 6.3		
4	1.6 1.8 1.9	2.2 2.4 2.5	3.5 3.6 3.7	4.2 4.7	5.1 5.2 5.5	6.1 6.2 6.3		
5	1.5 1.6	2.2 2.4		4.3 4.6		6.1 6.2 6.3 6.5		

THE chugging of two drilling rigs, making trial borings, is steadily marking out the limits of a zinc bonanza 300ft under a wind-swept hillside in Ireland.

If it is present in commercial quantities, the high quality (almost pure) zinc will cause an economic boom for the tranquil farming community at Galmoy, 80 miles south of Dublin and make a fortune for the Dublin-based prospector, *Conroy Petroleum and Natural Resources*.

Source: *The Sunday Times*, 30 November 1986

11

THE AVAILABILITY OF FINANCE AND EFFICIENT RESOURCE USE

Organisations use resources throughout the process of *production* (the creation of 'things' which satisfy wants) but this is only possible with the existence of finance as a resource. Without the necessary finance organisations would not be able to purchase the services of labour, lease or purchase property, or purchase required raw materials. We are also concerned, as students of organisations, to find out whether such resources are used efficiently.

This chapter is not intended as a definitive guide to all that is available in terms of finance for organisations but as the catalyst which encourages you to obtain data on what is available *today* in the business world.

Purpose of finance

- *List six activities to which financial resources will be put in an organisation*

Finance will be used to purchase or rent/lease raw materials; labour; know-how; property (buildings); machinery; vehicles; electricity; telephone services, etc. Since money is a medium of exchange, we can use it to satisfy all demands for settlement made on the organisation by those who provide us with goods/services.

If we follow logically the sequence of beginning and running an organisation it will become apparent for what purposes finance is used:

1. *Setting up the organisation:*
   All organisations will require initial capital (start-up capital), which will range from the required authorised minimum (working) capital which public limited companies have to raise (see Fig. 3.3) to the much smaller though just as important sums which the sole trader and partnership must obtain to begin business. Finance required to start a business will be needed for equipment, stock, to pay wages, and

to pay bills which are paid in advance (rent, rates, insurance, vehicle excise duty, etc.).

- *Assume you and two of your colleagues decide to go into business for yourselves offering a photocopying/ reproduction/printing service in the High Street of your nearest town. Locate suitable premises and investigate the sites to obtain data relating to rates' costs and the costs of a lease. Calculate approximately the initial start-up cost of such a venture in terms of rates and rental value only.*

2. *Obtaining resources:*
   In order to obtain the services of labour, and to obtain the component parts required for production, the organisation must offer money in exchange for such resource use. The rate at which labour will be paid will be a function of the demand for labour, its supply, nationally agreed wage-rates, local bargaining, and the relative importance of and extent of 'perks' connected with the position offered. The price of raw materials will be the subject of consultation between the contracting parties, but will also to a large extent be influenced by the pressures of supply and demand and quantities purchased (it being usual to expect a discount when purchasing in bulk and/or for cash).

- *What is meant by 'liquidity'?*
- *What is meant by debt factoring? How does this help to maintain liquidity in an organisation?*

3. *Marketing:*
   In Chapter 13 we will meet the various components involved in marketing but, at this stage, let us take the simplistic view that we are concerned only with advertising. Advertising requires finance, which we will not yet have generated since sales will be zero (hence the reason for advertising). This, and many other expenses associated with undertaking business, will require finance.

- *What would be the cost of taking out a full-page advertisement in one of your local newspapers?*

4. *Expansion:*
   It would be wrong to assume that businesses expand merely by ploughing back their profits. All profit belongs to the owners of an organisation, not the organisation itself. Profits may only be retained by the organisation with the consent of owners who, in the case of the public limited companies, will be concerned about the

Fig. 11.1 Some of the uses to which financial resources will be put

level of dividend payments. To expand it may be necessary to look to other sources of finance.

Sources of finance

Just as there are a number of uses to which finance can be put, there are also many sources of finance. Most people tend to think of the major banks as being a source of finance, particularly for the small- to medium-sized organisation. The Report of the Wilson Committee in 1980 stated in part, 'There had undoubtedly been more visible rivalry between banks for the custom of small businesses in recent years, with an expansion ... in the range of specialised services provided for small firms ...' Report of the Committee to Review the Functioning of Financial Institutions, (HMSO Cmnd 7937, June 1980).

- *Obtain literature from the major banks in your area and produce a checklist showing what each offers the prospective businessman, in terms of finance.*

The banks are not the only source of finance for organisations, such sources vary according to the nature of the organisation and the nature of the finance required. At one extreme we have the sole trader, content to borrow funds from friends and relatives, while at the other we have the multinational corporation financing expenditure by issuing new shares or funding projects by borrowing from merchant banks and pension funds.

Although the high street banks are not the only source of finance, they are nonetheless very significant. Some lending takes place under a scheme of loan guarantees operated by the Department of Trade. Under the Loan Guarantees for Small Businesses scheme the Department of Trade guarantees repayment of 80% of medium-term loans over two to seven years. Other sources of funds include other banking and financial institutions, such as the Allied Irish Bank, Royal Bank of Scotland, Standard Chartered Bank, and United Dominions Trust, among others.

- *Outline the main differences between a bank loan and an overdraft.*

Businesses operating in specified rural areas can benefit from the assistance given by the Council for Small industries in Rural Areas (CoSIRA) which loans finance and helps prospective borrowers draw up funding propositions which can be presented to the banks.

The larger organisations (public companies) that can sell shares in order to increase finance are free to do so, although this does affect the ownership of the organisation.

- *What is a gearing ratio? What is the significance of a gearing ratio?*
- *Make brief notes on each of the following methods of issuing shares:*
  a) public issue,
  b) offers for sale,
  c) placings,
  d) a Rights Issue.
- *Differentiate between loan capital and risk capital.*

Although it was stated earlier that profits do not belong to an organisation but to the owner(s), it is true that 50–60% of the capital funds of many of the larger 'quoted' companies comes from retained profit.

- *What is a 'quoted' company?*
- *Make brief notes on (a) the activities of and (b) the ownership of Finance for Industry Ltd.*

When we consider finance and the sources available we tend to overlook the fact that many organisations are able to generate sufficient resources from within, and thus not tie up capital. Such organisations will, for example, make use of leasing and hire purchase, which reduces the need for owner's capital to be committed.

Many organisations are making more and more use of trade credit, so much so that the total amount outstanding as trade credit is always much greater than the total of bank loans to industry. By taking goods on credit I can pay when I have sold them, thus I do not need to borrow money (on which I would have to pay interest) in order to obtain stock. And, as a creditor, I can factor my debts in order to obtain liquidity.

Finally, organisations ought to consider the benefits which can accrue from the workings of the tax system. There are specific tax reliefs (capital allowances) on many items of capital expenditure which can be set against taxable profits – thus reducing these profits and thereby reducing tax commitment; during periods of inflation organisations may also qualify for stock relief, which further reduces tax bills. Added to this are incentives offered through schemes such as the Business Start-up Scheme and the Venture Capital Scheme. The Business Start-up Scheme provided an incentive to encourage individual investors to buy equity shares in small companies, while the Venture Capital Scheme gave protection to an investor if his or her investment turned out to be unsuccessful. The Business Expansion Scheme, open to most people who pay income tax, gives tax relief for investment in new ordinary shares issued by companies not quoted on The Stock Exchange or dealt in on the Unlisted Securities Market. Such schemes encourage investment in companies that might otherwise have found great difficulty in attracting investors.

- *What and where is the* Unlisted Securities Market? *How does it differ from The Stock Exchange?*

Efficient resource use

Since this chapter has been concerned with finance, we will consider efficient resource use to imply efficient use of finance, or how financially efficient the organisation has been. We could consider other aspects of efficiency, such as that associated with labour (see mention of qualitative and quantitative measures in connection with labour in Chapter 12), particularly in connection with organisation structures and the total number of subordinates a manager has (span of control – see Chapter 2), and the point when efficiency is affected by size, though that would be inappropriate here. In the section concerning appraisal in Chapter 12 you will see how performance appraisal can be used to increase a firm's efficiency.

- *What do you think a manager should do (what are his functions)? What do you therefore understand by managerial efficiency?*

Organisations must continually strive for efficiency; the benefits to be gained from cutting costs (provided standards and sales are maintained) will be seen in improved profit positions; the identification and subsequent removal from the organisation of surplus capacity or inefficient units or departments will provide finance in the future for investment elsewhere in the (more efficient) organisation.

I find that on many occasions students work very efficiently at what they are doing, although what they are doing may not be what they were told to do. I often remind people prior to examinations to answer the question or deal with the task which is set, not one which they think is set or one which they wish had been set. The importance of discipline such as this lies in the fact that:

a) we need discipline in organisations at least as much as we need it in our private lives. In our private lives we need to be disciplined in our spending of money, in our hygiene, in our punctuality at arriving for work. This may seem very authoritarian but it is true that life does move along much more smoothly when we have an idea of who is doing what, when, where and why.

b) if we are slapdash, inefficient, or undisciplined we may spend a lot of time (and other resources) doing something that does not need to be done at present.

We have to accept that people are never going to be 100% efficient, even though we *can* ensure high degrees of efficiency. Indeed, it may not be to anyone's advantage if someone is 100% efficient. By way of example, consider the situation where you are the most efficient person in the country at making left-handed candles. If no-one is buying left-handed candles this year, what is the point? Does it really matter how efficient you are in a field where no-one wishes to buy what you have made?

Let me give you a simple example of an increase in efficiency and the resulting saving. Several years ago I became involved with a small company in the motor trade which dealt with sales of new and used cars and which also carried out mechanical and electrical repairs to vehicles. The organisation had been formed some years before my appearance by two brothers and their father, and the accounting devices used had been constructed when they initially set up the business. None had formal training in management or accountancy, or in any of the disciplines which might have prevented a number of inefficient activities with which they had become involved. This was one of my first experiences of the motor trade, and the problem and its solution showed that outsiders often see the root cause of organisational problems much more easily than those directly involved – this is the reason why many organisations use the services of outside management consultants. Whenever the mechanics completed a car service or performed a mechanical/electrical repair they also completed a *job card*. The job cards were numbered and their format is shown in Fig. 11.2.

When the time came for each job card to be entered into the account books, the relevant page had been drawn up as shown in Fig. 11.3.

- *Where does the inefficiency lie in the above example?*

When whoever was responsible had to transfer the

JOB CARD

Customer's Name:
Number ..
Date ....

Details of job to be done ....

Parts used ....
Labour cost ....
SUB TOTAL ....
VAT charged ....
Zero rated items ....
TOTAL ....

Fig. 11.2

Customer's Name	Labour	Parts	Sub Total	Zero Rated	VAT	Total

Fig. 11.3

details from the job cards to the record book, he would do so as follows:

1. Move the index finger of the non-writing hand to the second figure on the job card (labour cost) and copy this figure into the book.
2. Move finger up to figure immediately above (Parts used), copy this down.
3. Jump the next figure, find the Sub Total figure, and copy this down.
4. Jump the next figure and pick up the Zero rated number, copy this into the book.
5. Move back up one figure to the VAT charged amount, and copy this down.
6. Ignore next figure and move down to Total, copy this down.

It seemed to me that whoever completed this task was almost bound to make some mistakes because of the constant movement around the card, and it was very time consuming to work in such a way.

My solution was to merely rearrange the account book as shown in Fig. 11.4.

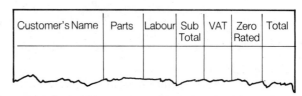

Customer's Name	Parts	Labour	Sub Total	VAT	Zero Rated	Total

Fig. 11.4

The process of transferring data from job cards to the account book was thus much simpler, and fewer mistakes were made since one merely had to follow the job card data and write this down as one came to it (without jumping around searching for relevant figures). I roughly estimated the saving in time to be:

| 6 seconds per job card | $\times$ | 300 (average number of jobs done per month by three mechanics) | $\times$ | 12 months per year | = | 21,600 seconds |

A saving of 6 hours may not sound like a great deal but to a small business, already inundated with paperwork (particularly those organisations that are VAT-registered and have to employ someone to act as an agent for the Customs and Excise – for which the Excise do not pay – to complete necessary forms and VAT returns), anything which made a saving in time, anything which increased efficiency, was to be welcomed.

In order to consider efficiency and resource use we need to be able to measure components and make sense of the data we obtain; organisations will use various qualitative and quantitative measures of performance to do just that.

Assessing performance

Accounting is one of a number of quantitative methods of analysis which have applications for business problems. The source of the information concerning measures of performance is to be found in the finance section of organisations. When measuring performance we do not concentrate entirely on 'business' organisations, since all public and private sector organisations need to be able to measure resource use and assess performance in a given time period. (See page 12 on assessment in the public sector.)

- *Why should it be necessary for an NHS hospital to measure resource use and assess performance? Should hospitals, which carry out a necessary function be concerned with finance and economics? Or should they be concerned solely with health care? Discuss this statement in groups of four or five.*

To the layman, efficiency in a public-sector organisation such as the local authority housing department may be measured in a number of ways. For example:

a) How long does it take them to answer the telephone when I call on a Monday morning to complain about vandalism on my estate?
b) How long does it take workmen to arrive to fix the leaking gutter and replace the missing tiles on my roof?
c) When workmen do arrive, how long does it take them to get the job done, how many men does it take, how many of the men actually work, and how many stand around 'supervising'. How many tea-breaks do they have?
d) How long was it before the repairs that were done needed to be done again?

These are the criteria that many people use to measure inefficiency.

- *Find out what members of the public think is a good indication of inefficiency in say, road repairers or workmen. Note down the comments of ten people and compare your notes with other members of your group. What is the most common complaint among the public which leads them to conclude that some workmen are inefficient?*

It is all very well thinking about efficiency and performance in terms such as those already mentioned but we do need to be more scientific and more technical when it comes to considering performance in organisations. It would serve little purpose for us merely to reiterate individual instances of inefficiency. We need to be more precise; we need to be able to prove that inefficiency exists; and we need a measure of performance so that we can compare performance now with performance after we have made changes that we hope will lead to improvements. Organisations require performance appraisal, that is, a review of results to ascertain the efficiency of that performance.

Although this may make performance appraisal in the public sector a little difficult in some areas (since such organisations are not intended to be profit maximisers) and just about impossible in others (e.g. education, health care, etc.) there *are* methods, though their use and the effectiveness of the results obtained are open to some debate.

- *In what way(s) could we assess teacher performance?*

How could we measure the performance of an NHS hospital? The speed with which they can amputate a limb, perhaps, or the number of patients they can cram into a ward, or the number of babies a gynaecologist can deliver in a day?

The measures used to assess performance will vary according to the organisation. The remainder of this chapter will consider the methods used in the assessment of business organisations.

- *Organisations such as British Coal and British Steel are expected to achieve a given real rate of return. What is meant by this? Is the expectation realistic?*

Qualitative and quantitative measures of performance

A qualitative measure is one concerned with quality, while a quantitative measure is concerned with quantity. Quantitative techniques include probability theory, linear programming, the mathematics of compound interest and annuities, and calculus – all of which are beyond the scope of this book. We shall therefore consider the use of accounting ratios to illustrate techniques involving the use of accounting data in measuring performance.

A quantitative approach will treat an estimate or an expected result as being certain; management must, however, evaluate subjective and qualitative factors to allow for the uncertainty which exists in the real world. When we evaluate performance, therefore, we must bear in mind that decisions had to be taken as to the direction that the business would take in the light of what was known at the time. Management is expected to make decisions, using managerial judgement, based on data which consists of quantitative and qualitative estimates.

Many of the factors concerned with the operation of an organisation cannot be quantified; it is not possible, for example, to measure how effective a particular organisational structure.is in relation to another. This does not prevent those concerned with the implementation of production (operational researchers) from creating situations/models which enable them to create more effective methods – though at the end of the day these must be assessed in some way.

- *If you were asked to assess two well-known public companies and to compare their performance over the past four years, how would you do this quantitatively?*

The crucial factor when assessing performance is *perspective*: for example, shareholders will be concerned with profits because dividends are directly related to these; managers, on the other hand, tend to be more concerned with cash and liquidity – many so-called profitable companies have gone out of business because they ran out of cash.

The interpretation and analysis of financial statements will be conducted via *ratio analysis*, which will be used in areas such as:

a) liquidity
b) capital structure
c) activity rate
d) profitability and asset utility
e) employee productivity
f) shares, share values and dividends.

Liquidity

There are a number of liquidity and working capital ratios in use, not only because they are useful to management for assessment purposes but also because creditors often need a guide of credit worthiness. First, the ratio concerned with meeting short-term obligations is the *current ratio*:

$$\frac{\text{current assets}}{\text{current liabilities}} = \text{current ratio}$$

Current assets must be sufficient to cover current liabilities – though it is not desirable to have high levels of current assets, since these are not in themselves profitable; there are times when organisations need to take risks (to allow liabilities to exceed assets) to increase the returns they hope to make. Current ratio of assets to liabilities enables us to see if an organisation can meet current obligations with a margin of safety to allow for possible shrinkage in value of current assets.

- *What may cause a decrease in the value of stocks held?*

It would be improper to give a figure and suggest this as a good guide for the current ratio. This ratio ought to be interpreted by consideration of the components which form it (cash, debtors, nature of and demand for stock held, etc.) as well as the type of business, the current position of the industry which the business is in, and future economic expectations.

Another ratio commonly used is the *liquidity* or *acid-test ratio*, which is calculated as follows:

$$\frac{\text{Current assets} - \text{stock}}{\text{current liabilities}} = \text{liquidity}$$

This is a more rigorous test of a company's ability to meet short-term obligations since it excludes stock. It therefore uses the measure of liquid assets which represents the source of funds from which such obligations would in reality be met – it takes time to convert stock into debtors and then into cash.

Liquidity is all important. There are two ratios which help to monitor liquidity position and improve cash flow:

$$\frac{\text{Average debtors}}{\text{Sales}} \times 365 = \text{Credit given in days}$$

If this can be reduced the liquidity position of the organisation is improved.

$$\frac{\text{Average creditors}}{\text{Purchases}} \times 365 = \text{Credit taken in days}$$

If this can be increased it reduces the demand on liquid assets.

Capital structure

The ratio under consideration here is the *debit/equity* ratio which makes use of the fact that finance for an organisation can come from the owners in the form of a shareholding, and from outside the organisation, in the form of debt. Borrowing finance has the advantage that organisations are able to offer greater returns to shareholders (provided their investments pay off) without asking them to contribute any more money.

Activity rate

There are two ratios which show how effectively a company manages its assets, *stock turnover* and *average collection period*. Stock turnover measures the number of times a year stock changes (on average); generally we would expect to see rapid stock turnover in retailing with perhaps much slower rates in manufacture.

$$\frac{\text{Sales}}{\text{Stock}} = \text{Stock turnover}$$

- *Obtain the company accounts for two national retailers and compare their stock turnover figures. What does this tell you about the two organisations?*

The average collection period refers to the average number of days' credit given to debtors and represents the amount of time during which the debtors are making use of this finance. Again, it is usual to find retailers with very short collection periods (credit sales being avoided in the main) but manufacturers may have collection periods of two months or more.

$$\frac{\text{Debtors/Average}}{\text{collection period}} = \frac{\text{Debtors}}{\text{Sales per day}}$$

Profitability and asset utility

Under this heading we can consider the ratios which relate the returns of the company to what had to be invested, or to effort (sales/turnover) needed to achieve those returns. Here I will include a rate of return on investment ratio and a number of profitability ratios. Consideration will also be given to ratios which indicate the efficiency of use of assets by comparing sales with various assets.

The key to any profitable enterprise is to achieve a good rate of return on capital employed.

Capital employed	= total current assets (cash, debtors, stock, etc.)	+ fixed assets (premises, machinery, etc.)	− current liabilities (creditors, loans, etc.)

The ratio is: $\dfrac{\text{Profit before tax}}{\text{Capital employed}} \times 100\%$

This indicates the efficiency with which the assets are applied within the business.

There are a number of other ratios concerned with profitability. A few of the more common ones are shown below:

$$\frac{\text{Gross profit}}{\text{Sales}} \times 100$$

This gives an indication of the total profit in relation to effort expended.

$$\frac{\text{Net profit}}{\text{Sales}} \times 100$$

This (when viewed in relation to the previous ratio) gives an indication of a) profit after expenses in relation to effort expended and, b) the extent to which profit is lost on expenses.

This is a general indicator of relative efficiency which is used when making intra-industry comparisons.

- *What is the difference between gross profit and net profit?*

Profitability related to investment $= \dfrac{\text{Net profits}}{\text{Net worth}}$

This measures the return to the owners of the business after taxes and interest have been paid. It appraises the earning power of the ownership investment.

- *What is meant by the 'net worth' of an organisation?*

$$\text{Net profit margin} = \frac{\text{Operating profit}}{\text{Sales}} \times 100\%$$

This ratio indicates the ability to generate profit from sales.

The ratios which indicate efficiency use *sales* as the base. In order to achieve sales effort needs to be expended; thus, in using turnover or sales we are using a figure which represents the amount of effort used. Variations in efficiency can be highlighted by looking at the relationship of the following:

$$\frac{\text{Cost of sales}}{\text{Sales}} \qquad \frac{\text{Selling and distribution expenses}}{\text{Sales}}$$

$$\frac{\text{Administrative expenses}}{\text{Sales}} \qquad \frac{\text{Financial expenses}}{\text{Sales}}$$

The first of these ratios (Cost of sales/Sales) is significant in that it includes all direct production costs, the component parts of which can be watched carefully through investigation of the following relationships:

$$\frac{\text{Direct materials}}{\text{Cost of sales}} \qquad \frac{\text{Direct labour}}{\text{Cost of sales}} \qquad \frac{\text{Direct factory expenses}}{\text{Cost of sales}}$$

Management will be concerned with any major differences that may occur from year to year in these relationships.

Sales can be related to any type of asset to assist in the assessment of performance, and there are ratios which allow one to check effective use of assets. For example:

$$\frac{\text{Sales}}{\text{Fixed assets}} \qquad \frac{\text{Sales}}{\text{Average stock}}$$

$$\frac{\text{Sales}}{\text{Plant and Machinery}} \qquad \frac{\text{Sales}}{\text{Average debtors}}$$

These guides will indicate the frequency with which assets have been converted into sales – which is a measure of efficiency.

Employee productivity

Since the labour element makes up the largest single cost figure in British industry, it is vitally important that organisations maintain a close watch on the efficiency of labour. In order to do this we must consider measures aimed at keeping management informed of the productivity and profitability of this resource.

Those ratios concerned with profitability and the sales generated per employee are perhaps the easiest to consider since they are fairly straightforward (see Fig. 11.5).

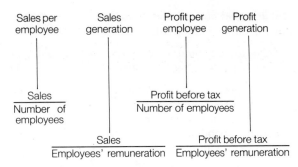

Fig. 11.5

It is often useful to compare wage levels between various companies since such a measure might give an indication of why there may be differences between the quality of staff. If we are concerned with efficiency we would need to consider all of the possible variables and the quality of labour must therefore be very important. The easiest way to do this would be to obtain the wage rate details of the firms concerned, though this may not always be possible.

- *How could you arrive at a rough estimate of the average wage rate for a firm if all you had was the annual report and accounts?*

When we are concerned with the productivity of labour we are interested in what that labour can do for an organisation. Organisations do not employ people because they like the look of them, generally speaking. Organisations employ people because their efforts enable the organisation to achieve its objective(s). This is not as bad as it sounds! We do not operate a slave market for labour. All labour services are paid for, thus the owners of those services (employees) earn remuneration, and the hirers of labour (employers) can obtain labour services. At the end of the day, if I have to pay someone £200 per week to work for me I will only do so if he at least earns (for the business) as much as it costs me to hire him (£200 + National Insurance contributions + any other costs of my employing him), I am interested in how much value a prospective employee can bring to my organisation. When assessing the efficiency of employees we can therefore follow this principle and consider the value added to products as a result of hiring labour services. The two ratios commonly used are:

$$\frac{\text{Value added}}{\text{Employee remuneration}} \qquad \frac{\text{Value added}}{\text{Number of employees}}$$

There is, however, a drawback with using these ratios. It is not, as might be expected, in measuring value added but in taking into account the quality and level of capital used.

- *How would you attempt to estimate value added in a manufacturing organisation?*

Value added is relatively simple to calculate: it is the difference between the cost of components used in manufacture and the value of these parts when sold as finished goods.

The quality and level of capital used is significant in as much as variations in output could be explained by differences in that capital; I am using the term *capital* here as being synonymous with plant and machinery.

Shares, share values, and dividends

It was mentioned earlier that one significant group interested in the efficiency of the organisation would be the shareholders (owners). These would be interested in the return on their investment (though this may be greater in the long run if they forfeit the chances now of making short-term gains), and there are a number of ratios which deal with this issue. Such ratios include those shown in Fig. 11.6.

- *What is the difference between a 'preference share' and an 'ordinary share'?*

We thus have a number of ratios which can be used to establish various measures of efficiency and performance and thereby enable an organisation to assess its position in relation to last year's performance and in relation to competitors' performance. However, conclusions reached will depend on the accuracy of data supplied. We may find, for example, that while the information contained within the balance sheet is technically correct it may be inaccurate in a number of ways. For example:

1. Stock figures may contain outdated stock.
2. Value of assets in the books may bear no relationship to their replacement value.

A brief mention was made earlier in this chapter of qualitative measures of performance. There are unfortunately no easy ratios or formulae which can be applied to such subjective valuations. Qualitative factors are those which are often difficult to express in quantitative terms. Examples include:

1. The effects of proposals for price increases on customer goodwill.
2. The effects of proposals for price cuts on relations with competitors.
3. The effects on staff-employee relations of certain proposals.

We can generally only deal with these issues on the basis of subjective valuation, which itself comes from our views/beliefs, our experience, and the experiences of others, etc. Your ability to weigh up considerations of a qualitative nature will increase as you progress through your career and will be

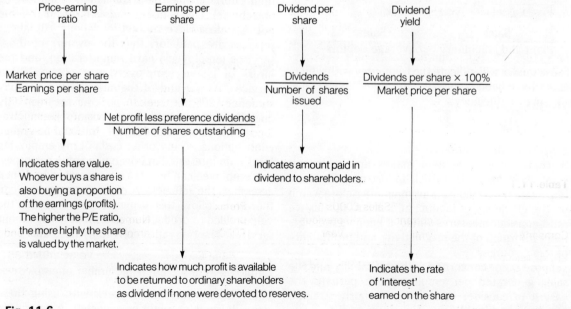

Fig. 11.6

enhanced by the use of role-play, case studies, and simulation in learning.

Assignments

Student activity 11.1

This is an assignment for groups of four or five. Your group has decided to go into business in an area not far from your college. The business will retail badges, T-shirts (either plain or with the design of the customer's choice), and 'pop memorabilia', such as posters and tour sweatshirts.

To begin trading you need to obtain a loan from your bank and you realise that, in order to impress upon the bank manager that you are a worthy investment, you must prepare a statement showing how you will be able to repay the loan. Your task is to estimate the start-up costs for such a venture and to suggest the probable size of your market. To attempt this realistically you will need to discover the figures relating to rent and rates for property similar to that which you would require, in the same area. You will also need to be aware of the costs involved in obtaining stock and equipment.

To be able to say something about the potential market you will need to be aware of factors such as the number of people who may be interested in such a shop (how many people live in the area and are of the age which you think would be interested in such stock?) and whether or not they have sufficient funds to enable them to be buyers of your merchandise (extremely high rates of local unemployment may, for example, preclude purchases of this nature since insufficient funds would be available for such purchases). Prepare the statement for your bank manager.

Student activity 11.2

This is an individual assignment.

In order to investigate the resource use of the organisations in Table 11.1, calculate:

a) pretax profit as a percentage of (current year) sales;
b) pretax profit per employee;
c) sales per employee (current year);
d) percentage change in sales between the two years shown.

Analyse the figures obtained from the calculations and produce a short report showing either:

a) which you think is the most efficient organisation, or
b) why it is not possible to select one organisation as being the most efficient.

Student activity 11.3

This is an individual assignment. Read the article overleaf (left) and give as many reasons as you can why an issue such as the TSB flotation should be heavily oversubscribed.

Make brief notes on the activities of 'stags' in the new issues market and the way in which 'bulls' and 'bears' make their money on The Stock Exchange.

Student activity 11.4

This is an individual assignment. Read the article overleaf (right) and carry out necessary additional research to enable you to prepare an oral presentation on what you consider to be the meaning and implication of wage inflation. In your presentation you must also demonstrate an awareness of other possible causes of inflation.

Student activity 11.5

This is an individual assignment. As a full-time student or as an employee who is tackling the BTEC course on a part-time basis, you no doubt have limited funds at your disposal. In order to ensure

Table 11.1

Company	Sales £000s		Pretax profit £000s	Number of employees	Year end
	current year	previous year			
British Telecom	8,387,000	7,653,000	1,810,000	233,711	31/3/86
Marks & Spencer	3,715,000	3,213,000	364,000	63,144	31/3/86
Ultramar	2,357,800	3,260,400	255,300	3,719	31/12/85

Source: *Business* Top Thousand 1986

Stags run risks in TSB race

VIDEO cameras, handwriting experts and a network of computers are being deployed to thwart illegal multiple applications for the £1.5 billion TSB share sale, which closes on Wednesday.

Already several hundred stags have been identified by Peat Marwick, the firm of accountants which is policing the issue. The stags face prosecution for fraud under the Theft Act and could face fines of several thousand pounds.

Source: *The Sunday Times*, 21 September 1986

FOR at least three decades British management has been able to blame the trade unions for most of this country's industrial and economic ills, and with good cause. Now they no longer have the unions to blame, for the Thatcher government has tamed them. Strikes are at record lows. Even the Fleet Street unions are succumbing to technological change. And union leaders have been banished from the corridors of Whitehall.

Yet Britain continues down the path of relative economic decline. For that, British managers now have nobody to blame but themselves. The poor quality of British management is now the main impediment to Britain's economic renaissance. The lack of a dynamic, confident business class is why the industries of America, West Germany and Japan continue to outpace Britain's.

Mark these figures well, for they contain the main symptom of this country's continuing economic decline. In the past 12 months, prices in the United States rose by 1.6%, wages by 2.2%. In West Germany, prices have actually fallen by 0.4% compared with a year ago, while wages have risen by 4.1%. Japanese prices have risen by a mere 0.1% in the past year, pay by 3.9%.

And Britain? Here prices have risen 2.4%, which is a bit higher than those other three economies, but not bad all the same. Wages, however, have risen by 7.5%, which is over twice as fast as the other three. Britain's rate of wage inflation is crippling our hopes of becoming competitive with tragic consequences for those on the dole – when labour costs are rising that fast, extra workers are simply not hired.

Source: *The Sunday Times*, 21 September 1986

that you get the best value for money you probably (subconsciously) weigh-up the potential gains from spending your money on particular ventures. It may come as a surprise to know that many organisations go through a similar process, because of limited resources. In their case the processs of weighing-up gains from expenditure against the costs involved may generally be referred to as *cost-benefit analysis*. Take a sheet of plain A4 paper and begin by writing down all the items on which you expect to spend money next week. As you do so, ask yourself if you really need to spend each particular sum, weigh-up the benefits and compare these (on paper) with the cost involved.

At the end of next week, check actual expenditure with the list prepared at the beginning of the week.

Answer the following questions:

1. Did you spend money on items *not* on the list at the beginning of the week?
2. Did you *not* spend money on items that you had anticipated buying? (If 'yes', note which item(s) you failed to buy and note why.)
3. Were you surprised by your buying habits? If so, in what way(s)? (For example, many people are surprised at the number of 'impulse' buys they enter into.)

What does this process tell you about the way in which you allocate your scarce resources? Will you continue to spend irrationally in the future, having experienced a little discipline in spending for a week?

Skills assessable

	Skill							
	1	2	3	4	5	6	7	8
Assignment								
1	1.6	2.4	3.5	4.3	5.1	6.1	7.1	
	1.8		3.6	4.6	5.2	6.2	7.2	
	1.10		3.7	4.7	5.3	6.3	7.3	
			3.8		5.5	6.4	7.4	
			3.9		5.6	6.6	7.5	
			3.11		5.8			
					5.10			
2	1.4	2.2		4.3	5.1			
		2.5		4.5	5.2			
				4.6	5.3			
					5.4			
					5.5			
					5.10			
3		2.2		4.3		6.1		
		2.4		4.5		6.2		
				4.6		6.3		
4	1.8	2.2		4.2	5.1	6.1		
		2.4		4.3	5.2	6.2		
		2.5		4.5		6.3		

5 This is a relatively simple task which does not lend itself to assessment.

12
THE ORGANISATION AND ITS EMPLOYEES

People are employed in organisations as managers and managed; as those who lead and those who are led. This chapter will consider specific areas of concern for management and worker alike through issues such as manpower planning, personnel policies, and industrial relations. The area of employment law will be discussed, albeit very generally since this is an area subject to almost continual change. In considering the suitability and efficiency of labour, (personnel) appraisal will also be discussed.

Manpower planning

When organisations are formed, particular objectives are set. Similarly, those orgnisations that have been around for some time will also have objectives. When such objectives are formulated, factors likely to affect the organisation, such as the external environment (see page 34) and (for existing concerns) performance (for measurement of this, see Chapter 11), are considered and alternative courses of action are devised and evaluated. Those responsible for the operation of the organisation, for example the directors, would construct a *strategic plan*, during the process of which they would take into account considerations of manpower.

Manpower planning is concerned with securing a supply of manpower which is able to undertake the organisation's activities: this does not necessarily always involve hiring more staff. We could also consider moving some staff to different organisational positions or even firing staff.

There are four stages involved in manpower planning:
1. Determine the demand for manpower.
2. Complete a manpower audit.
3. Determine external supplies of labour.
4. Reconcile demand for with supply of labour.

1. Demand for manpower

This is primarily determined by market forces in that, if demand for the product is good, demand for the labour that produces it will also be good.

- *If you had responsibility for ensuring that sufficient supplies of labour were available when required, what would you need to know from the production department? (NB you would have to ensure that employees were 'suitable'.)*

Faced with the above problem I would need to know *when* the labour was required, *how many* and with *what skills, where* they would have to work (which site), *what was involved* with the job, etc. (How could I interview for a job unless I know what it entails?)

2. Manpower audit

It was mentioned earlier that we do not always have to hire more people; staff mobility may help to solve a manpower problem. Our first task would be to analyse existing manpower resources within the organisation using both quantitative and qualitative measures (for quantitative and qualitative measures of finance as a resource see Chapter 11). The quantitative information which would be used in a manpower audit includes details such as:

a) ages of employees in particular departments, plus length of service;
b) specific details about individual employees, such as
    amount of time absent from work
    number of accidents and days lost as a result
    amount of training received;
c) labour turnover;
d) days lost through industrial action.

- *What is meant by 'labour turnover'?*

The qualitative information used in an analysis of manpower resources includes items such as:

a) level of skill attained by employees
b) potential shown at task undertaken and suitability for promotion
c) satisfaction shown with payments system
d) degree of satisfaction with administrative organisation and organisational culture.

After the analysis of manpower undertaken by the organisation we may find that hiring more resources is not necessary. We may be able to make better use of existing labour – we may even improve job satisfaction in the process.

The Trader Group of Newspapers consists of 10 titles distributing over 820,000 copies per week. Due to expansion, we are looking for two, top flight Sales Professionals to lead and develop our Classified Departments.

GROUP CLASSIFIED MANAGER
Responsibilities including organising, motivating and recruiting what will rapidly become the best Classified Department in the Midlands.

GROUP SALES TRAINER
Responsibilities including day to day training and motivation of staff.

Salaries for both positions are negotiable commensurate to experience and include a company car and usual large company benefits.

If you think you can fill either of the above important positions and relish the challenge of working for Britain's premier independent free newspaper then send full c.v. to:—

Doug Price,
National Sales Manager,
Trader Group of Newspapers,
Key Accounts Unit,
Abbot's Hill Chambers,
Gower Street,
DERBY DE1 1SD

Business Traveller

ADVERTISEMENT SALES EXECUTIVE

We require a Sales Executive capable of selling to both agencies and clients.
Previous experience in international travel, luxury goods and duty free products would be an advantage but is not essential.
Salary £12,000 plus Commission.
Apply in writing with CV to:

David Hammond
Advertisement Director
Perry Publications Limited
49 Old Bond Street
London W1X 3AF
Tel: 01-629 4688

SENIOR FREELANCE FINISHED ARTIST

We urgently require an experienced **Heavyweight** finished artist to supervise artworking on a new merchandising project. You would be expected to produce fast accurate high quality paste-ups, type mark-ups and lettering and, control and co-ordinate the workflow of other artworkers on the project. Would suit someone with an interest in science fiction or comics. Terms negotiable.

Please ring Leigh Baulch on 01-836 9807
Titan Books, 58 St Giles High St., London WC2H 8LH

Fig. 12.1 Some of the ways in which an employer can contact prospective employees

3. External labour supplies

If the organisation needs to hire more labour, the problems confronting those responsible are:

a) are there adequate supplies of labour?
b) do those available have the right skills?
c) are those available, with the right skills, living within commuting distance of our organisation?

Whether or not the type of labour, in sufficient numbers, is available is determined by factors such as:

a) occupational mobility of labour,
b) activities of those responsible for transmitting job information, such as Job Centres,
c) activities of training bodies, training establishments, and bodies such as the Manpower Services Commission,
d) level of unemployment,
e) accessibility of the organisation/local housing facilities.

- *What is meant by (a) occupational mobility of labour and (b) geographical mobility of labour?*
- *What are the objectives of the Manpower Services Commission?*

4. Reconcile demand for and supply of labour

When it has decided what resources are required from the external labour market the final task of the organisation is to reconcile the demand for labour services with what is on offer (supply). Manpower planning is thus concerned with forecasting the demand for labour, analysing available internal sources of labour services, and analysing the external supplies of labour. Alongside this the manpower plan initiates work on:

1. Retraining and staff development as part of the process of increasing the mobility of existing resources.
2. Management development, as an extension of the retraining requirements brought about by changes in the demand for specific labour services.
3. Revision to payments schemes and productivity plans.
4. Redundancies.

Whenever there is a change in production, or in the marketing of the organisation's products, technology, or economic conditions, those responsible for the manpower plan must go into action. Any of the factors mentioned above are likely to bring about changes (increases or decreases) in the demand for labour.

- *How will the technological revolution affect manpower plans?*

Performance appraisal

During the manpower audit the organisation attempts to analyse the human resources it employs using qualitative and quantitative data. One of the processes which people-orientated, far-sighted organisations are conducting, on a periodic (individual) basis, is that of performance appraisal; this is a systematic evaluation of an employee's performance at work and his potential for further development.

It is with the manpower audit in mind that we can appreciate two benefits which result from performance appraisal; such schemes provide the organisation with a database of skills and potential held by employees, *and* they also provide a *mechanism* for assessment of performance. As far as the individual is concerned, performance appraisal will provide him with feedback on his performance and on what are perceived to be his strengths and weaknesses as well as helping him to plan personal and job objectives and also ways of achieving them. There are also benefits to be gained from the point of view of motivation; giving feedback on performance and setting targets are in themselves motivators.

Performance appraisals are normally conducted via an interview with an immediate superior and very often an employee rating form is completed; there is considerable diversity in the content and format of such forms since most are created by individual organisations to suit their own needs (see Figs. 12.2, 12.3 and 12.4, opposite and on page 128).

- *Construct a rating form to be used by students in their appraisal of (a) staff and (b) their own performance as students.*

Since performance appraisal tends to rely heavily on interviews with employees it is not always possible to give them feedback which is useful, or to help them plan objectives, because an interview may not yield the information which would enable you to do this. For example, it would be expecting a great deal of employees for them to admit to deficiencies since they may feel that to do so may adversely affect their chances of promotion. Without the type of information employees may be reluctant to give, one of the benefits (to employees) of appraisal will be lost.

If employees are open and admit to deficiencies

Employee name			Job title		
Department					
Appraised by			Date		

Factor	Outstanding performance	Very satisfactory	Satisfactory	Developing performance	Not satisfactory
Knowledge of job					
Standard of work produced					
Administrative ability					
Personal organisation					
Communication skills					
Motivation					
Appearance					
Adaptability					

Fig. 12.2

Employee name			
Job title		Appraised by	
Department		Date	

Factor	Acceptable	Barely acceptable	Unacceptable
Presentability			
Behaviour to colleagues			
Behaviour to customers			
Motivation			
Time-keeping			

Fig. 12.3

	Outstanding	Good	Satisfactory	Fair	Poor	Not observed
Job knowledge						
Quality of work						
Relationships with subordinates						
Initiative						
Appearance						
Potential						
Leadership qualities						

Name ....   Department ....

Position ....

Appraiser ....   Date ....

Fig. 12.4

the exercise does not seem to yield much in the way of positive response. When made aware of deficiencies (by management) people tend to act very defensively rather than using their resources to improve their performance.

- *What do you think is the best way to let someone you work with know of a skill deficiency which you perceive them to have? Would your method be different if you had to tell someone that you socialise with? If the methods vary, why do you think that is so?*

One final problem with appraisal interviews is the interview itself. When we hear things about ourselves that we do not like, and when we are made aware of our shortcomings, we tend to be suspicious of the interviewer rather than keen to improve our ways. This is particularly so if we have had disagreements in the past with the interviewer; the fear is that personal issues will affect the interviewer's perception. Nevertheless, performance· appraisal can confer benefits on employees if they let it. It is for this reason that the issue is considered.

The appraisal interview tends to be linked to other personnel practices such as career structure and promotion, which are mentioned in the following section along with other personnel policies. Although performance appraisal can never

be regarded as a precise measuring technique (since there is no mathematical precision), it clearly has a valuable place in staff development programmes.

- *Construct a career plan for yourself which shows what you would like to be doing, and when, in the development of your career.*

Personnel policies

Since policies translate objectives into general statements which guide an organisation about its business, they are concerned with how the organisation deals with issues. In the context of this chapter we are concerned with how the organisation deals with *labour* issues.

The attitudes and philosophy of management with regard to personnel will be indicated in personnel policy and we must bear in mind that such policies are vitally important in building favourable attitudes among the workforce. Personnel policies are the means by which the organisation can establish guidelines for the interaction of the various components at work. Although these policies deal with relationships between management and workers, such relationships are generally much wider than is sometimes indicated if we simply view personnel policies in isolation. The relationships between workers and managers (who are in fact only another form of worker) are influenced by each other's perception of the other, by their perception of events, communication between the parties, contact between the parties, and so on.

The Personnel Department of an organisation is concerned with the human aspects of work; duties range from the physical and social welfare of employees, through to recruitment, devising incentive schemes, negotiating, dealing with discipline, and advising on employment legislation. In some organisations the Personnel Department no longer covers such a wide range of duties – a number of the above functions being delegated to other, specialised, departments. However, it is normally Personnel which is responsible for negotiations in most organisations, and in general the negotiations will concern industrial relations issues.

- *Contact four local organisations and try to establish the main areas of concern of their Personnel Departments. Compare your notes with others in your group and draw up a chart showing the six most common duties of local personnel departments.*

Personnel departments

Industrial Relations concerns the relationship between management and the workers (via their representatives, normally trade union members) and will encompass issues such as:

> employee participation (both in ownership and management)
> grievances
> discipline
> consultation and negotiation between managers and workers' representatives

As it steers an organisation to success, management needs personnel policies which it can follow concerning issues such as:

1. Recruitment and selection.
2. Training and development.
3. Pay and productivity.
4. Promotion and career planning.
5. Retirement, redundancy, and dismissal.

Recruitment and selection

Policies concerning these issues will include statements about how we ensure that needs are catered for by adding to our workforce, and the number of appointments to be made from outside the organisation. Organisations have to develop policies covering issues such as whether to recruit trained and experienced people from outside or whether to recruit someone with the capacity to learn and train him/her themselves.

- *What would you say are the benefits of hiring capable, though perhaps unskilled, employees, with the objective that the company trains them itself?*

The way(s) in which we recruit, that is, where we advertise our vacancies and whether or not we use recruitment consultants, are again issues which the organisation should have a policy for. As far as selection is concerned, we may need to establish common criteria throughout the organisation for the selection of similarly placed employees; our selection procedures may need an overhaul; and it will have to be decided who will do the interviewing and selection.

Training and development

Training and development policy of the organisation is probably a reflection of the way in which management views its 'resources'. That is, if management values its labour force and believes its workers have pride in their work and a desire to work well, it will probably reflect this view in its policy towards staff training – by devoting resources to training and making provision for attendance at courses. Organisations consist of many individuals, all with a role to perform. Training will often need to be provided, therefore, so that employees can adequately fulfil role expectations. Training policies will also contain guidance as to whether or not such training should be in-house or whether specialised (outside) courses are to be used.

- *What is meant by 'in-house' training programmes?*

Induction programmes should also be included in personnel policies, as well as retraining.

Pay and productivity

Writers concerned with motivation theory have tended to play down the importance of money as a motivator, while at the same time recognising that poor pay will act to demotivate employees.

- *What motivates you to work on assignments when the sun is shining and you could be otherwise engaged?*
- *Would you work for an organisation if the work was stimulating, you met interesting people, and you learned a great deal but the pay was very poor? If your answer is 'yes', can you say why?*

What organisations must do is ensure that their payments system is such that it attracts and keeps the calibre of employees most in demand. Policy should therefore be concerned with issues such as:

a) differential payments to specific groups,
b) linking of rewards to productivity increases,
c) the attitude towards regular overtime,
d) acceptable methods in dealing with pay negotiations,
e) attitudes to productivity throughout the entire organisation.

Promotion and career planning

There should be a policy towards internal promotion and the development of existing staff – remember, personnel policies reveal the attitudes and philosophies of management towards employees. Such policy can therefore be a potent motivator. It has often been suggested that the movement of personnel to various departments, with different responsibilities, is a contributor to the motivation of those members of staff. To this effect, organisations need to operate personnel policy in order to ensure that internal procedures facilitate such movement. This not only adds a new dimension to the experiences of the employee but will also improve and increase skills and awareness and, thereby, promotion potential.

The organisation should develop policies which give guidance and direction in career planning, with the prospect that the career development that is sought by employees can, potentially, be fulfilled.

- *What drawbacks can you imagine there may be to planning your career development over the next ten years?*

Retirement, redundancy, and dismissal
(see pages 107–108 on termination of employment)

The final issues concern leaving the organisation, and in all cases an organisation must devise adequate policies for dealing with the situations that may arise.

The official age for retirement in the UK is established by law but many organisations operate policies which allow certain employees to retire early without this adversely affecting their pension rights. It is often in the interest of the organisation to do this as well as being of benefit to the employee.

- *Name four things you would have to consider if you were given the opportunity to retire early.*
- *What are the advantages to an organisation of permitting employees to retire early, given that the organisation will have to meet the financial consequences of this?*

Policy in connection with redundancy and dismissal will follow legal requirements to a large extent, though individual organisations will establish systems which will deal with issues such as:

a) procedures for dealing with absenteeism,
b) appeals against disciplinary action,
c) procedures to be followed in the case of dismissal,
d) explaining benefits and entitlements due on redundancy,
e) amending individual records and safe storage of such data.

In order to deal with this aspect of redundancy and dismissal in more detail we will conclude this chapter by considering Employment Law and the implications of legislation in this area.

Employment law

In Chapter 10 (p. 107) I mentioned that the area of employment-related law was the subject of frequent change. To give an idea of just how much change has taken place in this field consider Table 12.1. Fortunately, BTEC courses are as much concerned with skills as with knowledge and, to that end, we emphasise the importance of being able to find relevant pieces of information, analyse them, draw out the implications and, perhaps, present your findings or produce a report. Thus, you ought not to be expected to 'learn' the contents of Table 12.1 or memorise chunks of specific Acts. There are some sections of particular Acts which will have much relevance to you as young employees or prospective employees and for this reason it will be useful to consider some of these areas in a little more detail at this stage (see also page 107 ff 'Termination of Employment').

Table 12.1 Employment-related law since the late 1950s

1958	Disabled Persons (Employment) Act
1963	Contracts of Employment Act
1963	Office, Shops and Railways Premises Act
1964–73	Industrial Training Acts
1965	Shops Act
1965 and 1969	Redundancy Payments Act
1965, 1973 and 1975	Social Security Acts
1965, 1968 and 1976	Race Relations Act
1967, 1968	Prices and Incomes Acts
1969	Employers' Liability (Defective Equipment) Act
1969	Employers' Liability (Compulsory Insurance) Act
1970	Equal Pay Act
1971	Industrial Relations Act
1972	Contracts of Employment Act
1973	Employment of Children Act
1973	Employment and Training Act
1972	Employment Medical Advisory Act
1974 and 1976	Trade Union and Labour Relations Act
1974	Health and Safety at Work Act
1975	Sex Discrimination Act
1975	Industry Act
1975	Employment Protection Act
1975	Pay Restraint (Social Contract) Phase I
1976	Pay Restraint (Social Contract) Phase II
1977	Employment Protection Act, Codes of Practice – Disciplinary Procedures
1977	Pay Restraint (Social Contract) Phase III
1978	Employment Protection Act Codes of Practice – Time-off for Trade Union activities
1978	Employment Protection Act
1979	Wages Council Act
1980	Companies Act
1980	Employment Act
1980	Industry Act
1982	Employment Act

(This list may now be out of date. Perhaps you could update it?)

Table 12.1 does not include the many statutory instruments which have been enacted to ensure the law is operative. Even so, you can see that there is a wealth of knowledge and legislation in just this one area.

- *What is a 'statutory instrument'?*

Let me emphasise at the outset that, although the law is there to protect employees and regulate relationships between them and employers, going to court is the *final* resort when we are attempting to resolve a conflict. Very often disagreements can be resolved amicably in discussions between the manager and the worker concerned (or their representatives in more formal situations). This is an interesting point, and one which many people overlook when studying law for the first time. As soon as we discover what rights we have under contract law, employment law, or torts we may automatically think that the solution to any problem concerning these issues is to go to court – a big mistake (except from the point of view of solicitors and barristers!), since this will involve you in costs and inconvenience. The time taken for a hearing may mean that by the time the issue comes to court you and the other party may already be on better terms and a court appearance will do more harm than good to your relationship. Also, going to court *may* not leave you with the outcome you would prefer. Even the Small Claims Court, where hearings are informal and you do not need a solicitor to represent you, can involve you in a non-compensatable cost, i.e. the use of your time. To take an action in this court will involve you in preparation and in a court appearance – you will thus be using time that you might have put to better use (*opportunity cost*, see pages 79–80).

- *What type of cases are heard in the Small Claims Court, and where is your nearest Small Claims Court?*

In the real world we do not run along to a court every five minutes in order to resolve a conflict. We try to establish communication links with the other party and iron out differences.

The resolution of differences between management and workers over working conditions, treatment at work, or any other work-related problem will sometimes be impossible. When this happens the two parties can use the services of the Advisory, Conciliation and Arbitration Service (see page 27) and, ultimately, an Industrial Tribunal.

- *What is an Industrial Tribunal? What powers do*

such tribunals have and who presides over cases brought before them?

One of the most important pieces of legislation is the Employment Protection (Consolidation) Act 1978, which is divided into a number of significant parts:

1. Entitlement to a written statement of terms of employment and itemised pay statements.
2. Rights arising from suspension of work on medical grounds.
3. Trade union activities and time off for trade union and public duties.
4. Maternity rights.
5. Rights to a minimum period of notice.
6. Unfair dismissal.
7. Redundancy payments.
8. Insolvency of employers.

- *Below are a number of situations which may occur, the result of which would render dismissal 'fair'. Make brief notes explaining each.*
  1. Misconduct.
  2. Incapability.
  3. Redundancy.

(The task on page 107 asked you to identify situations when a dismissal could be said to be *unfair*; any reason falling outside of those given as 'fair' may be unfair, though there are also a number of others.)

Let us consider just one of the Parts of the 1978 Act in a little more detail for a fuller understanding of this important area of law.

Employers must give employees a written statement within thirteen weeks of their joining the organisation, which must show certain details:

1. The amount of pay or the method of calculating it.
2. When payment is to be made.
3. Terms and conditions concerning hours of work.
4. Terms and conditions relating to:
   holidays
   pensions
   sickness or injury and provisions for sick pay.
5. Grievance procedure.
6. Date on which contract is to end if the employment contract is for a fixed term.
7. Job title.
8. Period of notice to be given either by the employee when he wishes to leave, or by the employer when he wishes to terminate the contract of employment.

Employees are also entitled to receive either a copy of any disciplinary rules which may apply to them or information about where to inspect such a copy.

- *What rights do pregnant women have with regard to employment and the provisions contained within the Employment Protection (Consolidation) Act 1978 and the Employment Act 1980?*

The Employment Act 1982 contains a number of important provisions as far as trade union and non-trade union members of organisations are concerned, and in Chapter 10 your attention was drawn to the more important items. As with any contract, both parties have to give something (consideration), and so you will not be surprised to find that in terms of the employment contract both sides have particular duties implied in that contract.

- *What is the difference between an **implied** and an **express** term within a contract?*

Employers' implied duties

There are certain duties employers have, even if these are not specifically mentioned in the contract of employment. They include the duty to

pay for work
provide work
provide a safe place of work
indemnify

Duty to pay for work. The first duty of an employer is to pay for employee services and, until the Payment of Wages Act 1960, this payment had to be made in coin of the realm (Truck Acts 1831–1940). Part of the reasoning behind the Truck Acts was that workmen should be protected against payment in kind and that they should be protected from interference with their freedom to dispose of wages as they thought fit. This was a problem in the days of the company store, when an employer paid in tokens, which could only be exchanged for provisions (at sometimes inflated prices) in company shops.

It is the case nowadays that if the employee agrees, payment can be made directly into a bank account.

- *Why would an employer want to take on the administrative problems of paying employees directly into their bank account when he could pay cash?*

One interesting point about the payment of wages and the risks of such wages being mis-spent is the clause of an 1883 Act which said that a workman's wages could not be paid to him in a public house (pub) – unless the workman worked in the public house!

Duty to provide work. Provided an employer pays his employees, it is generally not his *duty* to provide work, though there are exceptions.

- *Consider the cases of* Herbert Clayton & Jack Waller Ltd *v.* Oliver, *and* Devonald *v.* Rosser & Sons *and say what was interesting about the judgement in each case.*

While in the case of Langston *v* Chrysler/AUEW (1974) the court decided that there was no *right* to work 'for any particular employer or in any particular place', Lord Denning mentioned the 'right of a skilled worker to be given work to do in order to enjoy job satisfaction and to maintain his skill and expertise'.

Duty to provide a safe place of work. A major duty of employers, laid down in the the Health and Safety at Work Act 1974, is to ensure the health and safety of employees. The employer has to take reasonable care to prevent risks to health and safety – the breach of the statutory provisions being a criminal offence. Employers must also take out insurance cover to enable claims made by employees arising out of injuries sustained at work (due to employer's breach of duty) to be met.

Another important piece of legislation in this respect is the Occupier's Liability Act 1957, which established a duty 'to take such care as in all the circumstances of the case is reasonable to see that visitors will be reasonably safe in using the premises for which they are invited or permitted to be there' (see also page 104). The Employers' Liability (Defective Equipment) Act 1969 imposes a strict liability (see page 106) on the employer for injuries to employees from unsafe machinery (hidden defects). While the 1957 Act allowed an occupier to escape liability by having clearly written and visible notices, such liability can no longer be excluded or restricted for death or personal injury resulting from negligence (Unfair Contract Terms Act 1977). Other loss can no longer be restricted unless it is 'reasonable' to do so.

There is an onus on employers to select employees carefully and give adequate training and supervision.

- *Read the cases of* Qualcast Lyd *v.* Haynes *(1959), and* Hudson *v.* Ridge Mfg *(1957). What do they tell you about employers' liability?*

Duty to indemnify. An employee is entitled to be indemnified by his employer for loss or expenses incurred in the course of his employment.

- *Consider the case of* Re Famatina Development Corporation *for an illustration of this principle.*

Employees' implied duties

The law implies certain duties of employees and these include:

obedience
competence
faithful service.

Obedience. While it appears that the refusal to obey a trivial request is not serious, it is true to say that the refusal to obey an order does place one's job in jeopardy. Employees must be given an opportunity to explain why they are not complying with instructions, and employees have the right to disobey an order which is illegal.

- *Consider the details in the case of* Pepper *v.* Webb *(1969) and make notes on why the dismissal was said to be fair.*

Competence. Incompetence gives grounds for dismissal. Examples of what has been incorporated in the legislation as incompetence include:

persistent lateness
inefficiency
slowness.

Faithful service. A fundamental obligation of employees is to conduct their employment faithfully; thus integrity and honesty are important.

- *Consider the case of* Sinclair *v.* Neighbour *(1966) and say whether or not you think Sinclair's conduct was incompatible with his employment as the manager of the betting shop.*

An employee's actions are not to be contrary to the interests of his employer. Thus an employee must not:

take bribes
accept gifts
make secret profits
divulge information about the employer's
     business for gain or otherwise.

An employer even has the ability to prohibit any activity which he feels interferes with the employee's ability to perform his duties or endangers his professional position.

Finally, if an employee develops a process or product which is the result of his employment and the employment facilities and/or resources, it is the *employer* who has the right to all the proceeds·of the invention.

There is a great deal in employment legislation and a book such as this can only scratch the surface. Managers do not need to be experts in employment law – they can employ other people who are. What I have attempted to do is show that many areas are covered by legislation and the most important skills for you to develop are those concerned with retrieval of information, appreciation of detail, and the ability to communicate any information that is necessary.

Assignments

Student activity 12.1

This assignment has been designed on the basis that students will work in pairs to complete it. Your task is to produce:

a) a brief explanatory list of what you consider to be the functions of a personnel department (try for approximately a dozen);
b) a short document outlining what is involved (from liaison with managers in drawing up a job description to the checking of references) in the process of recruitment;
c) a list of what should be included in an induction programme.

Student activity 12.2

This is an individual assignment. One of the important functions of a personnel department is that of *Industrial Relations* (IR). Although this is an important area of contact between management and the workers, British industrial relations history leaves a lot to be desired. Many argue, for example, that the whole culture of management/worker relations in this country is archaic and thus outmoded. Whatever the causes of industrial unrest, both sides in a grievance will eventually have to sit around a table and resolve differences.

Prepare a document which illustrates what is included under the heading of 'Industrial Relations' and give three examples of poor industrial relations in Britain that have occurred within the last two years.

Student activity 12.3

This is an individual assignment. The article (right)

discusses the position employees can find themselves in when they have been in receipt of incentive prizes awarded by companies other than their employers. In the case mentioned in the article, the prize-giving organisation was a manufacturer whose products were distributed by another firm, for which the salesman works.

There are many examples of organisations which give their own employees benefits, hoping in the process to attract the best employees – and to keep them.

Let us assume that all benefits are to be taxable. You are to prepare a discussion document listing

---

GIVING up palm-fringed beaches to resume the rat race is a bit of a shock at the best of times, but how much more so if you later get a tax bill for your holiday.

Here's how such a horror story could unfold. Say you are a salesman working for a distributor of products made by another company. The manufacturer runs an annual competition for the distributor's salesmen with the prize of an 'all expenses paid' trip to some sunshine paradise. You win the prize and take your wife.

That happened three years ago and now you choke over breakfast on receiving in the post a tax bill for £1,200, plus interest and penalty charges.

How can this be? Well, employees are taxed under the PAYE system and deductions are made from each salary payment. At the end of a tax year the employer will make a return of benefits provided to employees and this information should be reflected in the employee's tax return. Any underpayment of tax will be separately assessed by the Inland Revenue in the following tax year.

The tax position over the incentive prize is clear – you, as an employee, had a free holiday which you won by reason of your employment. You are, therefore, taxable on the benefit received.

Source: *The Sunday Times*, 30 November 1986

examples of benefits offered by organisations and considering the implications for both employers and employees of the move to tax these benefits as though they were simply a part of the income of employees.

Student activity 12.4

This is a group assignment. It is hoped the issue will be discussed by the whole group (class) with the benefit of, perhaps, having local employers and union officials present as participants. It may be considered sufficiently beneficial to the operation of the assignment (and assessment) for students to be required to organise the meeting and invite the guests mentioned, plus others who may be considered able to enhance such a debate. In *Psychology for Managers*, Gary Cooper and Peter Makin (The British Psychological Society and Macmillan, 1985), the authors suggest that job stress has both (adverse) mental and physical health effects for employees, which are rarely considered in human or financial terms. The problem of stress at work is now thought to be commonplace. The

THE Department of Health and Social Security has been accused by one of the main civil service unions of operating a 'news blackout' by refusing to allow television companies to film inside local benefit offices.

Ministers have rejected a series of recent requests from BBC and ITV programmes for permission to take camera crews into local DHSS offices to film in areas where claimants are interviewed on benefit entitlements.

It is understood that no television crew has been allowed into claimant areas since a BBC *Panorama* film highlighted the stresses in DHSS offices in 1984.

The department says that the refusals are because of the need to protect the privacy of claimants. But the Society of Civil and Public Servants (SCPS) complained yesterday that the television companies were being kept out in order to cover up the 'chaotic conditions' in many DHSS benefit offices.

Source: *The Independent*, 5 December 1986

effects of stress on the employee on the one hand, and the resulting implications for the performance of the organisation on the other, ought to be sufficiently serious to warrant management attempts to reduce it. With this in mind, consider the article (below left) and discuss whether or not the attitude of the employer in this case (DHSS) has contributed to the stress of employees. You may also consider what other factors may lead to stress in employees and discuss what methods are available for relieving or coping with it.

Student activity 12.5

This is a group assignment for small groups of three. Your task is to produce a simple, clear, and imaginative pamphlet which will explain to people of your age what is meant by the various types of management style. You should consider enhancing your pamphlet with examples of organisations where the following management styles are employed or where people who employ such styles are individual managers. Amusing illustrations which will help to make the point are also to be included.

The styles are:

paternalistic management
laissez-faire management
democratic management
authoritarian management.

Skills assessable

	Skill 1	2	3	4	5	6	7	8
Assignment								
1	1.3	2.2	3.4	4.3		6.1		
	1.8	2.4	3.5	4.6		6.2		
	1.9	2.5	3.6			6.3		
2	1.6	2.2		4.6		6.1		
	1.8	2.5				6.2		
	1.9					6.3		
3	1.5	2.2		4.3	5.2	6.1		
	1.6	2.4			5.5	6.2		
	1.8	2.5			5.10	6.3		

4 This task does not lend itself to assessment unless the group are required to organise the meeting and invite outside speakers. Assessment will then be concentrated on general organisational skills.

5	1.6	2.2	3.4	4.3		6.1		
	1.8	2.4	3.5	4.6		6.2		
	1.9		3.6			6.3		
	1.10		3.7					
			3.9					
			3.11					

13
MARKETS AND DEMAND

The ultimate objective of all organisations is to satisfy customer demand. Whatever we may say about organisations tending to be profit maximisers, sales maximisers, or profit satisfiers (for organisations' objectives see page 9 ff) falls by the wayside if there is no customer demand for the product or service in question. In this process of satisfying customer demand organisations will make extensive use of *markets*. This chapter will therefore consider what markets *are*. There will also be a consideration of the notion of a marketing 'mix'.

Market types

A 'market' is an arrangement for bringing buyers and sellers into contact with one another to establish a price for a product. Let us consider this statement: *a market is an arrangement* – implies that markets do *not* have to be in a defined place or building; *bringing buyers and sellers into contact* – implies that the parties do *not* necessarily have to meet. To be in contact does not mean one party can actually see the other; *to establish a price* – implies that one party (sellers or buyers) *cannot* establish the price in isolation. The price is determined by the interplay of the actions of both sides in the deal.

A market is therefore an arrangement whereby the buyer and the seller get to know about one another, and the offers they are each making; they then agree to buy and sell at a particular price. This is clearly an important point for organisations since without markets their produce could not be sold.

- *Taking examples from the vicinity where you live/work/go to college, list as many instances of markets as you can.*

Everything that is for sale has a market, since there will be someone, somewhere, who is looking for that item and who is prepared to pay for it, just as there is likely to be someone who owns and wishes to sell that particular product.

- *From research into government statistics, find out what the size of the new-car market was in*

England and Wales last year (i.e. how many new cars were sold).

All organisations operate within markets, but there are many types of market. Some examples of the types of market in the economy are shown in Fig. 13.1.

- *What would you say the markets shown in Fig. 13.1 had in common?*
- *Produce a set of notes to be used during a verbal presentation of your explanation of the work of the major wholesale produce markets. For information about where these establishments may be, ask your local fruit and vegetable retailer, butcher, and fishmonger.*
- *Produce a brief, informal report on the workings of two of the commodity markets in this country.*

It is suggested that for any market to operate effectively a number of conditions must be fulfilled, these conditions are as follows:

1. Good communications, transport and other services (e.g. warehousing).
2. Inexcessive transport costs.
3. Standardised products.
4. Private property in goods. Having private property rights in goods implies that you have the right of disposal and transfer of ownership as you think fit. Having private property rights means you own, and can use or decide who is to use, and you can prevent other people from using or taking away. Without this right there would be little incentive in ownership since people could just help themselves to the property without having to pay.
5. Freedom to contract – backed up by a legal system that will enforce contract dealings, thus giving buyers and sellers security, without which such dealings would not take place so freely.
6. Price mechanism – a system by which goods/ services are allocated among competing consumers who demand the same. Based on the principle that those prepared to spend money can own private property rights in goods/ services. See section later in this chapter on establishment of a price via supply and demand.
7. Facilities for disseminating market information speedily and accurately.

- *Briefly explain why the seven items previously listed are said to be conditions of an effective market system. (Think in terms of what a market would be like without any of these conditions.)*

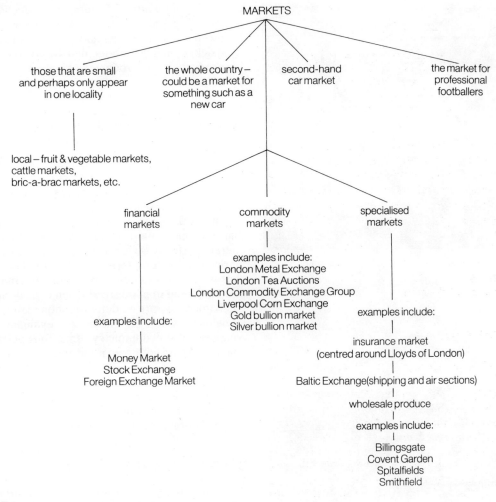

MARKETS

those that are small and perhaps only appear in one locality

the whole country – could be a market for something such as a new car

second-hand car market

the market for professional footballers

local – fruit & vegetable markets, cattle markets, bric-a-brac markets, etc.

financial markets

commodity markets

specialised markets

examples include:
London Metal Exchange
London Tea Auctions
London Commodity Exchange Group
Liverpool Corn Exchange
Gold bullion market
Silver bullion market

examples include:

examples include:

Money Market
Stock Exchange
Foreign Exchange Market

insurance market
(centred around Lloyds of London)

Baltic Exchange (shipping and air sections)

wholesale produce

examples include:

Billingsgate
Covent Garden
Spitalfields
Smithfield

Fig. 13.1

- *In what way(s) does the London Stock Exchange ensure speedy and accurate transmission of information?*

Markets are often analysed in terms of the degree of competition which exists within them and to this end economists use the concepts of *perfect* and *imperfect competition*. For perfect competition to exist a number of assumptions must be fulfilled and if we go through these briefly now we will then be able to make some sense of imperfect competition, and why things happen the way they do in the real world.

Perfect competition

For perfect competition to exist there must be:

a) *Large numbers of buyers and sellers*: this ensures that the price charged is determined by the pressure of so-called market forces (supply and demand interacting) and not by one or other of the two parties.

b) *Product homogeneity*: if products were homogeneous there would be no real or imagined differences between the outputs of different producers, that is, all products in a particular range would be identical. The implication of this is that there would therefore be no reason why you should buy from firm A rather than firm B, unless prices differed.

c) *Freedom of entry into the market for buyers and sellers*: if we wish prices to be established simply by the pressures of supply and demand, we must conceive of a situation where buyers or sellers

Fig. 13.2 Markets can take a variety of forms. Here are two extreme examples. One is a street market – similar to those you are familiar with – and the other is the London International Financial Futures Exchange

are not prevented from competing in the market.

d) *Responsive market*: no imperfections exist that would hinder an immediate response to price changes.

e) *Buyers and sellers have full knowledge of conditions within the market*: if this were not the case then we may argue that price differences merely reflected imperfect knowledge.

f) *Perfect mobility of buyers*: this ensures that people are able to travel to a bargain, rather than being forced through circumstances or cost to remain close to home and pay higher prices than those being charged elsewhere.

g) *Perfect mobility of factors of production* (see pages 90 and 91); this condition exists so that more of what is demanded can be produced quickly, that is, labour can be moved to the production of products which are in heavy demand.

(*Bear in mind that I am not saying that this is what happens in the real world. This is not what markets are really like, but merely an indication of what they would be like in ideal, perfect conditions.*)

We thus have a number of conditions which have to exist to give us the condition of perfect competition. What many people ask at this stage is, if perfect competition does not exist, why spend time considering it? In answer to this question we could say that an appreciation of what allows a market to operate perfectly is worth considering since perfect markets are considered to be of benefit to consumers. Knowledge of perfect competition will also stand you in good stead when considering the mechanics of price determination later; such knowledge will also enable an evaluation and comparison of economic systems, thus permitting you to make up your own mind about the efficiency of such systems.

If we consider markets in general we can see why they may be regarded as being imperfect. The condition relating to perfect competition will appear in brackets after each example.

Imperfect competition

Very often buyers or sellers are not aware of the offers being made by others because of the size and complexity of a market (*buyers and sellers must have full knowledge*). There are some ways of improving information, such as reading magazines like *Exchange & Mart* or the used car magazines, but these do not *eliminate* lack of information. A buyer may, for instance, pay appreciably more than the current market price for a second-hand car because it can be difficult to know what the market price is without closely following current transactions; not everyone will know of the magazine guides that are available which quote average prices; such prices may not, in fact, be available in certain areas, anyway. Even people who work in the motor trade need a guide (updated regularly) to average prices. The so-called *Glass's Guide* is, however, highly confidential and anyone not in the trade would find it very difficult to get hold of a copy.

• *Talk to a local motor trader and see if he will let*

you browse through his copy of Glass's Guide. *You may be in for a shock!*

- *What methods are there for improving information about vacancies in the job market?*

Ignorance of appropriate information regarding prevailing prices also restricts the mobility of buyers (*perfect mobility of buyers*).

One of the conditions for perfect competition may be impossible to attain because of restrictions imposed by government or other groups (*freedom of entry into the market for buyers and sellers* and *perfect mobility of factors of production*). We cannot simply set ourselves up as doctors and sell medical services – there are obvious restrictions on that. In the same way, we cannot sell a number of other services or work at particular trades unless we belong to a particular association, trade union, or professional organisation, membership usually being determined by academic qualifications and payment of a fee.

- *What occupations can you think of which require membership of an association before one can begin 'trading'? How does one become a member?*

Freedom of entry is also rarely possible for prospective producers in industries with very high capital costs.

Organisations take a great deal of time and trouble over differentiating their product from that of competitors, via product brands or logos, or other identifying trade marks (*product homogeneity*).

- *Consider examples of recent advertising campaigns which effectively tell you that the product of one organisation is better than that of its competitors. Make brief notes on the main differences between the competing products under discussion.*

In reality there are often situations where perfect competition would be thwarted because there are *monopolists* and *monopsonists* (*large numbers of buyers and sellers*).

- *What is meant by (a) a monopolist and (b) a monopsonist?*

Since markets are arrangements via which buyers and sellers can agree on prices and other conditions of sale, let us now consider how organisations and individuals are thought to interplay to set such prices. To do this we must first consider what *demand* and *supply* are in detail.

Demand

Demand is the number of items a person (an organisation) would be prepared to buy, at a given price, at a given period of time. You will notice that variables which you may have thought would influence demand, such as taste/fashion/income, etc., are held constant by considering the situation in a 'given period of time'. This is a technique employed simply because we are only able to consider the movement of one variable (price) when estimating what the level of demand is likely to be. If we attempted to take all possible variables into account we would not get far since the formula and method would be much too complex. The method most commonly adopted to consider the relationship between prices and quantities of a product consumed is a diagrammatic one. We will measure prices on the vertical axis and quantities on the horizontal (Fig. 13.3).

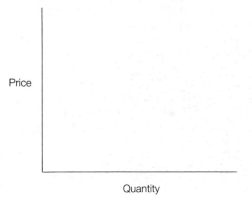

Fig. 13.3

- *What does an economist understand by the term 'consumption'?*
- *Consult friends and ask each to let you know how*

Table 13.1

Price (pence)	Quantity
40	
30	
20	
10	
5	
1	

Fill in the gaps under 'quantity'

many Mars bars they would consume per day at various prices. Armed with this data construct a demand schedule as in Table 13.1:

Demand diagrams are constructed from the data contained within demand schedules. What you have done in Table 13.1 is to collect demand data from a number of individuals. If we assume that all of the individuals you spoke to actually comprise the *total* market for the confectionery, then summing up all of the quantities that people showed a preference for at various prices would yield the 'market' demand (at various prices).

Market demand thus comes from the individual demands of consumer. For example, consider the demand for records. I accept that you all have particular favourites and would probably buy these records at prices which exceeded that of other groups/individual singers. I also accept that there are some fans who feel so strongly about their particular favourites that they would never buy other groups' material. However, there are also many people who, if prices of records were greatly reduced, would purchase more records than they do today. They would still have their favourites, and they could now buy all of their material, but they would also be able to sample the work of other groups. Let us assume, then, that the overall market demand for records is the sum of the individual demands of the only members of the record-buying public, who happen to number three: Mark, Helen, and Roxanne. The demand schedule is shown in Table 13.2.

Table 13.2

Price of single LPs (£s)	Number of LPs purchased per month by:			Market demand
	Mark	Helen	Roxanne	
9.00	2	2	0	4
8.00	3	2	0	5
7.00	3	3	1	7
6.00	4	3	2	9
5.00	5	4	2	11
4.00	7	4	3	14
3.00	8	5	3	16

- *Make sure you understand how the figures in the 'Market demand' column were calculated. If you are not sure, ask someone who is.*

A number of points to note about the schedule in Table 13.2 are:

a) As prices decrease people do sometimes spend more in total. Note for example, that when the records were £9 each Mark would spend £18 per month, but when they were £8 each he would spend £24. What would set a limit to the amount spent would be income, not necessarily logic.
b) As prices decrease people will generally buy more.
c) Each person exhibits a different preference in purchasing records, just as each will probably have different levels of income.

A diagrammatic representation of the market data shown above would give us a typical demand curve, as shown in Fig. 13.4. Demand curves are normally inverse, that is, as price *decreases* the quantity demanded *increases*.

- *What is meant by the term 'regressive demand'?*
- *Explain what 'goods of ostentation' and 'Giffen' goods are.*

Supply

Supply is the quantity of a product which entrepreneurs (and organisations) are prepared to make available at a given price, over a given period of time. You will notice that the conditions of time and price remain as they were with demand, for the same reasons. The quantity of goods being supplied to a market depends not only on the price which can be charged but also on such factors as:

a) *the state of technology* – the more advanced technology is, the greater the capacity to supply a larger quantity of goods;
b) *natural influences* – such as adverse weather conditions, which may affect the product itself (e.g. agricultural produce) or the distribution network (roads could become impassable, for example);

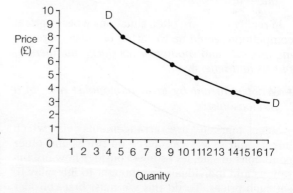

Fig. 13.4

c) *costs of production* – the cheaper it is to produce, the more likelihood there is that a profit will be made, and the greater the chances are for increased supply.

When we consider demand we tend to do so as consumers, since that is what we *all* are; when considering supply I would suggest you think of yourselves as entrepreneurs. As an entrepreneur you will be looking for the opportunity to make a profit and you ought to bear in mind that *price* is what you will *charge*, not what you have to *pay*. The higher the price, the greater the likelihood that you will not only cover your costs but also make a profit.

• *From what has just been said, what do you think will happen to supply when the price (which entrepreneurs can charge) is increased?*

As prices rise (as you charge more) the prospects of making a profit increase and it is thus more than likely that as the price rises, so does supply. This is a very simplistic way of looking at things; we all recognise that some commodities, such as agricultural produce, cannot be automatically supplied if prices should rise – it takes time to grow more crops. But, on the whole, as the price of a product rises this tempts more people to supply it.

Supply can also be represented diagrammatically, with the same axis as for demand curves (see Fig. 13.3). Such charts will normally show the supply curve as in Fig. 13.5. The indication is that as prices rise, quantity supplied also rises.

• *You should satisfy yourselves that you understand why supply also increases when the price increases.*

We saw that the market demand was the sum of individual demands for the product; in the same way the market supply curve is derived from the sum of the supply schedules of all of the producers

who are willing to supply products in a market at given prices, over a given period of time.

• *What is a 'regressive' supply curve? Suggest a situation in which a regressive supply curve could exist.*

If we assume, for simplicity, that there are only two producers of a particular product, then the market supply will come from both of these producers and the curve will be given by the sum of the output of each supplier (see Table 13.3 and Fig. 13.6).

Table 13.3

Price per unit (£)	Number of units produced by month by:		Market supply
	Firm X	Firm Y	
3.00	1	1	2
4.00	2	3	5
5.00	3	5	8
6.00	5	6	11
7.00	6	7	13
8.00	7	8	15
9.00	7	9	16

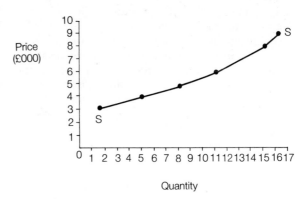

Fig. 13.6

Price determination

In perfectly competitive markets the price of a product is determined by the forces of supply and demand, and the best way to demonstrate this is by a diagram, since you are now aware of what a demand and supply curve generally look like.

• *Construct the demand and supply curves from the following schedules on graph paper.*

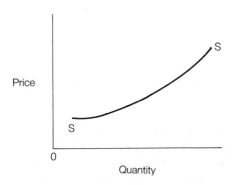

Fig. 13.5

Price (£)	Quantity demanded	Quantity supplied
3	160	20
4	140	50
5	110	80
6	90	110
7	70	130
8	50	150
9	40	160

Wherever the supply and demand curves meet, this indicates the point where the quantity supplied is equal to the quantity demanded. By reading across to the vertical axis, the price which is charged when this happens is said to be the market price or *equilibrium price*.

- *Can you see what the outcome would be if producers tried to impose a minimum charge of £7 in the above example?*
- *What would happen if, say, the Government imposed a maximum ceiling price of £3.50?*

In theory then, the establishment of a price as a result of the pressures of supply and demand appears to be a cost-free process requiring no form of agency to administer it. It would thus seem to be an appropriate and effective means of price determination. However, as we have seen during the discussion of imperfect competition, the real world does not operate on the basis of a perfect price mechanism governed only by supply and demand. Products are not homogeneous and organisations spend a lot of time and money emphasising the distinction between their goods and those of competitors. The activities of developing an image for an organisation and its product ranges, and of creating a distinction between the products of your organisation and those of competitors, are part of the task of *marketing*.

Before going on to the next section you are advised to read the first five pages of Chapter 6.

Marketing

The Marketing Department of an organisation, as we saw in Chapter 6, is concerned with developing a marketing plan which specifies:

    what has to be done
    when it is to be done
    who does what
    how it will be done

    what targets are to be achieved
    the expenditure budgets for each activity.

The marketing function, again as we saw in Chapter 6, should be concerned with:

1. Obtaining information relating to customer demand.
2. Disseminating this information to other departments as part of the overall communications mix.
3. Promoting the goods/services.
4. After-sales service.
5. Market research, decision-making, and defining information requirements.
6. Ensuring that Production, Personnel, Finance, etc., are aware of what is expected.
7. Branding, advertising, exhibitions, etc.
8. Maintenance of company market image.

The crucial aspect of marketing which I will tackle in this chapter is that of the *marketing mix*. The marketing mix is commonly referred to as the 'four Ps': **product; price; promotion; place**. Marketing is concerned with obtaining information in order to *find* customers; it is concerned with *enticing* those customers into purchasing the products of its organisation, and it is concerned with *keeping* those customers once they have been 'hooked'. By selectively changing the order of the marketing mix an organisation will hope to achieve the three objects of finding, enticing, and keeping customers. All of the functions in a marketing mix are variable and organisations are concerned that the particular group of variables offered to the market at any particular point in time have the desired effect on sales (in units) or turnover (£s)/profit (£s)/return on investment(%)/market share(%) or growth(%) in these measures.

When there are many variables it is often a problem to know *what* to change and *when* but, when the right mix of variables has been selected, the product will be right, it will be in the right place, at the right price, and it will be promoted in the right way. Let us therefore consider the 'four Ps' in more detail:

Product distribution

The product is whatever is offered for sale, whether it is a tangible commodity or a service and, for those organisations offering a range of products we have the term 'product mix'. The significance of the product itself, the utility it yields customers and, in recent years, the resources devoted to design are all important in terms of selling a product.

- *What is the meaning of 'utility' as far as an economist is concerned?*

Of particular significance to this aspect of the marketing mix is the way we view the product and those aspects that we consider important. We often consider product design, quality, and possibly brand names as important features, for example, but how often do we consider areas such as:

> modifications to products
> new product developments
> after-sales service
> guarantees and warranties
> the range of products on offer?

These are all important items under the general heading of 'product' and the benefits which will accrue as a result of some of these aspects are obvious. As an example, consider the quality of a product and its impact on the organisation and its customers. If we are considering a high-quality product then we would expect it to have a long life expectancy, to be reliable and relatively fault-free and, conceivably, to be a product whose value would appreciate over time. When an organisation considers product *quality* it is important to emphasise that it is not necessarily talking about *high* quality; it is, in fact, probably concerned with maintaining the same level of quality over successive batches of production.

- *Consider a product which you think was designed to have high-quality appeal and another which you feel is of inferior quality. How important would you say the quality aspect is in the marketing of each of these products? If you feel it is not a strong feature, say what is emphasised as a strong selling point for the product concerned.*

Few firms sell only one product, especially with the growth in takeovers and mergers in recent years. It is often to a firm's advantage to produce a range of products for a market. Thus Sony, for example, do not produce one personal cassette player (Walkman) but a range which extends with improvements in capabilities and quality.

One of the problems with product development was highlighted in Chapter 6 (page 62) during the discussion of compact disc players and digital audio tape (DAT). Product development has to be on a par with the market, if the development is too rapid, organisations cannot recover the costs of research and development, and the costs of tooling a production line before products become obsolete.

Some commentators argue that packaging is an important product consideration, as well as an important promotional aspect. The importance of packaging does not lie entirely in the advertising aspect, since it is also significant for protection (as with egg packaging) or for hygiene or safety (as with food or chemical packaging).

- *Consider half a dozen products where you think that the packaging is not only wasteful but also a nuisance. In these cases, why do the manufacturers package in this way?*

Finally, after-sales service was, for a long time, the one aspect of marketing which was ignored in the UK, or at best given insufficient attention, to the detriment of sales. In this respect, note the comment on Alan Sugar and Sir Clive Sinclair on page 62. Many durable products require some service arrangement, the beauty of which is that once a customer has purchased a product from your organisation you also have a service contract to operate, which increases revenue. Changes in consumer legislation, particularly in the area of inferior goods and poor services, has forced many organisations to spend more on service to the customer *after* the sale has been concluded.

Price

The price of a product has many variables:

> costs of production
> quality and performance of the product
> whether the product is new (untried) or well established
> prices of competitors' products
> size of market share aimed for.

We generally expect to pay more for better quality, though there are times when this does not stand us in good stead. A few years ago a friend had a Jaguar XJ6 for sale which he had bought cheaply, since he was in the motor trade. He used the car a great deal and after owning it for a year decided he wanted a change. He offered it for sale at about £500 less than the average price being asked for that model (same year of manufacture). No one telephoned so he decided he had advertised too cheaply and that many would-be customers were suspicious. He waited a few weeks and then advertised again, this time with a price which was about £300 *above* what it should have been. As soon as the newspaper was out people began to telephone and he had sold the car within a day to a customer who thought he had a good deal because he knocked my friend's price down by £200. Little did he know that he could have bought the same car three weeks earlier for £600 less! If people think the price is right, they will buy.

- *When I bought my first pocket calculator, in 1972, it cost the equivalent of about £23 at 1986 prices. It only had four functions ($+, -, \times, \div$) and no memory. In 1986 I could buy a seven-memory, scientific calculator for less than £20. Why do you think that that was the case?*

Promotion

Many promotion methods are listed on page 59. In effect, organisations attempt to convince us (consumers) that our lives would not be complete without their product. They will be concerned with a whole range of activities designed not only to familiarise us with their product range and create an interest on our part but to take that further; they will try to turn our interest into a need and will only be (momentarily) satisfied once we have purchased. The reason I say 'momentarily satisfied' is because organisations cannot stop there, having sold us one item; they all need to encourage us to buy more and more and more.

Earlier I mentioned that packaging was, to many, an important product consideration though it could arguably be a promotional aspect. Packaging may be a significant factor in the battle to get consumers to choose one product rather than another.

- *Look at the packaging used for various brands of shampoo, hair conditioner, and deodorant. What do you think is interesting and significant about the variations in packaging?*

The area of promotion includes, among others, sub-areas such as:

advertising
personal selling
sales promotion
competitions
free gifts
special offers, etc.

- *Select three from the above list and make short notes on each specifying what is involved and the advantages/disadvantages of each.*

Place

This is a wide issue in that organisations are not only concerned with the actual location in which sales are likely to take place (i.e. which shop, which town, etc.) but also with the distribution problems concerned with moving products from the point of manufacture to the point of sale.

In answer to the question of 'Where do we sell?', any organisation will have to complete market research to enable it to decide where it should launch its products. The major problem is one of distribution, but first an organisation must discover whether they ought to sell direct to the final consumer, or through intermediaries.

- *What is the difference between a wholesaler and a retailer?*

There are four channels of distribution:
1. The MANUFACTURER sells direct to the CUSTOMER.
2. The MANUFACTURER sells to a WHOLESALER, who in turn sells to a RETAILER, who then sells to the CONSUMER.
3. The MANUFACTURER sells via a WHOLESALER to the CONSUMER.
4. The MANUFACTURER sells direct to a RETAILER, who in turn sells to the CONSUMER.

- *Differentiate between an industrial market and a consumer market.*

In the first example the customer (note the term 'customer' – probably not a consumer like you and I but an organisation) is usually operative in an industrial market, buying expensive, sometimes large, items. In the second example we have the typical situation for mass produced consumer goods, with wholesalers buying in bulk from manufacturers.

- *What are the functions of a wholesaler?*

In the third example you will note the absence of a retailer; examples of such ventures are mail order and some cash-and-carry outlets.

- *What are the attractions of buying goods from a catalogue rather than shopping in the High Street?*

The fourth example includes retailers who are large enough to purchase direct from manufacturers, that is, they have the resources to be able to survive without the services of a wholesaler.

- *Name three High Street stores who buy direct from the manufacturer.*

One final point concerning these methods of

distribution is that they are channels that involve institutions (manufacturers, wholesalers, and retailers). We cannot leave distribution without recognising that the physical process of moving goods around the country to points of sale involves various activities. Distribution then is about the institutions involved *and* their activities.

- *List as many services as you can think of that involve physical distribution.*

Sometimes, sending goods direct from the point of manufacture to the point of sale is not practicable. For example, distances between the two sites may be too great. In these situations manufacturers and retailers will have to make use of a wholesaler, who will have storage facilities.

- *As far as commercial transport is concerned, what are the advantages and disadvantages of transporting goods by (a) road (b) rail (c) inland waterways, and (d) air?*
- *Assume you have the responsibility of dealing with the dispatch of a very large consignment of silicon chips from Manchester to Watford. Part of your task involves deciding which means of transport to use. What factors would influence your decision?*

Discussion in this chapter has primarily concerned the situation faced by competitive firms in imperfect competition, though there are situations where such organisations attempt to eliminate competition by entering into *voluntary agreements*. Since such agreements reduce competition, and since many countries have agencies designed to encourage competition, we must spend time considering this aspect of market activity.

Voluntary agreements and competition policy

For the purposes of this section I will take voluntary agreements to imply a relationship between suppliers which aims to reduce competition between them. Such agreements tend to be concerned with the price of the product which is for sale, with all participants in the agreement refusing to sell at a price above or below the agreed price. Firms operating in this way are said to be a *cartel*. Cartels can also be involved with limiting output instead of or as well as price agreements.

- *What is meant by the term 'cartel'?*

It is not always the case, however, that firms get together to simply agree on price or output levels. A variation on this theme is the example of what happens when contractors 'bid' for construction work when contracts are open to tender.

- *What type of construction work is generally 'open to tender'?*
- *What is meant by the term 'open to tender'?*

A number of firms would normally compete over the tender offer but, if a voluntary agreement is in force between them, the firms in the market would agree to take turns in offering the 'lowest' price for the job (collusive tendering); such a price would invariably be higher than that which may exist if the firms were in competition so each contractor would benefit from this situation.

- *Who 'loses' as a result of the action of the contractors mentioned above?*

One of the best known cartels is the Organisation of the Petroleum Exporting Countries (OPEC), which was formed in 1960 in order to unify and coordinate policies of its members with respect to the supply of oil.

Voluntary agreements seek to limit competition between suppliers with the objective of creating more for each supplier – at the cost of the consumer. It is for this reason (consumer loss) that we have agencies designed to combat the activities of those undertaking so-called restrictive trade practices. Because such practices are considered to be against the public interest they are generally prohibited unless the parties to the agreement can show that they do not injure the public interest. Organisations have been successful in combating such charges by arguing that their agreement has or would lead to a more efficient service or protects employment from overseas competition (and thus indirectly also offers some protection to the Balance of Payments) or helps or will help to improve production standards.

In some situations producers agree to supply only one dealer in an area provided that that dealer does not stock a competitor's products. Such an arrangement is referred to as 'exclusive dealing' and is common with petrol companies.

- *Review the case of* Esso Petroleum Company Ltd *v.* Harper's Garage Ltd *(1968) and say what the case demonstrates in terms of restrictive practices.*

Since, arguably, the consumer is likely to be the loser whenever an organisation has monopoly power, or several organisations group together to limit competition between them, the state takes it upon itself to regulate such activities. The term 'monopoly' is generally thought to refer to a situation of a single supplier, with the inherent capability of market control. However, the Fair Trading Act 1973 was much more stringent in its definition since it regards control of 25% of the market as potential monopoly; thus a firm which accounted for 25% of market output would be subject to the surveillance of the Monopolies and Mergers Commission (see task on page 100).

Alongside legislation concerned with the size of organisations we also have statutes concerned with the activity mentioned earlier of price and output regulation – the Restrictive Trade Practices Act 1976. The law has also acted, through the Resale Prices Act 1976, to prevent the once common policy of suppliers fixing a minimum resale price, the enforcement of which led to a serious inability to compete on price terms.

Organisations thus have to face a situation of a market-place which, although not perfect, has seen many attempts to encourage competitive activity. It is generally thought that the advent of money as a medium of exchange facilitated the extremely large number of transactions which take place in all markets throughout the year, year in year out. It will thus be somewhat surprising for you to find that a great many transactions (particularly in terms of international trade) do not take place for money but for 'barter'.

- *What is 'barter'? What are its main disadvantages?*

The activity of swopping, for example, jet airliners for oil takes us back to the very early days of difficulty over trade – that of trading without the medium of money to settle debts. Estimates as to the size of world trade generated by countertrade vary from 4.8% (Organisation of Economic Co-operation and Development – OECD – figures) to 8% (General Agreement on Tariffs and Trade – GATT – figures), though a number of commentators argue that world trade in total has not increased as a result of this activity – it is merely being 'financed' by bartering goods. Such activity as countertrade confuses the student of market-places since it appears to do little more than make negotiations for products even more complex than they might otherwise have been. An additional confusion is that the term 'countertrade' and others of the same ilk, such as 'counterpurchase' or 'offset deals', are not commonly understood and tend to mean different things to different people, depending on where you happen to be at the time!

An offset deal is quite different from a counter-trade arrangement but the terms are sometimes confused; offset deals occur when the buying country requires part of the contract to be fulfilled in that country. For example, if my (British) company wins an order to supply goods to China, the Chinese Government may insist that Chinese firms are allowed to produce some of the desired output. In 1986 the British Government faced a similar situation when, in negotiations with Saudi Arabia for the supply of UK fighter planes, the Saudis wanted the British to invest in factories and plants in Saudi Arabia before the Saudis would place the offer with Britain.

Markets ought to be places where goods/services can be bought and sold relatively cheaply, with little fuss and at little cost. We have seen what supposedly makes a market perfect and considered why it is that in reality markets are far from perfect. We have also seen that some markets appear unnecessarily complex because money is not used as a medium of exchange (barter takes place). What you must do at this stage is satisfy yourself that you appreciate what a market is; how the process of supply and demand generates prices; what part marketing has to play in an organisation's activities; and note that there are many imperfections in the real world which affect the complexity and nature of markets.

Assignments

Student activity 13.1

This is an individual assignment. There are a variety of types of market in this country, ranging from those with near perfect knowledge, such as the Stock Exchange, to those where knowledge is very imperfect, such as the market for second-hand cameras. An interesting move towards the improvement of knowledge, in the field of computers, has been the use of electronic bulletin boards for sending information via computers. The retail trade in this country is also experiencing the effects of computerisation, with a number of stores installing computer-aided equipment which will permit purchases to be made via a plastic card, which, when processed by the shop assistant, will automatically deduct the money from your bank account.

With the prospect that such immediate cash transfer is likely to catch on, plus the fact that Britain has the highest average number of personal computers held in private hands, it may not be long

Post Office warning on increased charged

By Michael Smith
Industrial Editor

HIGHER postage charges are threatened over the next few years unless the Government relaxes the tight money controls over the Post Office.

Post Office chairman, Sir Ron Dearing, is to ask Trade and Industry Secretary Paul Channon to take less money off the Post Office during the coming years to permit the organisation to undertake a huge new modernisation programme.

Sir Ron said the present Government demands were 'a very severe restraint.'

The Post Office paid £78 million to the Treasury under the Government's negative cash limit and the payment will rise to nearly £100 million in the current year. In addition, the Post Office will this year for the first time pay corporation tax to the Treasury.

But the Post Office is to embark on a five-year investment programme worth around £300 million to automate the counters network, introduce more information technology and modernise the parcels division.

Sir Ron explained yesterday that the Post Office could only raise the extra money by increasing prices, selling unwanted assets, cutting costs or retaining some profits. He said that selling assets would be difficult at a time of rapid expansion for the Post Office, while it was pointed out that the organisation had attracted growing volumes of mail by holding down prices.

Source: *The Guardian*, 22 July 1986

before we see the day, predicted so long ago, when we can remain in our homes and complete our shopping without leaving our armchairs.

Prepare a short discussion document in which you argue that armchair shopping (for most of the weekly, family purchases) would never become a reality. You must put forward at least four reasons why such shopping will not catch on, on a large scale.

Student activity 13.2

This is an individual assignment. Read the article (left) and any additional information which is necessary. Prepare an article which illustrates the relationship between the Post Office and the Government. The services of the Post Office have long been thought of as having a relatively inelastic demand. If this is the case, say what the implications of increased postal charges are likely to be. In the light of possible privatisation of postal services, what would you say would be the effects on postal charges of competition in this field?

Student activity 13.3

This is an assignment for students working in pairs. Consider the article overleaf (top). Prepare an oral presentation to explain why you believe the Amstrad computer company has been so successful, even in the face of severe competition from the computer giants, such as IBM.

Student activity 13.4

This assignment is for groups of four or five. Having read the article overleaf you are convinced that establishing a branch of a national bank in your college would prove very successful. Your group have the following tasks in this respect:

a) conduct a market research programme to discover who is likely to use such a bank, the preferred opening times, and the facilities required, as well as to provide you with the information to make the decisions required for items (b), (d) and (e);

b) agree on the best location for the branch within the college (assume there are no restraints on which room(s) you can use);

c) prepare the argument which you would present to the college governing body and to the bank which clearly shows that the site selected would be the best from a banking point of view;

IT is the most improbable business confrontation of the decade. On the left, 39-year-old Alan Sugar, East End van salesman made good: on the right, IBM, world's biggest corporation and heavy-weight computer power, forced to respond to Sugar's attack on the £34 billion world personal computer market with his cut-price PCs.

Sugar has already made an impact with his cheap word processors and his company, Amstrad, now claims 35% of the European home computer market. But this is modest besides his plan to bring computing to the masses with the PC1512, a machine with a performance that belies its rock-bottom £399 price tag.

There is always a danger that Sugar could take a bruising. The competition is wicked and even though Amstrad ranks fifth among British electronics companies, it is still puny compared to IBM. But there are good reasons why Sugar deserves to succeed, and why the rest of British industry should take a lesson from him in exploiting technology.

Source: *The Sunday Times*, 7 September 1986

Coping with overdrafts will join reading, writing and arithmetic as basic skills in the classroom if efforts by the big banks pay off

THE battle by the major banks to get through to the man in the street has moved into the classroom.

This month, Midland, TSB and Yorkshire Bank all launch campaigns to increase their shares of a lucrative and rapidly-expanding section of the youth market.

At a time when the banks are facing a strong challenge for customers from the building societies, success in recruiting schoolchildren could be vital to future profitability.

The most aggressive newcomer to the scene is Midland. Last week the bank began a national television advertising campaign to promote its imaginative and successful strategy of setting up bank branches in secondary schools.

The banks, which are managed by pupils on prevocational education courses, now provide Midland with 80,000 customers, offering individual deposit accounts for students at more than 750 schools in England and Wales. At the start of the new school year, no fewer than 100 new branches opened, which is not bad for a scheme started on a pilot basis three years ago.

John Collings, head of Midland's youth market division, says: 'We're absolutely astonished at the interest shown by schools in the scheme.

Source: *The Sunday Times*, 21 September 1986

d) prepare a list of the type of services you think the bank ought to provide;
e) select the national bank which you would prefer to operate in your college;
f) contact the bank concerned (locate the Head Office address and prepare the letter you would send) and invite a representative to your college.

There is no reason why you should not regard this as a 'real' task and, provided you can get the necessary permission from the college authorities, complete the project by attempting the following task:

g) when you have the bank representative at your college your task is to convince him or her that the bank should open such a branch and allow the students to operate it as part of a programme designed to increase work experience.

Student activity 13.5

This assignment, which has been designed for groups of three or four, concerns the issue raised in the article opposite. You are to assume the roles of British Rail Public Relations officers and your task is to prepare the explanation, to be given at a press

British Rail spares getting there – by road

By David Felton
Labour Correspondent

BRITISH rail has decided to let the road take the strain when it comes to distributing spare parts to its maintenance depots.

As part of a cost-cutting exercise BR is centralising all its storage of spares at Doncaster, and has awarded the £1.5m contract for distribution to more than 100 depots around the country to a Wakefield road haulage firm.

To add insult to what rail union leaders saw as a serious injury to the railways, the BR board decided to reject a bid for the business from its own Freightliners road/rail subsidiary and instead offer the contract to Swift Transport Services.

Andy Dodds, assistant general secretary of the National Union of Railwaymen, said last night: 'It is the height of folly for the railways to rely on private road haulage for the movement of vital traffic.'

The 12-month contract starts in January. For the first three months Swift will move spares from workshops and maintenance depots into the Doncaster depot and the new centralised system will swing into action in March.

BR said last night that the Freightliner tender had been rejected because it was too high. The problem was that the volume of traffic in spares was unpredictable.

A spokesman justified putting the business on to lorries rather than trains by arguing that unpredictability made planning ahead difficult, and forward planning was vital in moving freight. 'It's not such a silly idea as it seems on first sight. When you look into it, it's entirely logical,' he said.

But the NUR, which has shed several thousand members as a result of BR's efficiency drive, failed to see the logic. 'What a kick in the teeth for those struggling in BR's own freight business to promote the increasing use of rail. The board seem to be saying that they can't trust the railways for their own business.'

Back to an increasingly harassed BR official, who said the contract was not the kind of business which the railways were keen to attract.

As additional problem was that Doncaster was not close to a Freightliner terminal and many of the depots which would need the spares were also not near terminals.

Another possibility would have been to use BR's own Red Star fast parcels service, but this was discounted because it could not handle large components. In the meantime passengers can take comfort from the fact that broken down trains will now be repaired courtesy of a fast, cheap and reliable road service.

Source: *The Independent*, 11 December 1986

conference, of why British Rail is taking the steps indicated in the article. You are to make the presentation to the press, and so it may be worthwhile if you prepare not only the oral presentation but also some maps to illustrate part of the problem.

Skills assessable

	Skill							
	1	2	3	4	5	6	7	8
Assignment								
1	1.1	2.2		4.3		6.1		
	1.2	2.4				6.2		
	1.5			4.10		6.3		
	1.8							
2	1.8	2.2		4.3	5.1	6.1		
		2.5		4.5	5.2	6.2		
				4.10	5.10	6.3		
3	1.5	2.2	3.4	4.2	5.1	6.1		
	1.8	2.4	3.5	4.3	5.2	6.2		
		2.5	3.6	4.5	5.5	6.3		
			3.7	4.6	5.10			
			3.11					
4	1.3	2.2	3.4	4.3	5.1	6.1	7.1	
	1.4	2.4	3.5	4.5	5.2	6.2	7.2	
	1.6	2.5	3.6	4.6	5.4	6.3	7.3	
	1.8		3.7	4.10	5.5		7.4	
	1.9		3.9		5.6		7.5	
			3.11		5.10			
5	1.1	2.2	3.1	4.3	5.1	6.1		8.3
	1.2	2.4	3.2	4.6	5.2	6.2		
	1.6		3.6	4.10	5.5	6.3		
			3.7			6.5		
			3.9					
			3.11					

14
GOVERNMENT OBJECTIVES AND POLICIES

The government machine, which consists of central government, local government, quasi-governmental, and quasi-judicial bodies, affects organisations in a number of ways. Some of these include the regulation of activities, the encouragement of activities, charging for services, and giving grants, etc. Such local and national institutions affect the workings of all organisations. It is therefore important that any study of organisations takes note of the objectives and policies of government and the impact of governmental activities, together with the tools for their evaluation.

Government objectives

Government today assumes responsibility for the running of a variety of aspects of our lives, though this did not use to be the case. From the mercantilist doctrine of the seventeenth century, which attempted to introduce central governmental regulation of agriculture, industry, and trade, we moved towards a *laissez-faire* government after the Glorious Revolution (1688).

- *What was the Bill of Rights (established as a result of the Glorious Revolution)?*

The objectives of laissez-faire government were as follows:

1. Maintenance of a standing army for external defence.
2. Maintenance of a judicial system for internal law and order.

In the early part of the nineteenth century political thinking favoured the abolition of customs duties to stimulate trade, and by the 1860s free trade had been accomplished – with a consequent growth in the nation's wealth. At this time it was still maintained that the state had no part to play in economic affairs except that of encouraging competition and enterprise.

Philosophers such as Jeremy Bentham and John Stuart Mill were suggesting that the nation should be guided by the principle of 'the greatest good of the greatest number', a criterion for economic action which would involve the state in provision of specific benefits for those who could not afford to buy them. The government became involved in the lives of people through legislation such as the Education Act 1870 and the Public Health Act 1875. In the early part of the twentieth century the Old Age Pension Act (1908) and the National Insurance Act (1911) saw the state becoming involved in social issues.

Over time the state has become more involved in the lives of the people to the extent that, today, government policy reflects the encompassing nature of state provision and intervention. Such policies are concerned with the areas shown in Fig. 14.1.

- *List as many policy areas as you can think of under the heading of 'internal' and 'external' political (see Fig. 14.1).*

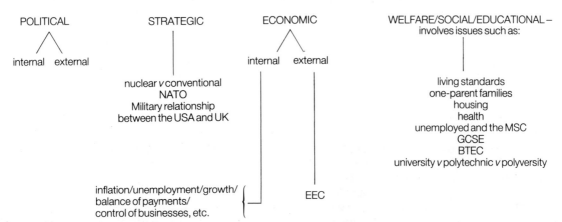

Fig. 14.1

Of primary concern are the economic objectives (since, if they do not get these right no other policies can be financed in the long term), which governments have had since the 1930s. There are four main policy objectives of governments (though they may be *mutually exclusive*, which means that the pursuance of one objective may make attempts to attain others impractical/unattainable). These are as follows:

1. Maintenance of balance on the Balance of Payments (see Chapter 15 for an explanation of the Balance of Payments).
2. Low levels of unemployment.
3. Low levels of inflation.
4. Good rate of economic growth.

- *In what way(s) may such objectives be mutually exclusive?*
- *What are the main social objectives of (a) the Conservative Party (b) the Labour Party, and (c) the SDP/Liberal Alliance?*

As with all policy objectives, each political party would have differing strategic objectives if they were the government of the day, if their manifestos are anything to go by. Let us consider a variety of issues which concern the major parties.

Defence

The Labour Party favours a withdrawal of nuclear weapons. The Conservative Party argues for the retention of nuclear weapons. The Social Democrats/Liberals would recognise the potential benefits in having nuclear weapons but would prefer it if all countries had none.

Military relationships with the USA would appear to be radically different if we viewed each political party in turn. For example, the Conservatives tend to favour strong ties with the USA while the Labour Party is generally suspicious of such links. To give an indication of how far apart the Conservative Party and the Labour Party are on defence spending, the Conservative Party Recess Brief (13), produced in the summer of 1986, revealed that since 1979 the Conservative government had spent £3 billion more *in real terms* on the Navy alone than Labour had planned for.

While the Conservatives talk of replacing Polaris by spending £9.87 billion on Trident, the SDP adamantly propose to cancel Trident. The SDP view is that strategic NATO shifts in conventional forces and the possibility of a different Polaris replacement (which would not make us so technologically dependent on the US) would be the better option.

Voting

While the Conservative Party and the Labour Party would both prefer to stay with the 'first-past-the-post' system for elections, the SDP/Liberal Alliance favour a form of proportional representation – primarily because, more than any other variable, it would ensure their re-election.

- *What is meant by a 'first-past-the-post' electoral system?*
- *There are a number of systems of proportional representation. The SDP Party proposes 'Community Proportional Representation'. How would this operate?*

It is true that our present system of electing MPs gives us governments who come to power with the support of a minority of the electorate. In 1979 for example, the Conservatives gained 43.9% of the total votes cast and yet held 339 seats in the House of Commons (slightly more than 53% of total seats). Another way of looking at these figures is to say that slightly more than 56% of those eligible to vote voted 'against' the Conservatives by voting for another party. It is argued that such an electoral system permits the election of a Government which could pursue extreme policies which were rejected by a majority of voters. This has led to 'adversary' politics – a system in which the Opposition opposes Government decisions and then reverses these decisions when in power.

- *What measures have been taken by the existing Government, which the Opposition claim they will reverse if elected at the next General Election?*

Housing

The main thrust in this area for the Conservatives is the sale of council houses to tenants, while the Labour Party oppose this and would reverse legislation giving tenants the right to buy. The SDP prefer to invest in expanding council housing programmes, while at the same time helping more people to buy, with the proviso that councils with a severe housing shortage should be allowed temporary suspension of the right to buy while they build up their stock of homes to cope with demand.

The economy

It is in this field that we probably see the greatest divergence of views, particularly between the (capitalist) Conservatives and the (socialist) Labour

Party. Between the two extreme economic viewpoints held we have the whole range of economic issues, centring on private ownership versus state control (see 'value systems', page 29 ff). It is interesting to note that the public sector of the economy and state share in the national product both tend to grow under socialist governments, while conservative governments aim to reduce growth in public expenditure.

• *What is meant by the 'national product'?*

The prime consideration of governments since the Second World War has been to control the economy and, although they have not been entirely successful (in fact, they have met with varying degrees of success), this has not prevented successive governments from attempting such control by various policy measures.

Government economic emphasis has changed, however. In the 1930s the major problem was unemployment, so government pursued (Keynesian) policies designed to stimulate the economy. While in the 1970s and 1980s the major issue was high rates of inflation, with the Conservative Governments at the end of the 1970s and into the 1980s concentrating on (Monetarist) policies designed to reduce these rates.

• *What is the central economic theme of the present Government?*

We can therefore consider the approach to economic rationale from the point of view of what we may call the *Keynesian model* and the *Monetarist model*. These two have been selected because the Keynesian model was followed by governments since the Second World War and up to the late 1970s and the Conservative Governments under Mrs Thatcher which were elected at the end of the 1970s and into the 1980s were said to be Monetarist.

The Keynesian model
This model takes its name from the economist, John Maynard Keynes, who borrowed ideas from other people and, in the early part of the 1930s, turned them into a theory which would help governments out of the business cycle crisis. All economies suffered from the vagaries of business cycles – those events which saw the economy sometimes in a buoyant, spending mood, with much demand for goods, services, and labour, and, at other times, in a depression with high levels of unemployment and little demand for goods or

services. Such a situation is generally depicted diagrammatically as in Figure 14.2.

Before the development and implementation of Keynesian ideas on controlling the economy, governments operated what was referred to as a Balanced Budget. The implication behind balanced budgets is simply that a government only spends what it can obtain in tax revenues – no more, no less. A balanced budget rule was considered necessary in order to curb the tendency towards deficit finance.

• *What is meant by the term 'deficit financing'?*

If you and I have to live within our budgets we may find it a struggle, but we soon learn to cope with the situation. If we are then offered credit, it is quite a temptation, and many find that they are soon unable to cope with the credit facilities they are offered. There are so many organisations encouraging us to 'buy now and pay later' that living on credit becomes a way of life, with dire consequences for some people.

The constitutional conventions which governed budgets and government spending had been over-shadowed since the nineteenth century by the rule that budgets should balance. The consequence of this action was that governments tended to *follow* what was happening in the economy and not lead. When many people were in work, all paying taxes, government revenue was high and so government spending was also high. When the slump came and many people were out of work government tax revenue declined, thus government spending declined and as a result the consequences of the slump were exaggerated. Governments tended to roll with the economy rather than trying to determine the route the economy should take.

If we accept for the moment that the economy is inherently unstable; fluctuations occur from time to time which leave us with boom periods, followed by slumps. Keynes's view was that if the government did the reverse of what the economy was doing, this would help the situation rather than make matters

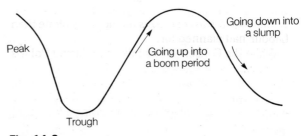

Fig. 14.2

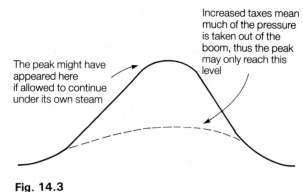

The peak might have appeared here if allowed to continue under its own steam

Increased taxes mean much of the pressure is taken out of the boom, thus the peak may only reach this level

Fig. 14.3

Business cycle without intervention

Cycle as a result of deficit and surplus budgets

Fig. 14.4

worse by following a balanced budget. The notion was to destabilise the budget in order to create a deficit or a surplus, depending on the state of the economy in relation to the trade cycles at any given time. For example, if the country was heading for a slump, Keynes argued that the government should operate a deficit budget – that is, spend what you do not have. The additional expenditure by government (sponsored by government borrowing) would be of the magnitude that would help to rejuvenate the economy. On the other hand, if the country was going into a boom period, the government could operate a surplus budget – that is to take more money out of circulation via taxes than it put back via, for example, subsidies. The effect of this would be to take some of the pressure out of the boom and thus the peak would be reached earlier, at a much lower level than might have been the case (see Fig. 14.3). The effect of government intervention of this type might be to produce economic conditions as shown in Fig. 14.4.

The peaks do not rise so high and the troughs are not so low as they might have been without the government intervention; such a situation is beneficial to the economy, and thereby to people in general.

Keynes appeared to believe that economic policy

would be produced by wise people who were not concerned with political pressures or political opportunities. In this sense, he certainly appears to have been over-optimistic concerning the possibility that politicians would exhibit enlightened management of the economy. However, in reality, such economic decision-making takes place in an environment of political parties which are striving for votes. It is thus quite practicable for governments to operate deficit budgets, since this allows them to spend without having to tax.

- *In what areas would you expect to see much government expenditure before an election?*

We frequently hear politicians proclaiming that the government should 'buy its way out of trouble' by injecting money into the economy (operate a deficit budget). We also hear others claiming that we tried for too long to 'live beyond our means'. What many fail to notice is that Keynesian ('full-employment') policies have appeared to lead to inflation. In fact, Professor Friedrich Hayek has been predicting for some forty years or more that the inevitable outcome of Keynesian policies would be inflation, which would progressively worsen and eventually collapse into massive unemployment.

It is true to say that early Keynesian theory has been greatly refined and elaborated, some would say beyond recognition. However, what has preceded has been a brief explanation of the basic approach, with some of the reservations people have about it.

Monetarist model

If one mentions the term 'monetarist', economists immediately think of the Chicago school of economic thought, the most influential member of which is Professor Milton Friedman. Monetarism gained an important role in British economic policy with the Thatcher governments at the end of the 1970s and into the 1980s, and Milton Friedman was a welcome guest of the Prime Minister. The basic contention of monetary theory is that inflation is caused by excess money supply. Before considering government policy in connection with the economy, in the light of monetary theory, let us first briefly look at the theory.

To appreciate in simplistic terms what the theory says about money and inflation you need first to be aware of how credit is created, since most of the 'money' in circulation is not coins and bank notes (these only make up about 20% of the total money supply). I like to exercise a little poetic licence at this stage and explain credit creation by taking events from history and somewhat compressing and slightly altering them. If this is not the way you have heard this before, don't worry – the explanation is for those who are not familiar with credit creation.

In the very early days of 'banking', the task of keeping valuables safe rested with goldsmiths – the only people with safe-deposit facilities. If I deposited gold (money) with the goldsmith he would give me a receipt. I would go home and, some time later, a creditor may call for the money (gold) I owe him; at this stage I may have to go back to the goldsmith, ask for my money (giving the goldsmith the receipt in return), pay the creditor and walk home. My creditor would then deposit the gold with the goldsmith for safe-keeping. In time, the goldsmiths tired of this and came to an arrangement whereby I could give my receipt for gold to the creditor, thus saving me from a walk to the goldsmith – and saving the goldsmith from the task of getting my gold from the safe, watching me give it to someone else, who promptly asked the goldsmith to look after it. The goldsmith had 'invented' the bank note. This was fine when my debt was equal to the value on my receipt – but what if the amounts differed? This is where we see the goldsmith's next good idea. If I want to transfer some of my money to someone else I can write a letter, addressed to the goldsmith and carried by my creditor, which instructs the goldsmith to let him have some of my money. Again, the goldsmith is not going to get my gold out of the vault and give it to the creditor, only to watch him redeposit it again, so he merely makes a book entry into the accounts which transfers some of my pile of money into the creditor's pile of money. The goldsmith 'invents' the cheque!

- *Would there be any major problem if there were more than one goldsmith?*
- *If the answer is 'yes', how do you think these problems could be solved?*

In time the goldsmith realises that not a great deal of the money deposited with him ever actually leaves his premises – though he is constantly making book entries and transferring money from one account to another. He thinks to himself, 'Why don't I lend some of this money which is lying around and charge interest on it? No one will miss it since few people ever take the money away, and if they do they will spend it and someone else will no doubt be back to deposit it for safe-keeping.' It isn't long before our goldsmith ('banker' if you like) is working out how much money is deposited and what percentage is withdrawn on average every week. He can then lend the rest at interest – much

better than running backwards and forwards carrying gold around.

- *In banking terms, what is meant by a Minimum Reserve Ratio?*
- *Bearing in mind how the goldsmiths operated (above), can you see how a commercial bank can 'create' credit? How can the government control such activities?*

Now that you see how easy it is for banks and other financial institutions to 'make money', you may begin to realise the extent of the problem facing a government trying to control the supply of money. There are several definitions of the money supply, the two main ones being M1 and M3. M1 is the so-called narrow definition and includes notes and coins, as well as sterling bank deposits on current account. M3, the broad definition, is M1 plus interest-bearing deposit accounts and certificates of deposit.

- *What is a 'certificate of deposit'?*

Since coins and banknotes only make up a small proportion of the total money supply, it would be pointless trying to control the money supply by restricting minting of coins and printing of notes. The main thrust must be aimed at those financial institutions capable of creating credit. Money is to be viewed just as any other commodity – the more there is available, the less valuable it becomes (the fewer the number of things which can be bought with it). In reality, we know that money is losing value when we see continual prices rises (inflation), since a rise in prices is just another way of considering a fall in the value of money – at the end of the day, we get less for our cash.

A government that is monetarist would therefore place considerable emphasis on controlling the money supply, that is, their main economic objective must be the reduction of inflation. Once inflation is down, the view is that the economy will be much healthier, businesses will be able to invest, consumers have price stability and, in general, the economic climate will prompt economic recovery.

We have therefore seen that governments can spend, stimulate the economy, and create employment (operate Keynesian policies) as an economic objective. Or, they can concentrate their efforts on bringing down the rate of inflation (via monetarist means) and then hope the stage will be set for economic growth.

It was mentioned in Chapter 1 that organisations are composed of various groups of individuals who share, or who appear to share, common objectives.

However, it is also the case that if we have a number of groups together, friction will eventually result. The state can also be regarded as an organisation with many separate, though often related, interest groups. The interests of the various groups in society sometimes coincide but on many occasions they conflict.

- *Consider a recent (local) example of conflict between competing groups. What was the nature of the conflict and how was it resolved? Can you now think of a better solution to this problem?*

Society therefore appears fraught with interest groups, whose objectives will be different, and who will all have leaders who believe in the right of their cause. The task for governments in such a situation is to maintain equilibrium between the potentially conflicting objectives of the various groups.

When we consider governmental organisations, the power held by the state, and the people involved, we often come across the terms *pluralist* and *élitist*.

Pluralism

Within a pluralistic frame of reference a country (an organisation on the largest of scales) is viewed as a complex system of inter-relationships between the overall objectives of the country and those of individuals within that country. Conflict is therefore inevitable and yet must be managed so that the overall governmental objectives can be reconciled with group beliefs and aims.

The very existence of competing groups acts as a built-in stabilizer in that there can be no rise to over-whelming power of any one group, since other centres of power would be inspired to strive for control, thus ensuring that a system of equilibrium reigns.

For a society to operate on a pluralist basis there must be the opportunity for access into the political system by both individuals and organisations. Without such access we would not be able either to support the issues we believed in or oppose those we felt were not suitable. It is important that there is not only provision for those who are interested to get involved, but that people do become involved. We are all aware of those groups that are 'run by the few – for the many'. You probably belong to several groups and enjoy taking part in the activities, but do not like to get involved with the administration!

- *Check the number of votes cast in the last five elections in your college for the Student Union President. At the time of each election, how many students were enrolled and eligible to vote? Does a comparison of each set of figures for each year tell you anything interesting?*

(If you happen to go to one of those rare colleges where people do get involved, get involved yourself. Don't lose the opportunity to be a part of a unique institution! Plato suggested that apathy killed democracy – it is as true today as it was two thousand years ago.)

Linked to this notion that people should get involved, and that there should be access to the political system, is the view that there should be free elections as a means of permitting participation in political decisions. In politics the term 'pluralism' means there must be at least two political parties.

Elitism

An élite is a group regarded as being superior in some way and therefore favoured; politically, an élite would be influential within society. Elitism implies that a few people will dominate the political process and that there will be little or no opposition. Linked to this would be the failure of most of those people who are entitled to vote (adults) to use their political power to influence decisions.

An élitist government would demonstrate very little consultation with interested parties and would control a disproportionate amount of scarce resources (in some cases it is their wealth that gives people membership of an élite). The term 'scarce resources' in this context does not only mean money, it could include skills and information – vital resources required by anyone who had aspirations to govern.

One does not need to be a young 'radical' to hold the view that 'they' run things; many of our older citizens will tell you it is the 'establishment' or the 'old boy network', or a few rich families, etc. who control the country.

- *What is meant by the 'old boy network'?*

I used to know a marvellous old chap who was convinced that the country was run by Martians (green élitists!) and another who thought all the important decisions were taken by a handful of industrial plutocrats (he was a young man during the Great Depression and never forgave his boss for making him redundant!). Such a view ('they' – whoever they may be – run things) is virtually impossible to disprove since it will be argued that the overt leaders constitute a ruling élite. If by some chance you can prove they do not, then you will be countered by the view that behind them is a covert (controlling) élite. (R. A. Dahl, 'A Critique of the Ruling Elite Model', *Decisions, Organisations and Society*, F. G. Castles, D. J. Murray and D. C. Potter, 1971, Penguin Books in association with The Open University Press.) Taken to its extreme, if we could prove they were not an élite, then no doubt another covert élite would be created who *were* behind the first covert group, and so on, ad infinitum.

Whatever the composition or the nature of government in this country, all governments have to choose; they must choose between one social policy option or another; they must choose between one economic policy or another; they must decide how to obtain money and where to spend it. All government activity, by its very nature, affects organisations or individuals in a country. We cannot begin to separate the many activities and decisions which, together, make us as individuals react in a particular way and make the organisations around us behave similarly. The best we can do is appreciate that neither the organisations nor the individuals in a society can be permitted to operate in isolation without their decisions adversely affecting others in our society. Government is there to keep the peace, to separate competing groups and to maintain an equilibrium by making decisions on behalf of us all.

Assignments

Student activity 14.1

This is an assignment suitable for groups of three or four. Governments of all political persuasion have a duty and a responsibility to the people of a country to plan for the future. It is in this respect that the present British Government is convinced of the need for electricity generation via nuclear means, in order that potential future demand can be satisfied.

Unfortunately, the use of nuclear fuel is greatly opposed by many people within the population, particularly those who have to live near sites where the waste from nuclear power stations is likely to be dumped. Consider the article below. Assume that you live near the proposed site and that you are determined to try all legitimate means open to you to prevent the dumping.

Your task is to prepare an action plan which will indicate what you intend to do to persuade the government not to permit dumping near your home. Bear in mind that your arguments may be

---

A drilling site in Cornwall funded by Nirex, the Government nuclear waste agency, will be invaded next month by a posse of men prospecting for tin – and claiming the protection of ancient Cornish laws. The United Kingdom Atomic Energy Authority (UKAEA), which runs the site, says it will fight back – using modern English laws.

The men are 'tinners', who claim the authority of a tin-miners' court, the Stannary Court, recognised by Edward I in 1305. The site is a former state quarry, so the chances of finding tin are slim; the tinners' aim is to drive away the UKAEA.

The quarry, at Reskajeage, near Camborne, was occupied this summer by a team working for the UKAEA's Harwell laboratory, for experiments, funded by Nirex, to test the movement of water through rock. Dr John Stubbs, the Harwell spokesman, has denied that this means Cornwall is being considered for dumping radioactive waste but his assurances fell on deaf ears, and the tinners decided to act.

The tinners have their own Stannary Parliament, which they believe predates and outranks Westminster. Carl Skewes, the Camborne tinner leading the campaign, claims that stannary law is still valid, even though the Stannary Parliament has met only once in the past 200 years.

Mr Skewes laid claim to the quarry by 'bounding' its corners with piles of stones, indicating that he intends to prospect for tin there. The bounds will be 'proclaimed' three times at the Stannary Court, and if unopposed, the court will issue a writ of possession on 7 January. The next day, Mr Skewes will lead two dozen tinners and about 200 supporters on to the site. Dr Stubbs is not impressed. 'We are just a harmless research organisation,' he said.

The UKAEA is taking legal advice, and will, if necessary, apply for an injunction against trespass.

The tinners are confident of success should the matter come to the courts. But Professor Robert Pennington of Birmingham University, an authority on stannary law, is not. He agreed that the original charter of 1305 has never been repealed, but pointed out that an Act of 1896 abolished the Stannary Court and transferred its authority to Cornwall County Court. He said, even by stannary law, the tinners had failed to give the UKAEA adequate notice.

Source: *The Independent*, 15 December 1986

countered. You will therefore need to outline the expected opposing argument and your own reaction to it.

Student activity 14.2

This is an assignment for students working in pairs. You recently overheard a conversation in which two neighbours appeared confused when it came to the governmental structure in the UK. Your neighbours did not seem to know, for example, where the responsibility lay for the provision of particular services. On hearing this you felt there may exist the demand for a short, lively, informative handbook outlining the organisation of government in the UK.

The intention is that you find a local printer who is prepared to back your judgement and to produce the handbook for you. To this end the completed version must show:

a) the relationship between central and local government;
b) the difference between a Member of Parliament and a member of a local council;
c) the sources of revenue for both central and local government;
d) the variety of services each is responsible for.

You must bear in mind the *market* this handbook will be aimed at and use appropriate language.

Student activity 14.3

This is a group assignment, suitable for groups of four. Consider the information (right) relating to proposed government action on jobs and trade union reform. Your task is to prepare a joint document which outlines the possible impact on unemployment of each of the four proposals given, detailing how each of the proposals is likely to affect the problem.

Student activity 14.4

This is an individual assignment. In a written reply to a Commons question in the week beginning Monday 15 December 1986, the Minister of Housing (John Patten) revealed that nearly three-quarters of a million council tenants had bought their homes in England since 1979. The figure for the whole country was more than 1 million.

There has, however, been considerable opposition to council house sales from the Labour Party.

In an article aimed at 16–18 year-old students of

Labour reform is top Tory target

Robert Taylor
Labour Editor

THE government is planning a controversial programme for action on jobs and trade union reform to be carried out if it wins the next general election.

Details will emerge during the next few months as the Conservatives seek to refute the charge of the opposition parties that they have failed to solve Britain's unemployment crises. The programme will include:

■ Moves to break up national pay bargaining in the public sector, especially the civil service;
■ Immediate legislation in a new Parliament to remove all rent controls from new private lettings as a way of easing labour mobility;
■ A further measure to make the trade unions more democratic, including postal ballots and legal rights for workers to leave closed shops and cross picket lines in strikes;
■ A job training scheme for the 500,000 18 to 25-year-olds out of work for more than six months.

Source: *The Observer*, 2 December 1986

British government, outline the reasons for council house sales as advocated by the Conservative Party, followed by the arguments against such sales, as advocated by the Labour Party.

Student activity 14.5

This is a group assignment, for groups of five or six. Successive governments have attempted to legislate to the benefit of those who may be disadvantaged through disability, or those likely to be otherwise discriminated against when it comes to employment opportunities. Find out if your local authority operates an Equal Opportunities Employment Programme.

If it does, prepare a presentation which demonstrates the components of the programme and its operation.

If it does not, investigate the area of Equal Opportunities Employment Programmes, and prepare guidelines for the introduction of such a programme by your local authority.

Skills assessable

Assignment	Skill 1	2	3	4	5	6	7	8
1	1.2 1.3 1.6 1.8 1.9	2.4 2.5	3.4 3.5 3.6 3.7 3.9 3.11	4.2 4.3 4.4 4.10		6.1 6.2 6.3		
2	1.3 1.6 1.8 1.9 1.10	2.2 2.4 2.5	3.4 3.6 3.9	4.3 4.4 4.6		6.1 6.2 6.3		
3	1.3 1.6 1.8 1.9 1.10	2.2 2.4 2.5	3.4 3.5 3.6 3.7 3.9 3.11	4.3 4.5 4.6 4.10	5.1 5.2 5.4 5.10	6.1 6.2 6.3		
4	1.6 1.8 1.9	2.2 2.4		4.3 4.6 4.10	5.1 5.2 5.3	6.1 6.2 6.3		
5	1.3 1.6 1.8	2.2 2.4 2.5 2.8	3.4 3.5 3.6 3.7 3.9 3.11	4.1 4.3 4.3 4.5 4.6		6.1 6.2 6.3		

INTERNATIONAL ACTIVITY AND THE ORGANISATION

Many organisations within the UK are involved in trading with organisations from other countries; some are buyers of foreign produce while others are sellers. International trade is important to any nation but especially so to a relatively small nation (in terms of land mass) such as ours. In this chapter we will consider why trade is thought to be so important, what agreements have been promoted to encourage trade, the technicalities of international trade, and the problems of developing nations.

Reasons for international trade

There are a number of reasons why trade is conducted between various countries:

1. It is economically advantageous – the *Law of Comparative Costs*.
2. Haphazard resource distribution over the world means that some countries do not possess what they want but may possess items which others want but do not have within their own boundaries.
3. Climatic differences mean some countries are unable to produce the variety of products they would like.
4. Demand outstrips that which can be produced in the home country.

- *Research the notion of comparative advantage and satisfy yourself that:*
  a) you can work through a simple mathematical explanation of the theory; and
  b) you fully appreciate the reasoning behind the Law of Comparative Costs.

Having completed the above task you ought now to be able to see why nations would want to specialise and trade with other nations. However, in reality nations do not specialise entirely. There are a number of reasons why nations would not blindly follow the principle enshrined within the Law of Comparative Costs. These include the following:

1. The example of comparative advantage you worked through probably assumed a two-country world. This is far removed from reality and thus, in the complexity of a multi-country world, the benefits from international specialisation may not become apparent.
2. Many countries insist on production of specific products for themselves, even though they may be able to purchase their requirements from a more efficient producer. Such insistence is sometimes the result of strategic (defence) arguments.
3. The principle behind comparative advantage assumes that factors of production can easily and quickly be moved to the production of another item. In reality we are plagued with the problem of occupational immobility.
4. The process of moving products across national boundaries is fraught with problems which force up transport costs. Such real-world headaches as transport costs were again probably not taken into account in the comparative advantage example you worked through previously. Their existence, coupled with the fact that they have to be financed, sometimes makes international trade less attractive than it might otherwise be.

- *What do you understand by 'occupational immobility'? How can this problem be eased?*

Trading restrictions

Not only do we have situations where countries do not follow the principle behind the Law of Comparative Costs but we also have countries that attempt to block the free movement of goods overseas; such countries are said to be *protectionist*. Those that exhibit behaviour typical of protectionism will often attempt to justify the action by claiming that:

a) they are protecting the interests of new, emerging (infant) industries that need protecting from overseas competition. The counter argument suggests that such 'infant industries' never learn to grow up, that is, they will continue to need protection from the vagaries of competition which exist in the 'outside' world.

b) they are merely erecting temporary devices designed to restore an imbalance in the Balance of Payments. The counter argument is that to do this one has to forego the advantages of unrestricted trade – advantages which could be accruing to the consumers of the nation as a result of their being able to buy competitively-priced goods.

c) they are preventing other countries from 'dumping' – the process by which the goods of one country are sold in another at a price which is below that attainable in the country of origin; many in fact argue that dumping implies selling goods at below their cost of production. The importation of such cheap items will seriously (adversely) affect producers in the importing country and it is these organisations which generally request restrictions on the free movement of such goods into their country.

d) there are social reasons why organisations should not be allowed to fail simply because the products they are responsible for can be obtained cheaper from another country. This argument, based as it is on the moral grounds of preventing unemployment in an organisation and consequent loss to entire districts, is often put forward to support the notion that we need an indigenous coal industry.

- *Consider a recently reported request for import restrictions anywhere in the world. What reasons were put forward to support such action?*

Subsidies act to restrict trade since they artificially

Embargoes	Quotas	Tariffs	Currency restrictions

an outright prohibition. Can be aimed either at a particular class of good or the goods of a particular country.

a tax on goods coming into the country. Not only raises the price of the good, thus making it less competitive in relation to home-produced items, but also earns revenue for the state (excise duty).

as with embargoes, can be aimed at particular goods or those of a specific country. Imports are limited to a permitted quota in either volume or value terms.

in order to purchase goods from a particular country, importers must be able to pay with the currency of that country. If the state (attempting trade restriction) limits the amount of currency that can be obtained trade cannot take place since payment cannot be made.

Fig. 15.1   Methods used to restrict trade

reduce the price of *home-produced goods*. A subsidy thus has the effect of making home-produced goods more attractive, which should increase the likelihood of sales (at the expense of imported – more expensive – items).

- *Differentiate between bilateral and multilateral trade.*

Trading agreements

Although many countries have at times initiated a programme of trade restriction, there have been a number of organisations established with the objective of reducing barriers to trade between members and encouraging the free movement of goods (and people – see the EEC below). Such organisations are not new and neither is the notion of free trade; proponents of *laissez-faire* in the nineteenth century were sponsoring the notion that the abolition of all customs and excise duties would stimulate international trade and thereby create prosperity for all. As far as organisations aimed at removing trade restrictions are concerned, the General Agreement on Tariffs and Trade was the first to emerge after the Second World War.

General Agreement on Tariffs and Trade (GATT)

The Agreement, signed in 1947, aimed to reduce tariffs and import quotas (trade barriers). When President Kennedy cut US tariffs in 1963 (on condition that other countries would do the same by 1967), this so-called Kennedy Round resulted in dramatic reductions of the tariffs of industrialised nations by 1967. Later agreements have further helped to reduce tariffs.

European Free Trade Association (EFTA)

This organisation was formed in 1960, primarily because the UK found the terms offered for membership of the EEC unacceptable. Membership included Austria, Denmark, Norway, Portugal, Sweden, Switzerland, and the United Kingdom. This group was referred to as the 'Outer Seven' since, although they were formed as a purely economic association (no political implications existed), they were often compared to the members of the EEC (as it was at the time). The original EEC membership ('The Six') was a body of countries with much more in common both culturally and geographically than the present EEC. When the United

Kingdom and Denmark eventually gained entry to the EEC they left the EFTA.

European Economic Community (EEC)

The EEC grew from what was initially a customs union (Benelux) established in 1945 by three European nations – Belgium, Luxemburg, and the Netherlands.

The Benelux countries were joined in 1952 by West Germany, Italy, and France to form the European Coal and Steel Community, which was an attempt to rationalise production of these items. The political boundaries of the countries concerned did not make economic sense in such a market (coal, iron, and steel).

The membership now consisted of six nations ('The Six') who agreed to take matters a stage further and establish an area which would have free trade within it; this was to be known as the EEC. It was also generally accepted that political union should be an ultimate objective. At this time the UK felt unable to join for a number of reasons. For example, it had special agricultural and trading ties with other nations of the Commonwealth (which would be lost on entry to the EEC), and the political aspects of the EEC made many people wary in the UK.

Economic growth within the EEC in its early days was greater than that experienced by other industrialised nations, and it became more attractive as a market-place for the UK as time went on. As a result the UK, along with Denmark and the Republic of Ireland, joined the EEC in 1973 (forming 'The Nine'). The Community was joined in 1981 by a new partner, Greece, and in 1985 Spain joined.

Ultimately the EEC market will be one where there is free movement of goods across national boundaries, and also free movement of labour. Any one of us could then take up employment in any of the member states without the need for a passport, visa, or other documentation. The EEC would effectively become one 'community'.

The potential benefits of free trade have also been recognised by countries outside Western Europe. Thus there are free trade areas in the Soviet Union, Africa, Latin and Central America, and the Caribbean.

- *Working in groups of four, undertake research on the following and produce a set of notes on each similar to that given on the European free trade associations and GATT, previously mentioned:*
  Comecon (Council for Mutual Economic Aid);
  Caricom (Carribbean Community);
  Latin American Free Trade Association (LAFTA);
  Central American Common Market (CACM).

Technicalities of international trade

International trade carries with it a number of problems which are not met in trade within nations. For example, trade with organisations from other nations involves the complexity of having to deal in foreign currency, the problems of dealing with nations which may have different customs and laws concerning trade, issues concerning the Balance of Payments, and so on. At this stage time will be spent on considering some of the complications associated with international trade.

Foreign exchange

To purchase the products of another country one must first obtain the currency of that country through the foreign exchange market. The issue would be a relatively simple one if the value of all currencies were *fixed*; businessmen could arrange forward contracts and know how much they will get, in terms of their own currency – fixed rates remove much of the uncertainty surrounding international trade. The major problem surfaces when market forces (demand and supply) are permitted to establish exchange rates on a *floating* basis. Such a situation brings with it much uncertainty, which is something businessmen try to minimise.

We saw in Chapter 13 how the pressures of supply and demand establish a market price. Such a situation will work exactly the same way when we are considering the establishment of the price of foreign currency (foreign exchange rate). Foreign currency can be regarded as just another product in a market place.

Two extreme possibilities were mentioned in connection with the establishment of the foreign exchange rate:

Fixed rate: this would be maintained at some specific relationship either with a precious metal (gold) or another currency, say, dollars ($).
Floating rate: the rate would be permitted to move, according to the day-to-day pressures of supply and demand.

Fixed exchange rates under the Gold Standard were the system we operated within until 1931, the currency value being defined in terms of a specific weight of gold. This so-called

Gold Standard stimulated the free flow of goods internationally because it carried with it stability, that characteristic loved by businessmen. The value of all currencies within the Gold Standard were linked to gold at a specific rate, which meant that because they were *all* linked to gold they were necessarily linked to one another. With the ending of the Gold Standard nations moved to a *Flexible-Exchange-Rate* system and then, in 1944, *Managed Flexibility*.

- *What was 'Managed Flexibility'?*

It makes sense to consider and compare the workings of a rigid system and the operation of a floating system of exchange rate determination. For the purposes of this discussion, fixed rates will be explained via the mechanism of the Gold Standard. The system worked in this way:

1. Suppose imports (goods we buy from overseas) were greater than exports (goods we sell overseas) and we paid in £s, which were exchanged by the other country with the Bank of England for gold.
2. Because more people would be changing £s into gold (since imports are greater than exports) rather than the other way (which is what our exporters would do with the gold they earned from overseas), gold reserves would decline.
3. As a result of declining gold reserves credit would be contracted.
4. As credit was contracted, interest rates would rise.
5. If interest rates went up, investment (if linked to interest rates) would decline.
6. Level of money incomes would thus fall.
7. As money incomes fall, the price of British goods should be reduced.
8. As British goods would be cheaper our exports should be stimulated (they now look more attractive because they are cheaper) and imports discouraged (since they would now appear expensive alongside British competition).
9. Thus the balance between imports and exports should be restored.

There was also the implicit assumption that those earning the export surplus (equivalent to our deficit) could expand credit in their own countries and thus create demand for goods (some of the supply of which could come from us).

The Gold Standard was thus said to have *Automatic Balancing* – the obligation to convert £s into gold implied credit in this country was tied to central bank gold reserves.

- *Why might the Gold Standard system not work as anticipated?*

There are two aspects to consider in answering the question above. On the one hand, there is the assumption that those with an export surplus could and would expand credit. However, countries in this position failed to do so for fear of creating internal inflation.

The second aspect rests on the assumption of price flexibility. If you refer back to the note on the working of the system you will notice that investment declines and the level of money incomes fall – thus workers have to accept lower money wages and entrepreneurs lower prices and profits. The system relied on employment remaining constant, with the same number of workers being employed but each receiving less. In reality, a smaller number of workers received constant money incomes since wage cuts were opposed. The end product was unemployment.

One of the main drawbacks of the system was the fact that a government's control of the money supply was dependent on whether or not gold was flowing into or out of the country. It is also regarded as being a misuse of resources to have to maintain gold reserves to back-up a note issue. People can no longer go to the Bank of England and give up their £ notes for an equivalent amount of gold. Thus, the Gold Standard would not meet the requirements of a trading nation today.

- *In connection with the issue of bank notes, what is meant by a 'fiduciary issue'?*

Floating exchange rates, as the name suggests, is the system whereby the value of a currency is permitted to fluctuate freely in relation to other currencies such that the rate of exchange (price of the currency) is determined in the foreign exchange market by the demand for the currency and the supply available.

The foreign exchange market is not *one* place – there are separate markets in most countries; it may be possible that the value of a currency in one country differs from its value elsewhere – though such a position would not continue for long.

- *What is meant by 'arbitrage'?*

The exchange rate actually depends on the relation between a country's exports and its imports. If imports increase we need to obtain more foreign currency to pay for them. Thus, if imports rise, the demand for foreign currency increases.

- *When demand for anything increases, what happens to its price, ceteris paribus? What is the significance of specifying 'ceteris paribus'?*

When a country increases its exports it earns more foreign currency, thus, as exports rise, supply of foreign currency increases.

When a country's currency loses value (depreciates), imports become more expensive in real and money terms, but its exports become cheaper for overseas buyers. Thus, imports should be reduced and exports increased.

- *Explain the difference between 'real terms' and 'money terms'.*

When currency appreciates a country's exports become dearer and imports become cheaper. If there is imbalance such that a country finds the value of its exports and imports differ (either exports are greater than imports or vice versa) then a change in the value of a currency could help remedy this situation.

A freely fluctuating exchange rate system does not suffer from the restrictions of the Gold Standard, though we often witness governments intervening *to regulate* the exchange rate of their currencies via what has become known as a 'dirty float'. To explain this point, let me first say that governments are interested in, among other things, either *maintaining* the value of their currency within fairly tight limits or having the ability to *change these rates*. There may be a number of reasons for this. For example, the stability assists businesses, or it may be important politically to maintain the rate at a specific point, or they may wish to devalue the currency to facilitate an export drive, etc. Whatever reason there may be for a government to determine the exchange rate of its currency, the fact is that the British government (and others) can and do enter the foreign exchange market.

- *We do not see the Prime Minister or the Cabinet or other members of the government working in the foreign exchange market. Who/what then is the British government representative in foreign exchange dealings?*

A reconsideration of demand and supply analysis (Chapter 13) should show you how a government can affect the value of its currency. Suppose, for example, that the value of sterling was falling.

- *What would happen if a representative of this government went into the market and began buying up £ notes?*

On the other hand, suppose there was a run on £ notes and, as a result of excess demand, the value of a £ note *(its price)* began to rise. Since the government may have a vested interest in not letting the currency value rise, they could introduce more £ notes into the market (increase the supply of £ notes) which should have the desired effect of reducing the price of sterling (to the point where the government want it to rest).

One final point about exchange rates concerns their use in helping to correct a trade imbalance. All countries must aim to achieve a balance between the value of exports and the value of imports, primarily because we can only afford to buy imports if we earn enough from the sale of our exports. Also, if we were to sell more overseas than we bought from foreign producers, there would be a great deal of money flowing into the country and this would go to the factors of production for their productive efforts (see Fig. 9.2). On the face of it, it sounds fine that factors of production will earn more, though we should recognise that if more money flows into the country in this way it may only lead to inflation – which would present the government with yet more headaches.

If a country's imports are continually greater than exports, then that country will eventually have problems over payment. Initially it may be possible to use accumulated assets (savings), just as you and I would if our expenditure was greater than our income, or the country (again, just like you and I) could go into debt. However, neither of these options go to the root cause of the problem nor would a country be able to rely on them for long; savings would eventually expire and going into debt would only be possible if you could at least hold out the hope of ultimate solvency. Thus, neither using assets (savings) nor borrowing can continue indefinitely. If imports are greater than exports we need to:

(Option 1) cut imports
and/or
(Option 2) boost exports.

This could be where exchange rate movements might help.

The prices charged for goods traded overseas have two components: (a) the price in the country of origin, and (b) the rate of exchange between countries.

Option 1, the cutting of imports, could be facilitated by changing the exchange rate such that the £ became more valuable. For example:

Assume the rate was £1:$2

British consumers would pay £22.50 for a good which was produced to sell at $45 (assume no transport costs).

If the British government could influence the exchange rate such that it became £1:$1.50, then the $45 good would cost the British buyer £30 (an increase of £7.50).

This increase in cost may be enough to persuade the consumers in this country not to buy, thus reducing imports.

Option 2, the boosting of exports, could also be facilitated by altering the exhange rate. For example:

Assume the rate was £1:$2

A British produced commodity costs £500 to manufacture and therefore sells in the USA for $1,000 (assuming no transport costs).

The British government influences the exchange rate such that it becomes £1:$1.50.

The British good will now cost the American consumer 750 dollars (a saving of $250).

This 'reduction' in price may be enough to persuade overseas consumers to buy more British products.

This all sounds very nice but if it were as simple as that countries ought never to have balance of payments problems, yet they do.

- *Given the previous examples of how exchange rate movements could help a country with trade balance problems, why don't countries employ this solution?*

For those of you who could not see the reason why in the above task, think of the impact on other countries' trade balances if we devalued our currency. If they were to find themselves in trouble how could they get out of it?

Finally, in connection with foreign currency and the activities of organisations which deal in international trade, brief mention ought to be made of the issue of 'currency hedging'. Since organisations which want to buy from overseas producers need foreign currency, it makes a great deal of sense for them to obtain that currency at favourable rates. Currency hedging works in much the same way as hedging in any other market and for the same reason – to mitigate fluctuations in prices.

Investors may hedge against inflation by holding wealth in the form of shares or a precious metal rather than money. Those people with the responsibility for buying grain will deal in futures markets, where contracts to buy and sell at a future date are arranged and where a gain on a future deal may offset a loss incurred by a price change. Those concerned with obtaining foreign currency will do so while attempting to get as much as they can for their money.

The drawback of foreign currency is that organisations must spend a great deal of time and money trying to obtain the currency of another country in order to facilitate deals. These are resources which could be put to better uses. Hedging is a means of trying to protect against a loss.

Balance of payments

I have mentioned the fact that goods flow into (imports) and out of a country (exports) but have not said anything about non-goods which people pay for, such as the services of banking, insurance, and shipping, or that great money-earner, tourism. If we only traded goods we would be concerned to keep a check on the value of goods sold and the value of goods bought; in other words, we would be concerned with the Balance of Trade. This Balance of Trade concerns things we can see (goods) and is sometimes referred to as the *visible* balance; it represents a part of the Balance of Payments.

- *Obtain figures showing the Balance of Trade in the United Kingdom for the past ten years and plot this data on graph paper. What does this chart tell you about the Balance of Trade position in the UK?*

Just as any trading organisation has to keep an account of where money came from and where it goes to, nations also have to keep a record of income and expenditure. The Balance of payments shows the relationship between a country's total payments to all other countries and its total receipts from them.

The term 'balance' implies an equality and, in an accounting sense, the Balance of Payments always balances. However, although it must always balance, it need not be in equilibrium, that is, we may have a deficit or a surplus balance.

- *What is the implication of a deficit balance on any type of account?*

The Balance of Payments consists of three sections, which we can think of in this way (see Fig. 15.2):

a) *current account* ... the visible trade and invisibles taken together. The invisibles were the items referred to on page 165 as 'non-good' items.

b) *currency flow* ... lending to other countries, borrowing from other countries, or the transfer of assets.

c) *official financing* ... the record of changes in foreign currency reserves.

When total receipts are greater than total payments the Balance of Payments is said to be *favourable*; when payments are greater than receipts, this is said to be *adverse*.

It is somewhat misleading to suggest that a balance is favourable or adverse. For example, a country may continuously import more goods than it exports and yet still have a current account surplus if receipts from invisibles are more than sufficient to offset a trade deficit. Before coming to the conclusion that a situation is favourable or unfavourable one must examine the cause of a debit or credit balance.

We could argue that while a country is in deficit on its Balance of Payments it is better off than when in surplus because while in deficit it must be receiving more imports than it parts with in exports and these imports will increase living standards (we do, however, have to pay for these items eventually).

It was mentioned earlier that if we sold more overseas than we bought, that is, if the Balance of Payments were 'favourable', we would not necessarily be better off as a nation. The influx of money may only lead to inflation.

* *Using the same layout as in Fig. 15.2, obtain the current data for the Balance of Payments and complete the account.*
* *Obtain the figures for the Balance of Payments*

BALANCE OF PAYMENTS

UNITED KINGDOM LIMITED

YEAR ENDING 1988

CURRENT ACCOUNT

VISIBLE TRADE ....

+   INVISIBLE TRADE .... _____

CURRENT BALANCE

CURRENCY FLOW

CURRENT BALANCE ....

+ INVESTMENT AND OTHER CAPITAL FLOWS ....

BALANCING ITEM .... _____

TOTAL CURRENCY FLOW

This is money available for adding to reserves, paying off foreign debt, or investing abroad. When this is shown as a loss (–) nations must borrow, use reserves or sell foreign assets.

OFFICIAL FINANCING

OFFICIAL BORROWINGS (+)
OR REPAYMENTS (–) ....

CHANGES IN OFFICIAL RESERVES
[ADDITIONS (–) or DRAWINGS (+)]..................... _____

Fig. 15.2   Balance of payments

position for the last ten years and plot this data alongside the data showing the Balance of Trade position (from the task on page 165). What is significant about the two lines now on the chart?

A final issue in connection with the Balance of Payments concerns the short-term capital movements between countries that are made from time to time when the owners of such funds are either looking for more favourable rates of interest or a more secure place for their assets. The movement of so-called 'hot money', which are generally quite extensive funds, can have a disturbing effect on the capital account of the Balance of Payments. Hot money is normally moved to financial centres offering better rates of interest that it is currently earning. There are occasions when such funds are moved at short notice by owners who want safety rather than higher interest rates. In these circumstances the money is referred to as 'refugee money' but the impact on the Balance of Payments is the same as for hot money. Because, for safety reasons, the money will almost certainly be withdrawn when a country is having difficulty with its Balance of Payments, such difficulties will be aggravated simply because large sums of capital have been withdrawn.

You will by now be realising that as far as a British organisation is concerned, there is much more to international trade than merely selling abroad or simply buying from abroad. Organisations will necessarily need to complete a mass of paperwork, be governed by specific legislation, be prepared to follow strange national customs, appreciate a variety of cultures when trading with organisations/consumers in foreign lands, and be prepared for the problems of dealing with foreign exchange.

- *What is an 'export credit guarantee' and how does it help international trade?*

As if this were not enough, the market for some organisations may well be the 'Third World' and this too will have its own peculiarities associated with trade. An issue of increasing concern to many people in recent years, in connection with trade to the Third World, has been the moral questions behind some deals. For example, the ethical questions surrounding deals such as Nestlé selling dried baby milk to the inhabitants of industrially backward and poor African states. Three main issues arose out of this incident which were significant. First, the use of dried milk as a substitute for breast feeding was condemned by many since powdered milk does not contain a vital ingredient which is only found in mother's milk and which is thought necessary for healthy babies. Secondly, the mixing of the dried milk with water has to be done in specific proportions and, since many of the users were illiterate, the correct amounts of water and dried milk were not being used. Thirdly, in many regions the water used to make up the milk was not itself pure and not adequately boiled.

Third World trade involves organisations in many complex issues and no study of international trade would be complete without a brief view of what the Third World is and which countries are thought to be developing as industrial nations – the so-called newly developing countries.

Trade and the Third World

We hear a great deal about economic development and the Third World, often without knowing what is meant by the 'Third World' or where exactly it is. For this reason, the remainder of this chapter will consider this, and we will begin by looking at some definitions of the First, Second, and Third Worlds as our standpoint.

In his book *The Three Worlds – Culture and World Development* (Weidenfeld and Nicolson, 1984), Peter Worsley describes a number of views of these various worlds in an attempt to clarify what and where the Third World is. First, it would be useful to differentiate between what appear to be *political* distinctions between the three worlds and *economic* distinctions. Worsley mentions the fact that the United Nations began classifying countries into one of three categories after 1951 and that two of these categories were of a political nature. We had, on the one hand, the so-called 'free enterprise' or 'market' economies which were economically developed and, on the other hand, we had the 'centrally-planned' economies.

- *Differentiate between a market economy and a centrally-planned economy, giving examples of each.*

Whatever fell outside this classification was grouped on a purely economic basis, that of 'primary producing countries'.

- *Differentiate between primary, secondary, and tertiary production.*

Worsley argues that logically four titles should have been contrived:

1. Developed, capitalist countries.
2. Underdeveloped, capitalist countries.
3. Developed, communist countries.
4. Underdeveloped, communist countries.

While this classification of the world into two types of communist and two types of capitalist system may be useful to some, it does little to further our knowledge of organisations at this level. Since we are referring to the Third World, let us assume that there are only the three classifications.

The First World

Composed of those countries which operate regimes whereby private individuals can own property and where there is competition between producers; a system whereby all citizens are equal in legal and political rights; a system where the state intervenes in economic and social aspects of life only for the benefit of society as a whole.

The Second World

Composed of those countries which have a collective economy with state ownership and direction of the means of production; a system where generally only one political party exists (and thus only one party governs); a regime which uses control of the media and communications to exercise control over the will of the people.

The Third World

Composed of the least economically developed countries; generally non-aligned and probably newly-independent; undertaking the process of industrialisation, often with the assistance of the developed nations of both the West (USA, Great Britain, Germany, etc.) and the East (USSR).

- *What is a 'non-aligned' country?*
- *Identify three countries on the American continent which can be said to be economically backward but developing.*
- *Identify three countries on the African continent which can be said to be economically backward but developing.*

Very often, because of the scarcity of human skills, the scarcity of material resources, chronic shortages of funds, and, quite often, shifts in political support which can lead to civil wars (as in Ethiopia and the Sudan at the time of the famines in the early and mid-1980s), developing countries must choose between the current consumption levels of the population or investment in the future. While this is a choice all nations have to face, the developing nations have an additional burden which we cannot lose sight of, that is, the fact that these levels of consumption refer to subsistence levels as far as a large proportion of the population is concerned. Thus, investment in the future will result in the death today of many people.

- *What can be purchased by someone with a subsistence level of income in say, a poor African state?*

As if there are not enough problems for the developing nations, they also have to contend with problems about the *way* in which development should take place. One characteristic of developing nations is the ready existence of low-cost, unskilled labour coupled with a shortage of capital. What tends to happen unless great care is taken is that emerging nations go for technology which is not appropriate to their capabilities and skills or which does not suit their cultural background.

An example of the realisation of this was the attitude of foreign industrialists towards industrial development in Iran during the early days of the oil boom. Development was paid for out of oil revenue, which many people believed would continue for many more years than it actually did. The point of the example, however, lies in the type of development which the foreign industrialists had recommended. The Iranians did not possess the technical skills needed for rapid industrial development and so their inexperience and organisational inability meant the foreign industrialists relied on selling goods for assembly. The process was one whereby commodities such as cars and tractors were packaged in crates and were assembled in Iran, a task which required the minimum of skill from indigenous labour.

- *Select one of the countries earlier identified as being an economically backward but developing American nation and say what type of investment is most likely to be of the greatest benefit to this country.*
- *Select one of the countries earlier identified as being an economically backward but developing African nation and say what type of investment is most likely to be of the greatest benefit to this country.*
- *In the two tasks above, do your recommendations differ? If yes, how do they differ and why? If no, why are they the same?*

It is from examples such as this that one begins to

appreciate that developing countries should use the technology which is 'appropriate' to their circumstances. The foreign industrialists saw that this was the best way of producing (particularly since it also yielded much greater profits for them!) for the Iranians. In those countries where, as mentioned earlier, there is often a surplus of low-cost labour and a shortage of capital it is suggested that the technology adopted is labour intensive.

Too many underdeveloped nations have, in the past, presumed that what is most modern in terms of technology will be the best for them. Those nations which have sought the advice of foreign consultants (who are presumed to know best) will often be given advice which is inconsistent with their needs, simply because the consultants will advocate technology with which they (the consultants) are familiar – rather than consider what would be best given the existing labour skills.

A great deal of trade has been generated with developing nations along the lines of provision of technology, machines, know-how, and skills in order to enable development to take place. It is in these areas that British organisations can at present best serve the needs of the developing countries and their own organisational objectives (profit, for example).

- *What is a 'primary' export?*

A sudden shift in the demand for primary exports has dire consequences on the economy of the producing country. This is a problem faced by wealthy countries as well as poor ones. Oil-rich Saudi Arabia experienced some difficulty in September 1986 as a result of the fall in the price of oil which had occurred in the previous few months.

Such events often lead to the problem of having to reschedule debt repayments and many countries find themselves in a position where the value of their annual production is just sufficient to pay the interest of their loans. There have in fact been a number of countries that have had to suspend repayments of foreign loans until they were able to repay – not all of them being poor Third World countries either. For example, Poland, South Africa, and Argentina have all been down this road in the recent past.

While a fall in the price of raw materials may help organisations in the UK we need to bear in mind that the impact of, say, debt rescheduling may bankrupt many countries. International trade is fraught with the problems faced by organisations dealing solely in internal trade – plus a few others for good measure.

Assignments

Student activity 15.1

This is an assignment designed to be completed by students working in pairs. Consider the article below. Produce an informal report outlining the Common Agricultural Policy of the EEC and go on to define the terms 'green' pound and 'green' franc. Say also why there is so much tension between British and French farmers.

EEC still deadlocked on green currency plan

By Tim Dickson in Brussels

THE EEC is still deadlocked on European Commission proposals to devalue the 'green' pound and the 'green' franc.

The package of agri-monetary measures – aimed primarily at defusing tensions among French lamb producers and British beef farmers – was discussed by agricultural experts from member states at their weekly meeting in Brussels yesterday but no agreement was reached.

The issue is likely to be raised again next week.

The Commission put forward its proposals – a 6 per cent green currency devaluation for UK beef, 2 per cent for UK lamb, 3.3 per cent for French beef and 3.2 per cent for French lamb – after initially turning down a plan inspired by Mr Frans Andriessen, the Farm Commissioner. The change of plan came after intense political pressure from France and the UK but when they were debated by the Community's Agriculture Ministers last Tuesday the measures ran into opposition from five member states.

Source: *The Financial Times*, 25 November 1986

Student activity 15.2

This is an individual assignment. The report in the article below centres on Mrs Thatcher's attempt to encourage the removal of trade barriers between EEC member states. Since the implications of free trade between member states would appear, in the long run, to be particularly attractive to participants, it is sometimes hard to imagine why a nation would erect trade barriers.

You have decided to produce a magazine article outlining the advantages to be gained from unrestricted international trade and discussing the drawbacks of trade restriction. You will also need to make it clear exactly what weapons are open to governments to prevent the free movement of goods between countries.

Student activity 15.3

This is an individual assignment. You work for a manufacturing organisation that has to import 85% of its raw materials. The Director of the Purchasing Department (Mike Smart) has just read the newspaper article concerning the balance of payments position. He asks you (as an employee in his department) to produce a memo for him outlining what you think will be the implications, for importing firms such as yours, of further deterioration in the balance of payments position. Justify any assertions you make in the preparation of this memo.

Thatcher plea to EEC over trade barriers

By Quentin Peel in Brussels

MRS Margaret Thatcher, the British Prime Minister, has appealed directly to her fellow heads of government in the EEC to break the logjam on removing trade barriers to a genuine common market in the Community.

In a letter sent last week, she has spelt out the problems about slow progress in scrapping national barriers to trade, and called for their political impetus to unblock decisions on 13 measures currently on the negotiating table.

These include a common regulation on counterfeit goods; measues to ease the cross-border trade in pharmaceuticals; agreement on what constitutes good laboratory practice; and common standards for the construction of and safety features on industrial vehicles, such as fork-lift trucks. They also include a new initiative to open up the whole field of public sector purchasing to freer EEC-wide competition.

Source: *The Financial Times*, 25 November 1986

Invisible 'wipe out' surplus

By Steve Levinson
Economics Correspondent

BRITAIN'S balance of payments surplus in the first nine months of this year was officially wiped out yesterday by new and lower estimates of the value of invisible earnings.

Only last week the Department of Trade published figures showing a current account surplus of £364m for the first three quarters, but the new figures show that the total surplus was only £43m.

The downgrading was due to lower invisible earnings in each quarter than previously estimated. Invisible earnings for the first quarter was shaved by £70m, in the second quarter by £104m and in the third by £147m.

The figures, from the Central Statistical Office, show that the Government has consistently over-estimated invisible earnings. The latest revisions also knocked £53m off 1985's invisible surplus.

Last week's publication of the monthly trade figures caused a political row due to an unprecedented rise in the invisibles estimate from £600m to £800m a month in the third quarter.

Source: *The Independent*, 5 December 1986

Student activity 15.4

This is an individual assignment. A careful eye on the national press will reveal not infrequent references to the World Court (the International Court of Justice in The Hague). This is an important arena for the settling of grievances yet little is generally known about the institution. To deal with this issue, your task is to prepare a five-minute oral presentation on the activities and jurisdiction of the Court.

Student activity 15.5

This is a group assignment. It is suggested that groups of three or four are large enough. Prepare a pamphlet which illustrates, in layman's language, what the following institutions have responsibility for and how they enforce their decisions:

1. The World Bank.
2. The International Monetary Fund (IMF).
3. The General Agreement on Tariffs and Trade (GATT).

Skills assessable

Assignment	*Skill* 1	2	3	4	5	6	7	8
1	1.6 1.8 1.9	2.2 2.4 2.5	3.4 3.6 3.7	4.3 4.10		6.1 6.2 6.3		
2	1.1 1.2 1.3 1.6 1.8 1.9	2.2 2.4 2.5		4.3 4.5 4.6 4.10		6.1 6.2 6.3		
3	1.1 1.2 1.6 1.8	2.2 2.4 2.5		4.3 4.4 4.6	5.1 5.2 5.3 5.5 5.10	6.1 6.2 6.3		
4	1.8 1.9	2.2 2.4 2.5		4.3 4.5 4.6		6.1 6.2 6.3		
5	1.3 1.8 1.9	2.2 2.4 2.5	3.4 3.5 3.6 3.7 3.9 3.11	4.3 4.4 4.6		6.1 6.2 6.3		

INDEX

INDEX